D1234704

HISTORY– THE HUMAN GAMBLE

HISTORY– THE HUMAN GAMBLE

REUVEN BRENNER

The University of Chicago Press ■ Chicago and London

A citizen of Israel and France, REUVEN BRENNER took his degrees from Hebrew University, was a postdoctoral fellow at the University of Chicago, and now teaches economics at the Université de Montréal.

The University of Chicago Press, Chicago 60637
The University of Chicago Press, Ltd., London

© 1983 by The University of Chicago
All rights reserved. Published 1983
Printed in the United States of America
90 89 88 87 86 85 84 83   5 4 3 2 1

Library of Congress Cataloging in Publication Data

Brenner, Reuven.
  History—the human gamble.

  Bibliography: p.
  Includes index.
  1. Social history—Methodology. 2. Social change.
3. Necessity (Philosophy) 4. Risk-taking (Psychology)
5. Creativity (Psychology) 6. Diffusion of innovations.
I. Title.
HN8.B69   1983   302   83-5780
ISBN 0-226-07402-1

Res, non verba. Facts, not words.
Distinguish the things from the noises that they
are making.
These are some of the things that my mother,
the noblest of all persons I have known, taught
me. This book is dedicated to her memory.

Contents

Preface

Life is a jest, and all things show it;
I thought so once, and now I know it.
JOHN GAY, *The Epitaph on his Monument in Westminster Abbey*

It is my hope that this book will present a novel, uniform approach to the examination of human behavior in a variety of contexts and situations.

Today human behavior is analyzed by psychologists, sociologists, economists, anthropologists, among others. Psychologists see human beings as suffering from stress, depression, obsession, oedipal complexes, and as trying to escape from freedom (according to Fromm). For economists the same human beings merely maximize their utility, have rational expectations, and are always better off when they have a greater freedom of choice. For anthropologists some human beings are bound by traditions, lack aspirations, and live near starvation. For some historians, history is made by kings, prophets, and revolutionaries, while for others the same history is made by the classes. Briefly, a look at the various disciplines in the social sciences will reveal both a rather schizophrenic human being and that very different interpretations are given to the same facts. How is this possible? After all, these fields are all supposed to deal with various aspects of behavior of the same human beings. Can it be that human beings are rational when they make their shopping lists but not when they go to a psychiatrist?

This book attempts to show that a uniform approach to *all* aspects of human behavior as well as to history may be possible. The approach is based on the view that people do their utmost to ensure their self-preservation, a view to which I shall give a precise, rigorous meaning, and from which all the verifiable implications that appear later in this book are derived. I should emphasize that the novelty of the approach is rather in the precision given to the term "self-preservation," the verifiable implications derived from it, and the way they are verified, rather than in the idea itself. For the idea that one can understand human behavior and history by assuming that, like all other creatures, human beings strive for self-preservation has been suggested in the past (by Hobbes in 1651) and more recently (by Wilson in 1978). But no writer, to my knowledge, has either given precision to this term, derived verifiable implications from this view, or looked systematically at the facts. These are the three things that I will try to do in this book.

Thus I will discuss neither the philosophical issue of why "self-preservation" is a goal, nor the question what is "good" for the human race. In general, no normative questions are raised in this book, in spite of the fact that some chapters deal rigorously with the issues of both the distribution of wealth and religion. But I hope to show that even these issues can be analyzed within a falsifiable framework.

In the first chapter I present my approach and some of its implications in order to shed light on the questions: Why do people gamble? Why do they take out insurance? Why do they commit crimes? And, perhaps most startlingly, Why do they "think"? That is, Why do they offer novel ideas and become creative? The somewhat surprising answer is that one's fluctuating position in the distribution of wealth leads one not only to gamble more, to commit more crimes, but also to gamble more frequently on new ideas in science, business, the arts, politics, and the ordinary business of everyday life. It was this conclusion that suggested the title of the first chapter: "Why Do People Take Risks? or, Was Inequality Eve's Apple?"

One of this book's additional central ideas is developed in the second chapter: namely, that the increase in population can explain the emergence of market institutions, government, and the accompanying legal system. While the way this view is presented may be novel, the idea that many features of modern societies can be viewed as adaptations to our increased numbers is not. Ester Boserup (1965, 1981) has suggested and presented evidence showing that developments in agriculture occur when population increases, rather than the contrary. That is, the evidence does not seem to support the view that people randomly invent a new agricultural technique and then population increases because more food is available. Rather, first population increases because of some exogenous reason (a change in climate or an immunization to a disease) and *then* the agricultural techniques are adapted. The same view is presented by Mark N. Cohen (1977) in his extremely well-documented book, *Food Crisis in Prehistory,* where archeological as well as other kinds of evidence suggest that the *emergence* of agriculture took place in response to an increase in population rather than some "revolutionary" outburst of the human mind.

The arguments presented in chapter 2 rely on this view of the world, and show that when population increases not only agricultural techniques will be adjusted but also human behavior in general, and contracts (or market and legal institutions) will emerge to replace exchanges based on family ties and trust. In the setting forth of this analysis two questions are raised: Why does this process happen? How does it happen?

The answer to the first question is based on the argument that when people live in relatively isolated communities, they expect to carry out most of their intertemporal exchanges with a stable population. In these circumstances agreements are reached and contracts are enforced by customs and by the trust among kin, which substitute for laws and police, institutions that fulfill the same roles today. However, when exchanges become more anonymous (and this word, by definition, implies a relatively large number of potential participants in exchanges) then written contracts, a legal framework, and the authorities enforcing them substitute for contracts previously based on trust.

The answer to the second question is based once again on the views presented in chapter 1. When population unexpectedly increases, at first wealth per capita diminishes and the distribution of wealth changes. These changes lead people not only to commit more criminal acts and gamble more, but also to gamble more frequently on novel ideas. Lucky hits eventually lead to the creation of new rules in the organization of social institutions and to technological innovations. How these arguments explain why Cain killed Abel will be, I hope, a surprise.

These, then, are the two central ideas developed in the first two chapters: first, that the perception of *inequality* makes people what they are (i.e., *thinking* creatures), and second, that markets, legal institutions, and literacy emerge in response to increases in human populations. These two ideas are combined in the rest of the chapters to shed light on a wide range of historical events: the first concept shows *why* people looked for new ideas to start with, and the second one shows why these ideas gained followers at one period rather than another.

Thus these two central ideas may be seen to shed light both on a series of daily activities (gambling, crime, creativity, occupational choices of minorities) and some "big" historical events (the "rise of the West," the emergence of the Protestant Ethic, anti-Semitic outbursts). The reason for choosing such apparently strikingly different topics is simple: it shows the greater explanatory power of the book's uniform approach.

This explanation for historical events is by no means deterministic. Quite the contrary: as the reader will be able to perceive, both my views and the evidence suggest that "chance happeneth to them all." The conclusion is even stronger: not only do the views and evidence suggest that life is a gamble, but also that much of what we think of as "progress" is actually either a sign of people's greater suffering or a regaining of standards enjoyed in the past.

I have had to pay a price for my ambitious plan, for I have had to depart sometimes from one of the principles of good scholarship by making use of secondary and tertiary sources, rather than relying on primary materials. Yet two arguments can be brought to my defense. One is practical: there are only twenty-four hours in a day. The second concerns the reader. Were I to use only primary sources, the reader could find it hard to know whether interpretations given to some facts are the product of my imagination alone or have also been put forth by scholars in other fields. Thus using secondary sources by writers from various disciplines ensures the reader as to the generality and relative neutrality of my approach.

One final note: in spite of the difficult subjects involved, my story will be simple and it will be described in clear language. Since what I deal with represents the ordinary facts and occurrences of everyday life, there is no point in using a jargon that completely baffles the ordinary literate reader. Economic, legal, and sociological abstractions mean nothing at all until they are brought down to earth, and if they cannot be, then they are probably irrelevant or wrong. But since many social scientists write down their arguments in mathematics and consider a knowledge of this abstract language as the standard in their fields rather than explicative power, my arguments are at times translated to mathematics, the translations generally appearing in the appendixes to the various chapters.

Acknowledgments

In spite of the fact that the central ideas in this book run counter to many of the ideas that members of the Department of Economics at the University of Chicago are perceived as standing for, the major influence on my ideas, the encouragement to write this book, to discard both traditional approaches in economics and traditional boundaries between disciplines, came from two members of this department, Gary S. Becker and Theodore W. Schultz, and from Richard A. Posner at the Law School of the University of Chicago. They provided me continuously with helpful and detailed suggestions. I also thank them for their intellectual honesty. Special thanks are due to James Buchanan and to Douglass C. North, whose comments helped me to sharpen the arguments, and to Colin Day for his encouragement.

Valuable comments were also provided by William Baumol, Jean-Pierre Béguelin, Antal Deutsch, Morris De Groot, Leonard Dudley, Jean-Marie Dufour, Roman Frydman, Marc Gaudry, George Grantham, Christopher Green, Barbara Haskel, the late Arcadius Kahan, Edi Karni, Nicholas Kiefer, Ruth Klinov, Robert Lafrance, Tadek Matuszewski, William McNeill, Jacob Mincer, Joel Mokyr, Frederic Pryor, Mark Schankerman, and William Watson. I would also like to thank my research assistants, Richard Guay, Michel Poitevin, and Maxim Trottier, for their dedicated work, and express my appreciation to Cathy Duggan and Nicole Laporte for their excellent secretarial assistance through the many drafts of this work.

I wish to thank the Memorial Foundation for Jewish Culture, the Ecole des Hautes Etudes Commerciales, and the Department of Economics at the University of Montreal for their support.

Finally, I would like to thank my wife, Gabrielle, not only for her direct contribution to some chapters in the book, but also for much more. I recognize that anything I may have accomplished not only in this book, but in general, is not my accomplishment alone, but ours together. I do not know what would have happened were it not for our partnership.

NOTE: Permission to reprint material from the following sources is gratefully acknowledged:

Reuven Brenner, "On Memory and Markets, or, Why Are You Paying 2.99 for a Widget?" *Journal of Business* 55, no. 1 (1982): 147–49, 153–57, copyright © 1982 by The University of Chicago.

Reuven Brenner, "Economics—An Imperialist Science?" *Journal of Legal Studies* 9 (January 1980): 180–84, copyright © 1980 by The University of Chicago.

Reuven Brenner, and Nicholas M. Kiefer, "The Economics of Diaspora," *Journal of Economic Development and Cultural Change* 29, no. 3 (1981): 523–39, copyright © 1981 by The University of Chicago.

Roger E. Brinner and Charles E. Clotfelter, "An Economic Appraisal of State Lotteries," *National Tax Journal,* vol. 28, copyright © 1975 by the *National Tax Journal* (tables 1.1 and 1.2).

Jack Goody, editor, *Literacy in Traditional Societies.* Reprinted by permission of Cambridge University Press. © Cambridge University Press 1968.

Melville J. Herskovits, *Economic Anthropology,* copyright © 1965 by Alfred A. Knopf, Inc.

Paul Johnson, *A History of Christianity,* copyright © 1976. Reprinted with the permission of Atheneum Publishers and of Weidenfeld Publishers, Ltd.

Eckerhard Kulke, *The Parsees in India* (p. 86), copyright © 1974 by Weltforum Verlag, Munich (tables 5.1 and 5.4).

Mark Twain, *Letters from the Earth,* edited by Bernard DeVoto, copyright 1942 by The President and Fellows of Harvard College. Copyright © 1962 by The Mark Twain Company. By permission of Harper and Row, Publishers, Inc.

"Very well, then, what have you to say?"
"That there is something better than logic."
"Indeed? What is it?"
"Fact."

MARK TWAIN, *Letters from the Earth*

Gambling, writing about new ideas, and committing crimes are all relatively risky activities in that their outcomes depend on chance more than the outcomes of customary activities such as performing a regular job or following others' ideas. In order to understand why people decide to perform risky acts, one must show what factors determine attitudes toward risks in general. In this chapter I hope to show that it is the perception of inequality that induces people to take risks.

> *Discouragement seizes us only when we can no longer count on chance.*
>
> GEORGE SAND, *Handsome Lawrence II*

Why Do People Gamble?

Theory

The traditional approaches to gambling have followed two lines. One views lottery tickets as just another consumer good that people buy because they derive direct utility from playing: lotteries represent a leisure activity, an entertainment (when done in Las Vegas, for example), or a "dream." This view focuses on the immediate pleasurable aspects of lotteries without taking into account the possibility that the holder of the lottery ticket may be interested in the prizes he may win. It also neglects the simple fact that the mathematical expectation of the gain must be smaller than the price of the lottery tickets, which is why governments can raise revenue from selling them. Thus, this theory assumes that in spite of the expected monetary loss, an increased expected utility must be associated with the holding of a lottery ticket, or with participation in games of chance in general. While such expectations might be plausible for games like cards (played among friends), horse track betting, bingo, or games played in the lights and glitter of Las Vegas and Monte Carlo, since these all possess entertainment values, it is hardly credible that buying a lottery ticket gives rise to enough entertainment that does *not* depend on the expected prize. Last, it must be noted that any theory that "explains" some events because of "tastes" cannot be falsified—"De gustibus non est disputandum."

This criticism has led social scientists to examine gambling by an alternative approach, namely, a theory of consumer choices in situations of risk. Friedman and Savage (1948) have offered such a theory. Their explanation is based on the premise that each consumer derives satisfaction, $U(W)$, from his wealth, W, only, and that he will choose to gamble only if the expected utility of buying a lottery ticket for a price h and with an expected monetary prize H is greater than his satisfaction from his current level of wealth. If p is the probability of winning the prize H, the mathematical translation of this statement is:

(1) $$pU(W - h + H) + (1 - p) U(W - h) > U(W)$$

If we assume that the lottery is "unfair," i.e., that the expectation of the gain, pH, is smaller than the price of the ticket h, then it follows that one will buy it only if the marginal utility of wealth is increasing (i.e., $U''(W) > 0$). This feature of the utility function is called "risk-loving"; it must be imposed in order to show why people participate in unfair gambles.

The problem with this approach is that it sheds no light on actual behavior, as can easily be inferred from the following observation: an individual whose marginal utility is increasing will never take out either "fair" or "unfair" insurance (the "unfairness" representing now the premium from which the insurance companies make profits). In order for someone to take out such insurance the marginal utility of wealth must be diminishing (i.e., $U''(W) < 0$). This argument thus implies that people would *either* gamble or insure themselves, but never do both (since the same utility function for the same wealth cannot have simultaneously a negative and a positive second derivative). But it is a fact that people both gamble and insure themselves.

In order to solve this inconsistency between the predictions of the model and the facts, Friedman and Savage have assumed that at relatively high and low levels of wealth the marginal utility of wealth decreases, while at middle levels it increases. This additional restriction on the shape of the utility function "explains" (in a nonverifiable way) the observation that people both gamble and insure themselves, but it leads to new inconsistencies. As both Alchian (1953) and Markowitz (1952) have pointed out, if this were the shape of the utility function, the relatively rich would never insure themselves against events in which large losses with small probabilities occur, and they would never gamble. But, of course, this is exactly what they do. Markowitz tried to eliminate these implications from Friedman's and Savage's model by another mental exercise, namely, by imposing further restrictions on the utility function. But he recognized that his views could not be verified either. My approach does not encounter these problems: it not only predicts that people, including the relatively rich, will *both* gamble and insure themselves, but it leads to many verifiable predictions. In order to arrive at them let us give first an alternative definition of and interpretation to the meaning of "individual satisfaction."

Let us assume that an individual's behavior is relative, that is, that his satisfaction depends not only on his wealth, W_o, but also on the fraction of people who are richer than he is, $\alpha(W > W_o)$, given that $\alpha(\cdot)$ represents his expected position in the wealth distribution:[1]

$$(2) \qquad\qquad U = U(W_o, \alpha(W > W_o)|\alpha(\cdot))$$

Let us assume further that an increase in one's wealth, holding the distribution of wealth constant, increases one's satisfaction (that is, the marginal utility of wealth is positive), but an increase in the fraction of people who are richer decreases his satisfaction. One may interpret this assumption as reflecting one's envy and ambition, but I would maintain that it reflects a change in one's success in the struggle for a kind of existence that one aspires to.

For one can argue that the probability that an individual, his family, or his offspring will either survive in such a struggle and not be hindered by opposition is greater if his *relative* wealth is greater. And, conversely, a decrease in one's relative wealth will diminish this probability. Without raising the philosophical (albeit not scientific) question of *why* we do the utmost to ensure such self-preservation, I assume that this is the way we are, and it is this goal that "satisfaction" (or the utility function) represents. The reader will be better able to judge whether or not this fundamental motive can explain human behavior once he or she becomes acquainted with both the implications derived from this assumption and with the evidence presented in this book.

I hope now to show that by giving this interpretation to an individual's "satisfaction", one can understand why people gamble and why they take out insurance.

Suppose that a lottery ticket costs h, an amount that is small relative to the individual's wealth and which he expects to lose with a probability p. Let H be the large prize one can win with a small probability of $(1-p)$. Assuming that h is small relative to both the individual's wealth and to the average wealth in the economy, losing it will not change one's relative position in the distribution of wealth (i.e., $\alpha(W > W_o) \approx \alpha(W > W_o - h)$). On the other hand, if the prize, H, is relatively large, winning it changes the individual's position, i.e., $\alpha(W > W_o) > \alpha(W > W_o - h + H)$. A numerical example illustrates these statements: if h, for example, equals $5, losing it will not make one poor, and not spending it on a lottery ticket will not make one rich. But if one wins $100,000, one's relative position in the wealth distribution changes considerably. Translated to mathematics, the decision to gamble is thus determined by this condition (a greater precision is given to the mathematical translations in the appendix):

$$U(W_o, \alpha(W > W_o)) < pU(W_o - h, \alpha(W > W_o))$$

(3)
$$+ (1 - p) U(W_o - h + H,$$

$$\alpha(W > W_o - h + H))$$

The term on the left-hand side represents the individual's position if he does not gamble, while the sum on the right-hand side equals the value of his expected satisfaction if he does. Condition (3) immediately implies that inequality in the distribution of wealth induces people to gamble on both fair bets and on unfair ones ("unfair" meaning that people know that on average the odds are against them), and that the more their satisfaction is affected by their relative position in the distribution of wealth the more they are willing to participate in unfair bets. In nontechnical language one would say that the more envious one is, the more one is willing to gamble. It also follows from (3) that if a state of "equality" existed (whatever that term means), there would be no gambling. This might appear to be not a bad thing. The problem is, as will be shown later in this chapter, that if there were "equality," the human race as we know it would not exist. Human thinking seems to be *due* to the perception of inequality.

In contrast to the view of Friedman and Savage, demonstrating that individuals who gamble may also take out insurance is a straightforward exercise. Assume that there is a small probability, p, of losing a large amount H (because of fire, for example) and a great probability, $1-p$, of retaining one's initial wealth (if fire does not occur). The consideration for taking out a fair or unfair insurance policy at price h that compensates the individual if the unfortunate event occurs is similar to the condition for the participation in a fair or an unfair gamble, the "unfairness" now representing the insurance premium:

$$\text{(4)} \quad U(W_o - h, \alpha(W > W_o - h)) > pU(W_o - H, \alpha(W > W_o - H))$$
$$+ (1-p) U(W_o, \alpha(W > W_o))$$

This condition implies that the *same* individuals who gamble may also insure themselves. They perform both acts for the same reasons: in both cases individuals expect to lose relatively small amounts, either the price of a lottery ticket or the insurance premium. But these small amounts are worth losing since these are the only ways by which people can either change or avoid changing their relative position in the distribution of wealth. Thus people gamble in order to try to become richer and change their relative position in the distribution of wealth, and they insure themselves in order to prevent becoming poorer, thus avoiding a change in their relative position.

In order to predict who the people are who are more likely to gamble, something must be said about the distribution of wealth in the economy. The distribution of wealth has been found to be positively skewed, that is, there is a relatively small "upper class," a larger upper middle class, a still larger lower middle class, and some fraction of poor (see Solow 1967). There are several arguments that explain this evidence: one of them is that since the ability and incentive to invest in one's skills and education (holding life expectancy constant) are positively correlated, even if the distribution of abilities in the economy is normal, the distribution of incomes will be positively skewed (see Becker 1975a). This means that as one's wealth, W_o, increases, the percentage of people who possess more wealth than W_o diminishes at an increasing rate. It thus follows that the wealthier one becomes the smaller is one's incentive to gamble on unfair bets, or the expected benefit of changing one's position in the wealth distribution diminishes. The converse holds true as well: the lower one falls in the wealth distribution, the greater will be one's incentive to gamble on unfair bets. (To Fitzgerald's observation, that "the rich are different from the rest of us," Hemingway added, "Yes, they have more money," which is similar to the point made above: the rich do not behave differently because they have different "tastes"; rather they behave differently because they have more money.)

The *incentives* to gamble and to take out insurance will thus depend on one's relative position in the distribution of wealth. People who are in the "middle" of the wealth distribution, that is, the middle class, will take out insurance against large losses that occur with small degree of frequency, will bet on unfair gambles that give away large prizes with small probabilities, and may be indifferent toward participating in fair gambles with small gains and small losses. The "upper class" will tend to insure itself, will be indifferent to participating in fair gambles with small gains and small losses, but will tend to participate less that the middle class in unfair gambles. In contrast, the relatively poor have greater incentives to gamble on unfair bets. These conclusions follow from the assumption that people's attitudes toward risks are affected by their relative position in the distribution of wealth, and not because they have different "tastes."

Evidence

Let us turn now from words to facts.[2] The more general implications of my argument may provide answers to the questions of why people both gamble and insure themselves, and why the relatively poor have a greater incentive to gamble than the relatively rich. The latter prediction holds *only* for those games in which a large prize can indeed change one's relative position in the distribution of wealth. Thus, if my view is correct, one would expect that people would prefer games in which a few large prizes are given away to those in which many more smaller prizes are given away. Indeed, both the *Report of the Royal Commission of Betting, Lotteries and Gambling* (1951) and the more recent *Final Report on Gambling in the U.S.* (1976) have found that expectation of a *large* financial reward is the reason people give for their purchasing of lottery tickets. They prefer this prize structure to one in which smaller prizes are distributed even though the probability of winning them is greater.[3] But while many lotteries are of this kind, some are not: in bingo games the maximum prize is around $5000, and participation in them does not seem to fit my analysis. However, the fact is that bingo, which requires one's physical presence during the game, is viewed by the participants as a social activity having entertainment value rather than as a means for getting rich. This contrasts with lotteries, where only the monetary outcomes seem to matter to the ticket buyers. If indeed people make this distinction between bingo and lotteries, one would expect that both the participants and their expenditure patterns would differ. They do, but in order to see how let us first verify whether the relatively poor indeed spend more proportionately on lotteries with a large first prize.

Surveys of these ticket buyers have found that poor people spend a greater proportion of their income on lottery tickets. Rosen and Norton (1966) have concluded that "lower income groups buy more than a proportionate share of tickets" in the New Hampshire state lotteries. Brinner and Clotfelter (1975), using data from Connecticut, Massachusetts, and Pennsylvania have also found that poor families spend a much higher percentage of their income on lottery tickets than higher income groups. Their results are presented in table 1.1. By analyzing a sample of winners in the Michigan lottery they also found that expenditures on lottery tickets as a percentage of income was decreasing (see table 1.2).

Similar evidence is quoted in the 1976 *Final Report on Gambling,* which concluded that the "lottery is one of the more regressive forms of gambling" (p. 155), this conclusion being based on the evidence presented in table 1.3. This table shows that poorer families spend 0.3% of their income on lottery tickets, almost four times more than the 0.08% that the relatively rich spend on them. The same report also found that the expenditures on bingo games and lottery tickets were different among different economic classes: while those with an income below $5,000 spent 0.3% of it on lottery tickets; those in the $5,000–$10,000 range spent 0.23%, while those in the $10,000–$15,000 range spent 0.13%. The respective percentages for the bingo games were 0.49%, 0.69%, and 0.18% (dropping rapidly for higher incomes; see table 1.3), suggesting that bingo is perceived as entertainment by the relatively poor. The report states that "middle-aged and elderly women, widows, and those earning under $5,000 a year are highly represented among the 'heavy' bingo players. . . . Bingo is viewed more in 'social' terms than other forms of gambling; most players play to have a good time" (p. 163).

Several investigations into how much people spend on gambling have gathered only one additional bit of information, namely, the buyer's income or that of his household. As has been shown, this information was already sufficient to arrive at the conclusion that lower income groups tend to spend disproportionately on lotteries. In other instances, however, the incomes seem too high to support this claim. But consider the following arguments: an income of $15,000 for a fifty-year-old is a different indicator of wealth than the same income for a twenty-five-year-old. The older man, knowing that he is almost at the peak of what he will earn, but still wanting to leave an inheritance to his children, is *poorer* than his younger counterpart with a similar income. The only way he can still become rich is not through his labor or the financial market but only through gambling. Thus one would expect that older and retired people would be disproportionately represented among the lottery ticket buyers. The second argument is more complex: a $15,000 annual income indicates a different position in the distribution of wealth for a single person than for a family with four children. Diverse studies have been made trying to compare and correct for these differences, one of their obvious conclusions being that the greater the number of children the poorer the family for the same household income.[4] By adapting the approach to cover this case, one obtains the prediction that families with more children will tend to buy more lottery tickets with a chance of winning a big prize than will families with fewer children.

In order to verify these two predictions, surveys of the winners of big prizes are used, since not enough information is available for the whole lottery-ticket-buying public. One survey was made of the big winners ($1,000,000) in Michigan for the years 1973–80. There were forty-six such winners. The survey included their age at the time of winning, their occupation, and for some the number of children and grandchildren. In New York there were eight winners in 1977–78, and for each of them age and occupation were given.

If one assumes that the winners of the big prizes are an unbiased sample of the lottery-ticket-buying population (and this will be the case if the lottery is not rigged), one can determine whether or not my views are false by comparing some of the winners' sample characteristics with the total Michigan and New York population characteristics as given in the 1970 Census. The average age of the Michigan and New York winners was fifty-four, while the average age of the Michigan and New York population above sixteen was 27.9. Among the winners 10% (seven, to be precise) were below the age of thirty-five, while 60% (thirty-four of the fifty-four) were above the age of fifty. This comparison enables us to reject at the 1% level the possibility that the winners are an unbiased sample of the general population. Further, the winners' average number of children was five (for the twenty-nine winners that this datum was given), while the average number of grandchildren was six (these averages do not include one winner who had seven children and thirty-two grandchildren). Occupations, when not retired, were all characteristic of the poor or the lower middle class: janitors, factory workers, and so forth. In conclusion, the probability that such a sample is a random one for the population above sixteen years old is very small. Thus the facts seem consistent with my views: the lottery-playing population tends to be older and poorer than the rest of the population. This evidence suggests that one must be careful when analyzing the gambling population: looking only at its income might lead to inappropriate conclusions. For if it is found that its average income is, let us say, $20,000, that might only imply that older, poorer people gamble more often than the relatively rich.

Another fact worth noting is that in some developing countries state lottery officials want to appeal to the poorer strata of the population. In Mexico, for instance, a state lottery has existed for 203 years in which the top prize is $2 million. When a wealthy man wins—a rare occurrence—lottery players and officials are dismayed (see Weinstein and Deitch 1974: 88–89), suggesting that everybody recognizes that this market exists mainly for the redistribution of wealth among the relatively poor. This observation has also been made by Foster (1967), who notes that in the past in traditional peasant societies an increase in wealth was often seen as due either to the discovery of treasure or the making of a pact with the devil. But he continues:

Modern lotteries are very much functional equivalents of buried treasure tales in peasant societies, and at least in Tzintzuntzan the correlation is clearly understood. One elderly informant, when asked why no one had found buried treasure in recent years, remarked that this was indeed true but "Today we Mexicans have lotteries instead. . . ." This, I think, explains the interest in lotteries in under-developed countries. . . . The man who goes without lunch, and fails to buy shoes for his children in order to buy a weekly ticket, is not a ne'er-do-well; he is the Horatio Alger of his society who is doing what he feels is most likely to advance his position. . . . The odds are against him, but it is the *only* way he knows in which to work toward success." [P. 318; italics in original.]

This precisely reflects one implication of my views, which would predict an increased interest in lotteries in developing countries.

"Moral" authorities as well as some social scientists have had rather negative attitudes toward gamblers, arguing that gamblers are unstable, destroy their family lives, and overestimate their chances of winning. It is not very clear on what evidence these views are based: according to the *Final Report on Gambling in the U.S.* (1976), these aspects of leisure activities characterize gamblers and nongamblers alike (see p. 68 in the *Report*): gamblers watch slightly less T.V. (hardly a mortal sin), read more newspapers and more magazines than nongamblers, and read about as many books. Gamblers devote much more time to opera, lectures, museums, nightclubs, dancing, movies, theater, and active sports. They also socialize more with friends and relatives and participate more in community activities. The few things that they spend much less time on include home improvements, gardening, knitting, sewing, and, yes, going to church (but then this is to be expected: some of us gamble on a better life on earth while others on a better afterlife—but is there any reason for forbidding either form of gambling?). This same result was found by a Swedish survey, which reveals that gambling does not lead to the disastrous consequences suggested by the opponents of gambling and its legalization. Bettors and nonbettors in the Swedish sample discharged their familial, occupational, and social duties in similar fashion. Moreover, there was no positive correlation between crime and *legal* gambling; Cornish (1978) summarizes the evidence. In 1951 in England a study carried out by the Principal Medical Officer in Wakefield Prison showed that out of 800 consecutive admissions examined in 1948, it was reported that in only 2% of cases was gambling "a factor in the offender's downfall." Even among this 2% gambling was considered to be merely one aspect of the "generally slack and dissolute life," while only in seven cases was betting a significant factor. Similar studies of criminal populations have been carried out more recently: Sewell (1972) conducted a survey to determine the prevalence of frequency of gambling for a sample of short-term prisoners at Penton-ville, and found little evidence that prisoners were any more likely to bet than comparable social groups from national samples, such as provided by Gallup (1972) or Borill's (1975) surveys. Of course, if one examines the relationship between crime and gambling where gambling is outlawed, the results would be tautological and could shed no light on the discussion of whether or not gambling and crime are correlated.

In their recent book *Gambling, Work and Leisure* (1976), Downes and his associates provide little evidence to support the view that the majority of gamblers squander their money recklessly, whether it is money spent on stakes or money earned from winnings. There is evidence that many people budget for their expenditures, that participants intend to use any large win thriftily and sensibly (Gallup 1972, Cornish 1978) and in fact do so, spending the money by preference on home-centered items if and when they win (Smith and Razzell 1975, Downes et al. 1976). In horse-race betting, too, small wins are rebet more often than large ones, while rebetting itself is largely confined to regular punters, although even among this latter group three times as many save their winnings or spend them on household goods as rebet them (Downes et al. 1976). These data sup-port the implications of my approach, for they do not imply that people gamble because they are "obsessed" with games or that they are born with this "taste." Rather, they gamble in order to become richer; once they succeed, they gamble less. Finally, as to some social scientists' asumption that gamblers overestimate their chances of winning,[5] the Royal Commission concluded that gamblers were as aware as nongamblers of the unprofitable nature of gambling.

Since gambling redistributes wealth among the relatively poor by vol-untary exchange, we have to ask why there have been and continue to be so many restrictions imposed on this specific sector by governments. If one agrees with Stigler's (1975) view that the content of legislation depends on the power of some interest groups, the answer seems to be straightforward. Restricting gambling increases the demand for alternative means of redistributing wealth. Since redistributing wealth is what poli-ticians do, restrictions on gambling increase the demand for their services in order to increase the level of relative wealth: the fact that governments that forbid the private sector to operate lotteries do so themselves might support Stigler's views. This is an amusing view, but there seems to be a more fundamental reason for restricting gambling. In order to discover it, let us turn back to the beginning of the analysis and determine what human sentiments can be defined where the distribution of wealth in the economy is not equal.

The assumption that an increase in the percentage of people whose wealth is greater than one's own diminishes one's satisfaction can be translated into everyday language as reflecting either one's envy or one's ambition. Economists, who derive their conclusions by assuming that people's satisfaction stems only from monetary wealth have been unable to understand the motives behind gambling. Their misunderstanding is due probably not only to the fact that they look at human behavior through the lenses of their abstract models, but also to the fact that those who have elaborated these models and the politicians who have adopted their implications have been relatively successful. For economists, therefore, the motivation for gambling may seem strange and irrational. Indeed, as my views imply, people's beliefs and the sentiments they share are *not* independent of their wealth and their relative position in its distribution. Thus it is not very surprising that one finds that some economists have uttered such statements as the following:

> The overweening conceit which the greater part of men have of their own abilities is an ancient evil. That the chance of gain is materially overvalued, we may learn from the universal success of lotteries.
>
> [Adam Smith 1776]

> The pleasures of gambling are likely to engender a restless, feverish character, unsuited for a steady work as well as for the higher and more solid pleasures of life.
>
> [Alfred Marshall 1890]

> It is usually agreed that casinos should, in the public interest, be inaccessible and expensive.
>
> [John Maynard Keynes 1936]

> Gambling is certainly not a meritorious taste, but if people want to gamble, let them.
>
> [Milton Friedman, interview in *Business Week,* 4 August 1975]

But as the views and the empirical evidence presented here suggest, all four writers may be wrong: Keynes because he does not recognize that the restriction may be costly, since people may decide to gamble illegally, thus necessitating expenditures for jails and law enforcement; and Smith, Marshall, and Friedman because they consider gambling only as a matter of taste. The facts seem to indicate that people know very well that the odds are against them, yet they also know that through gambling they have a chance to become rich, that is, to change significantly their relative position in the distribution of wealth (something that welfare programs, however generous, cannot do), at the slight expense of the price of a lottery ticket. Restricting gambling therefore imposes a tax on the hopes and dreams of the relatively poor. Unfortunately, we do not know enough about human behavior to be able to predict how will people behave when faced with such restrictions. As George Sand noted, "Discouragement seizes us only when we can no longer count on chance." And who knows how discouraged people behave?

Criminal Acts

Crime and Inequality

The characteristic feature of a lottery ticket is that the potential gains and losses it represents depend on luck alone. The rationale for the existence of such tickets is that by selling and buying them wealth is redistributed in the society through a voluntary exchange.

There are other methods, voluntary and involuntary, for redistributing wealth: crime, taxation, charity, and family transfers, for example. If my views are correct, then one can understand why doing one's utmost to ensure self-preservation can lead to either gambling, crime, or the attempt to change the distribution by decreasing others' wealth through compulsory transfers.

Increasing one's relative wealth through criminal acts can take many forms: stealing, destruction of property (by vandalism or war), destroying another's reputation, or killing.

Consider the decision to commit a crime, to steal, for example, where by the term "crime" I refer either to an illegal act or to an act not in accordance with existing custom. W_o denotes wealth, H the amount one expects to steal, and P the value of punishment, of paying a fine or going to prison if one is caught. Let p be the probability of being caught; then the expected satisfaction from committing a crime, denoted by EU, is

$$(5) \qquad EU = pU(W_o - P, \alpha(W > W_o - P)) + (1-p) \cdot$$

$$\cdot U(W_o + H, \alpha(W_o + H))$$

The sum on the right-hand side shows the expected outcome, the first term of being caught and the second of being undetected. Assume that one did not commit a crime when one's wealth was W_o, that is,

$$(6) \qquad U(W_o, \alpha(W > W_o)|\alpha(\cdot)) > EU$$

Now let us assume that one's position in the distribution of wealth worsens either because one's wealth diminishes unexpectedly to W_1 or stays constant but many other people who were previously poorer become suddenly richer. One then becomes more likely to commit the crime that one was previously reluctant to perpetrate; the inequality in (6) may be reversed because one has been outdone by one's "fellows" (i.e., members of one's own class).

The conclusion is simple: one's incentive to commit the crime that one was previously reluctant to commit increases when one's relative position in the distribution of wealth diminishes significantly. One can also say that in this model the man who suddenly finds himself with relatively little and cannot continue his customary way of life is the man who is more likely to begin committing crimes.[6] Let us contrast this conclusion with the ones reached by social scientists who have tried to explain crime rates.

Economists have depicted the criminal as one who divides his time between legal activities with certain rewards and illegal activities with risky, uncertain rewards (see, for example, Becker 1974, Ehrlich 1975, and Block and Heineke 1975). Changes in the distribution of wealth have been assumed to have no direct effect on criminal behavior, since economists have assumed in their models that behavior is shaped only by wealth. Thus, according to their approach, lower average incomes have been the predictors of participation in criminal acts.

The economists' approach has been applied to the analysis of only a very limited range of crimes, and its results have often been criticized (for a summary of the criticism see Carr-Hill and Stern 1979). Most social scientists have indeed emphasized the role that *changes* in the wealth distribution play in criminal acts, although in contrast to the economic models they have not provided a uniform theoretical background for their analysis. But the evidence of these social scientists seems to support my approach: Danziger and Wheeler (1975), for example, have introduced in their empirical analysis a measure of the distribution of wealth in the economy. They used time-series data for the United States in the period 1949–70, and cross-sectional data for U.S. cities in 1960. They remark that recorded offences rose through the 1960s when aggregate income was rising and declined in the 1930s when income was falling, which supports their argument (for which, however, they do not provide theoretical grounds) that it is low relative income and not low average income that generates offences.

Sociologists have offered three main hypotheses in an attempt to explain crimes; the theory of anomie (by Durkheim 1911, Merton 1957), of culture conflict (Sellin 1938), and that based on family background (Walker 1965). The first theory is based on the observation that modern societies differ from medieval ones in the way in which an individual's status, a relative concept, is ascribed and achieved. But since Durkheim gives no explanation for the different structure of society, no testable implications can be derived from his theory. Merton (1957) revised Durkheim's theory and argued that individuals can accept or reject institutional means and goals and may try to change them. He argues, but presents no empirical evidence, that the most frequent form of adjustment is "innovation," and when material wealth is concerned this means fraud and theft. While no testable implications can be derived from Merton's approach as it stands, some similarities between his and my approach will become evident later. The theory of cultural conflict was developed from the suggestion that when one group imposes its own code of behavior on another by force, there is likely to be a large increase in crime (Sellin 1938). This hypothesis approximates mine: imposing restrictions on one group *decreases* both its wealth and changes the distribution of wealth in the economy. Sellin's views are thus consistent with my approach.[7]

Psychologists frequently emphasize the effects that changes in family structure have on crime, and make use of the term "maladjustment" in their analyses. The conditions they most frequently discuss are broken homes and adolescent delinquency (see, for example, N. D. Walker 1965). Again, their approach approximates mine (but not one that defines behavior only in terms of wealth).

For a child, the meaning of a "broken home" is that, relative to other children, his wealth (a term that, as shown in chapter 2, includes the security and parental attention he gets) decreases. If the view presented here is correct, it follows that the probability that children from broken homes will commit criminal acts would be greater than for children from normal backgrounds. Glueck and Glueck (1950) studied 500 delinquent and 500 nondelinquent adolescents: 60% of the delinquents came from homes that had been broken by separation, divorce, or prolonged absence of a parent, as against 34% of the nondelinquents. In a study by Carr-Saunders and his associates (1942), out of 1953 delinquent boys and 1970 nondelinquent controls, 28% of the former and 16% of the latter came from families in which one or both natural parents were missing. (While these studies were written quite a while ago, they are still quoted by recent books, Carr-Hill and Stern [1979] for example, as the classical, best studies in the field, although many additional ones that present similar evidence have been carried out since these seminal studies).

I have put together my own set of data in order to determine whether or not it falsifies my views. It does not. The result of the statistical analysis described below is that as the fraction of people who become relatively poorer increases, the crime rate increases. From this evidence, along with that mentioned earlier and the evidence to be presented later, one can conclude that becoming relatively poor along with the expectation of staying permanently poorer seem to induce people to commit crimes.[8]

Data on Canadian crime rates provide the basis for the analysis. Since Canada has only ten provinces and data on inequality exist only at the provincial level, I could not make the type of cross-sectional analysis that has been frequently done in the U.S. Also, since data on inequality exist only from 1966 onward (not for all the provinces), neither could I use time-series analysis alone. Rather, I was obliged to pool together cross-sectional data and data from the same province across time and make the appropriate statistical adjustments.

The types of crimes analysed were breaking and entering; robbery; theft; and fraud. Rape and murder were omitted. In order to examine the implications of my views as extensively as possible, separate statistical analyses were done for each type of crime.

If my assumptions are correct, changes in crime rates should be affected by the following explanatory variables:

1. The level of inequality, here measured by the percentage of families below one-half of median income (this is also the measure of inequalilty used by Ehrlich [1974] in his empirical analysis of crime rates in the U.S.).
2. The number of policemen, which serves as a proxy for the probability of being caught.
3. Urbanization, which affects the probability of being caught, for anonymity becomes easier with greater urbanization; thus, it is easier for crimes to be undetected.
4. Unemployment rates. The reason for introducing this variable is to distinguish between two viewpoints concerning crime rates. According to my view, increased unemployment perceived as temporary should lead to diminished crime rates, for the incentive to keep one's record straight is increased and the opportunities to commit crimes are diminished. In contrast to this view, others argue that increased unemployment increases the crime rate, since the opportunity cost of one's time becomes lower when one is unemployed. As shown below, the facts seem consistent with my view rather than the alternative: an increase in the unemployment rate seems to diminish significantly the crime rate rather than increase it.

The statistical analysis was carried out by the following method: least-square regression equations were estimated for the pooled cross-sectional and time-series data. The equations were as follows:

$$(7) \quad CR = \alpha + \beta_1 PO + \beta_2 IN + \beta_3 U + \beta_4 URB + \beta_5 T + u$$

where the notations represent logarithmic transformations of these variables:

CR = the number of recorded offenses per 100,000 people above the age of 16

PO = the number of policemen, a measure for the probability of being caught

IN = inequality, as measured by the percentage of families below one-half of median income (in the statistical tests if the crime referred to 1970, the inequality measure referred to 1969)

U = unemployment rate

URB = urbanization rate, measured by the fraction of the population living in cities

T = time trend

$\alpha, \beta_1, \beta_2, \beta_3, \beta_4, \beta_5$ = the regression coefficients

u = the residual

In order to obtain consistent estimates the ordinary least-square method was used to all of the pooled observations. (Two transformations were then carried out: one to remove autoregression, the other to remove heteroskedasticity.) The dependent variable in the first equation is VT, total recorded thefts:

(8) $VT = -0.29 - 2.96\ PO + 7.5\ IN - 9.11\ U + 14.5\ URB + 0.225\ T$
  (-0.9) (-5.5) (3.07) (-3.3) (11.9) (7.2)

  $DW = 1.223$ $F(5/29) = 401.09$

where the numbers in parentheses denote the t statistics, DW the Durbin Watson statistic, and $F(./.)$ the F statistic.

All the coefficients are significant and in the expected directions: increases in the police force and in the unemployment rate (probably perceived as temporary) lower the crime rate, while increased inequality and urbanization increase it.

In the rest of the tests I have distinguished between the components of the term "theft" and tested each of them separately. The definition of theft included (1) "breaking and entering" (into apartments, hotels, shops, etc.); (2) theft of cars, bicycles, and telephones, shoplifting, and other forms of theft that do not involve either violence or breaking in; and (3) fraud, either at a workplace or in general. BE denotes breaking and entering, TH theft (including shoplifiting), and FR fraud. The respective results are:

(9) $BE = -.037 - 2.1\ PO + 2.94\ IN + 0.19\ U + 12.8\ URB + 0.15\ T$
  (-3.4) (-6.01) (1.48) (0.7) (15.41) (4.95)

  $DW = 1.38$ $F(5/29) = 429.5$

(10) $TH = 3.21 - 1.91\ PO + 8.74\ IN - 8.96\ U + 7.04\ URB + 0.13\ T$
  (6.05) (-7.26) (4.84) (-5.25) (9.67) (8.02)

  $DW = 0.96$ $F(5/29) = 32.26$

(11) $FR = 0.13 - 2.65\ PO + 12.9\ IN - 14.39\ U + 8.69\ URB + 0.18\ T$
  (0.4) (-4.4) (5.46) (-5.14) (9.00) (5.52)

  $DW = 1.83$ $F(5/29) = 171.8$

The coefficients of inequality and of urbanization are always positive and significant and that of expenditures on police negative and significant. But in the regression for breaking and entering, where unemployment is insignificant, in all the rest of the regressions it is significant and negative, which means that an increase in unemployment diminishes the crime rate. Let us reemphasize the interpretation given to this result.

If the result obtained were that increased unemployment diminishes only the number of fraudulent crimes but not the number of other criminal acts, the explanation would be straightforward: when unemployment increases, the opportunities to perpetrate fraud diminish. However, this interpretation suggests that a fraction of those unemployed are not merely the innocent victims of sudden variations in supply and demand, but can with good reason be suspected of committing fraud. Since one often encounters the charge that statistics can easily be manipulated to misinterpret the facts (which is true), I have checked this issue more closely. While no Canadian data could be found, the American Management Association has stated that on average 20% of the bankruptcies during the last few years have been due to employee fraud. Thus the assumption that there is among the first employees fired from a given firm a fraction that will commit fraud might not be altogether false.

However, one can give a more plausible interpretation to the negative and significant relationship between unemployment rates and crime rates. One would expect that people will commit fewer crimes when they perceive the increased unemployment as temporary, for people have greater incentive to keep their record straight and make greater efforts when they temporarily face either a smaller probability of finding a job or a greater probability of being laid off.

The distinction between temporary and permanent unemployment is crucial to this argument. If the increase in the duration of unemployment is perceived as temporary, then it will not be viewed as changing the wealth distribution significantly. In contrast, an increase in the duration of unemployment perceived as permanent will be viewed as leading to such a change. For this reason one must be careful in interpreting correlations between crime rates and unemployment rates. If one finds a positive correlation, it does not necessarily imply that increased unemployment results in an increased crime rate. What it might indicate is that the increased unemployment is expected to be of a longer duration, thus leading to the perception that the distribution of wealth has changed.

In conclusion, let me reemphasize the main point of this section: both the theory and the facts suggest that it is people's worsened position in the distribution of wealth rather than temporary fluctuations in unemployment that seems to increase the crime rate significantly.

Envy is a pain of mind that successful men cause their neighbors.
ONASANDER, A.D. 49

On Slander and Vandalism

The views presented here may help us understand the phenomena of slander and vandalism, acts that are considered to be criminal.

Few people have devoted so much attention to envy as Samuel Johnson. His view was that "envy may act without expense or danger. To spread suspicion, to invent calumnies, to propagate scandal, requires neither labour nor courage. It is easy for the author of a lie, however malignant, to escape detection, and infamy needs very little industry to assist its circulation." And, according to Johnson, of all vices envy is the closest to "pure and unmixed evil" because its object is "lessening others, though we gain nothing to ourselves."

On the contrary, I would contend that people perceive gains (albeit not monetary ones) when they destroy others' reputations. Since one's reputation is a part of one's wealth, ruining it changes the distribution of wealth that has shaped one's behavior by diminishing the fraction of people who are perceived as wealthier. Johnson also argued that "much . . . happiness of life would be advanced by the eradication of envy from the human heart." If the views presented here are correct, this statement is somewhat meaningless. For, as will be shown in this chapter, the same process that causes some to be envious leads others to think and become creative.

Yet Johnson's explanation of the fundamental motive behind envy is the same as mine: namely, the desire to relieve the sense of any unfavorable disparity between oneself and others. According to this view, slander can be viewed as an act committed in order to damage another's reputation, which is part of his wealth.

In this sense slander and vandalism can be compared: both change the distribution of wealth, one by damaging reputations, the other by making the rest of the society aware of one group's worsened position in the wealth distribution and demanding a redistribution. Vandalism and slander thus both represent a channel of communication by which individuals or groups announce their threat to society. As Epictetus puts it, "Envy is the adversary of the fortunate."

While acts of vandalism are more likely to occur in societies with large populations, slander is more likely to affect the distribution of wealth in relatively isolated communities. For unless public figures and scandal sheets are involved, slander can hardly have a significant effect when it makes its threats among a relatively large population. An act of vandalism, however, is a media event. When, on the other hand, one lives in a relatively isolated society, slander can achieve its goal. Lewis (1968), sharing the view of many anthropologists, has noted that in primitive societies people do indeed fight with words:

> The power of the tongue and of the spoken word in spreading hostility and enmity, in countering it, or in broadcasting conciliatory messages, in ruining reputations or praising men to the skies, is very evident in Somali culture. [p. 268]

Jane Austen's novels are good examples too of the role slander could play in the relatively small, closed societies of the eighteenth-century English countryside and of the way punishment for spreading slander was inflicted by custom. The information about public figures spread by today's scandal sheets needs only one further comment: as will become clear in the next chapter, when population increases scandal sheets substitute for oral slander, and libel suits and their outcomes substitute for the punishments previously inflicted by customary behavior.

Gambling, Crime, and Inequality: Further Evidence

By realizing that a significant loss in one's wealth increases the incentive to commit either criminal or rebellious acts, people may consider transferring part of their wealth by various methods. These methods will be discussed next.

As will be shown in detail in the next chapter, small, isolated communities establish norms of behavior and sets of beliefs concerning how to redistribute wealth, without the necessity of relying on a central authority for this purpose. In contrast, when the frequency of interaction among individuals is expected to diminish (and this happens when population or its mobility increases), family ties are weakened, customs become more difficult to enforce, and a central authority takes over the role of the redistribution of wealth. Thus one would expect that in primitive societies, which for hundreds of years have kept their population stable, custom will provide the guidelines for redistributing wealth. But when population increases and becomes more mobile, or communities become less isolated, central authorities are expected to take over this role.

An example of the mechanism behind the redistribution of wealth among tribes in the Nilgiri hills of India, which initially possessed different levels of wealth, is given by Herskovits (1940):

> The members of this tribe were musicians and artists for the three neighbouring folk of their area, the pastoral Toda, the jungle-dwelling Kurumba, and the agricultural Badaga. Each tribe had clearly defined and ritually regulated obligations and prerogatives with respect to all the others. The Toda provided the Kota with ghee for certain

ceremonies and with buffaloes for sacrifices at their funerals. The Kota furnished the Toda with the pots and knives they needed in their everyday life and made the music essential to Toda ceremonies. The Kota provided the Bagada with similar goods and services, receiving grain in return. They stood in the same exchange relationship with the forest Kurumba, but these latter, who could only provide meagre material compensation—honey, canes, and occasionally fruit—were able to afford the Kota supernatural protection, since the Kurumba were dreaded sorcerers, so feared that every Kota family must have their own Kurumba protector against the magic which others of this tribe might work against them. [p. 157]

In terms of the human attitudes discussed here, these relationships can be explained in the following way: since the Kurumba were initially relatively poor, they were more likely to commit criminal acts. Realizing the threat, the Kota, in an attempt to diminish this possibility, were ready to make payments to them. The threat might have been the source of the custom and of the belief that the Kurumba were "dreaded sorcerers." This example illustrates how the sentiments discussed here can be useful in the "bargaining" of the relatively poor with the rest of the society. Today the "dreaded sorcerers" are called "potential criminals" and wealth is redistributed by a central authority rather than on the basis of family acquaintance. But the patterns of behavior are familiar; only the terminology is different. Indeed it is a matter of semantics whether we use the term "criminal" or the term "sorcerer." We will return to the matter of language in later chapters.

Views similar to the ones outlined above are evident in many studies that describe how in relatively isolated small communities individuals or families who lose something and become relatively poor are viewed as a threat to the stability of the community. Their envy and jealousy are viewed as leading to aggression toward the more fortunate. At the same time it is also pointed out that individuals or families who become wealthy are also viewed as a threat to the stability of the community. These observations are consistent with the views presented here, since such events reflect changes in the distribution of wealth, which, by increasing the probability of criminal and rebellious acts, diminish the stability of the society.

Gluckman (1965) writes:

For though a man gains prestige by his productive capacities, if he outdoes his fellows too much, they will suspect him of witchcraft. Richards reports of the Bemba, that to find one beehive with honey in the woods is luck, to find two is very good luck, to find three is witchcraft. Generally, she concludes, for a man to do much better than his fellows is dangerous. . . . Here accusations of witchcraft and sorcery maintain the egalitarian basis of the society in two ways: not only is the prosperous man in danger of accusations, but he also fears the malice of witches and sorcerers among his envious fellows. [p. 88]

The mechanism that restores equilibrium by diminishing inequality is based on either a set of beliefs (in the passage by Gluckman a shared belief in witches) or on some agreed-upon norm of behavior.[9] Today we no longer believe in witchcraft, so exploitation has taken its place. Again, this change might be a matter of semantics only.

In primitive societies the practices of giving away or destroying goods during large feasts and of burying the dead with their property seem to be frequent (see Goody 1962, Gluckman 1965, Herskovits 1940, and Posner 1980). These traditions can be viewed as devices for maintaining the stability of the distribution of wealth and thus the stability of the society. Burying the dead with their property may be seen as decreasing inequality, thus preventing criminal and rebellious acts. The fact that "prestige" in primitive societies attaches to giving away goods during feasts and that people have the obligation to compete in doing so can also be viewed as a method of promoting equality. One of the most famous "feast institutions" of tribal society, the potlatch of the American Indians, is described in Gluckman (1965):

The *potlatch* . . . might entail vast destruction to shame competitors of equal rank. . . . Huge quantities of precious seal oil might be burnt. The more sumptuous the presents given away and the more lavish the destruction of property, the greater . . . the prestige accruing to the host, while the rival guest sank in public esteem correspondingly. To recover face, and regain prestige, he had to give presents in return, with interest, at a greater feast. [p. 89]

Physical property is thus traded for "prestige," which is viewed, with justice, as relatively harmless. For as evident both from Gluckman's statement and the previous discussion, one's prestige can be easily destroyed either by competition with others or by gossip.

These are only a few of the customs that serve to maintain the stability of the wealth distribution; there are many others that promote the same goal. Hoebel (1954) notes that the Eskimo sometimes kill ungenerous rich people, and Herskovits (1940) describes the process of redistribution among the Yokuts:

If a man, especially a rich one, did not join in a fandango, the chief and his doctor would plan to make this man or some member of his family sick. . . . [The doctor then] makes several successive attempts to cure his victim, each time being paid for his services. He withholds his cure until he has finally broken the man and got him into debt. . . . [p. 443]

Similar patterns of behavior can be found in traditional peasant societies that have evolved in relatively isolated small communities. In their book, *Behind Mud Walls* (1963), William and Charlotte Wiser note that dilapidated walls suggesting poverty are used as a strategy by the relatively rich to protect themselves against the jealousy of the relatively poor. Foster (1967), discussing the behavior of peasant societies in Latin America, notes:

In Latin America [a person who improves his position] is pressured into sponsoring a costly fiesta by serving as *mayordomo*. His reward is prestige, which is viewed as harmless. Prestige cannot be dangerous since it is traded for dangerous wealth; the mayordomo has, in fact, been "disarmed." . . . There is good reason why peasant fiestas consume so much wealth in fireworks, candles, music, and food; and why, in peasant communities the rites of baptism, marriage and death may involve relatively huge expenditures. These practices are a redistributive mechanism which permits a person or family that potentially threatens community stability gracefully to restore the status quo thereby returning itself to a state of acceptability. [p. 315; italics in original]

A similar point is made in Wolf (1959) in his description of a closed peasant community in Mexico:

By liquidating the surpluses, it makes all men rich in sacred experience but poor in earthly goods. Since it levels differences of wealth, it also inhibits the growth of class distinctions based on wealth. . . . In engineering parlance, it acts as a feedback, returning a system that is beginning to oscillate to its original course. [p. 216]

The evidence from these societies suggests that when population is stable and relatively small in size, various customs substitute for the role of a central authority in the redistribution of wealth. Obedience to these customs maintains inequality at a stable level, and thus incentives to commit criminal and rebellious acts are diminished and the stability of the society is ensured.

Evidence on changing methods of redistributing wealth in Europe supports the view that these methods are altered in response to fluctuations in the number of people with whom one expects to interact. Recall that the Middle Ages were characterized by a drastic reduction in Europe's population, and communities became much more isolated than they had been before. Then from the eleventh century the population grew continuously, with only one major interruption: the Black Death that swept Europe during the fourteenth century. If my views are accurate, one would expect that, beginning in the eleventh century, customs and family ties would be weakened, and the crime rate would rise until, slowly, a central authority would take over the role of redistributing wealth, thus substituting for the weakened customs and family ties. Historians have taken note of these features, but without providing a uniform approach within which to analyze them. We will now examine this process of substitution, and return to it in the following chapters, in particular chapter 3.

Cipolla (1976) describes some features of European societies before the Industrial Revolution:

> Chronicles and documents continually refer to voluntary transfers of wealth on the part of the Church, the princes, the rich, and the ordinary people. The tradition of charity was strong and the act of charity an everyday affair. . . . Feasts were also suitable occasions for charity. In Venice the Doges made large donations to the poor at election time. . . . In Rome at the election of a pope and subsequent anniversaries a half giulio was given to anyone who came to ask for it and the gift increased for each of the sons; pregnant women counted as two. People lent or hired each other their children, and pillows multiplied the pregnancies. . . . Transfers to the poor normally must have amounted to noticeably more than one percent of gross national product. . . . Until recent times hospitals, houses for abandoned children and foundations for the distribution of dowries to poor girls operated in Europe. [pp. 20–23]

On gambling as a method of redistributing wealth, he notes:

> In preindustrial Europe dowries and gambling had considerable importance [as forms of voluntary transfers of wealth]. . . . As in all underdeveloped societies, people thought of dowries and of gambling as sources for financing business. [p. 23]

He then goes on to summarize the evidence on other methods of redistributing wealth:

> Consider now the compulsory transfers of wealth. We think mostly of taxation, but plundering raids, highway robbery, and theft . . . belong to the same category. In medieval Europe political theorists saw a negligible demarcation between taxation and robbery. . . .
> Much has been written about theft from the legal and judicial points of view, but little from the statistical. We know however that it was a very frequent event. . . . It appears that the earlier the period under examination, the greater is the relative importance of transfers compared to that of exchanges. Indeed, for the Dark Ages Grierson

has asserted that "the alternatives to trade (gift and theft) were more important than trade itself. . . ." [And Duby has] observed . . . , "To rob and to offer: these two complementary acts covered a very large portion of exchanges." [pp. 24–26]

Evidence from the fifteenth to the seventeenth century in Europe, a period characterized by rapid population growth, shows that in nine of the eleven cities and areas sampled the percentage of poor in the total population was between 10% and 20% (see Cipolla 1976, who notes that the term "unemployed" did not exist, only the terms "poor" and "beggar," but this again may be just a matter of semantics). Accompanying this level of poverty historians have noted both the frequency of theft and robbery on the part of common and lower-class people *and* the emergence of the trend of central authority substituting for customs in regulating inequality. In sixteenth-century England the government developed the machinery for the administration and enforcement of charity—the great Elizabethan code of 1597 and 1601 (see Cipolla 1976)—thus producing an effective national system of poor relief. During the Reformation, one of Calvin's aims was to establish new institutions to centralize and coordinate welfare; some of the events related to this process during the sixteenth century will be examined in detail in chapters 3 and 4.

This section has had two purposes: first, to set the stage for the historical discussions in the following chapters. Second, to show how in societies with stable populations customs can diminish the crime rate by maintaining the wealth distribution stable. Why such customs result in less creative thinking will be discussed next.[10]

Before taking up this question, however, let us remind ourselves that what we have been discussing up to this point are what some view as the negative consequences of Eve's eating the apple: crimes and games of chance.

> *It is a law of nature we overlook, that intellectual versatility is the compensation for change, danger and trouble. An animal perfectly in harmony with its environment is a perfect mechanism. Nature never appeals to intelligence until habit and instinct are useless. There is no intelligence where there is no change and no need of change. Only those animals partake of intelligence that have to meet a huge variety of needs and changes.*
>
> H. G. WELLS, *The Time Machine*

Why Do We Think? Why Does One Become Creative?

In the first section of this chapter I suggested that human behavior may be viewed as the striving for self-preservation. If this is true, I must show that the aspect of human nature that leads us to take into account other people's wealth is also *beneficial*. Up to now it has been shown that this trait is merely costly and has thus no survival value, for both gambling and crime either simply redistribute wealth or destroy it. In this section I intend to show how this trait leads human beings to gamble on new ideas in business, science, the arts, technology, and the organization of social institutions. According to this scheme, people will think more when their *relative* position in the distribution of wealth fluctuates more. In turn, this trait ensures the survival of both the individual and the human race and sustains the perception that levels of wealth, on the whole, are held stable.

First, it is interesting to note that the first occurrences of gambling, criminal acts, and "thinking" in the Bible are associated with the danger of altering the distribution of wealth, although they are described in allegorical language. The serpent, tempting Eve, says: "For God doth know that in the day ye eat thereof, then your eyes shall be opened, and ye shall be as gods, knowing good and evil" (Genesis 3:5); Eve is then ready for the big gamble. This verse has been interpreted by biblical scholars as describing the trait of envy (see Kassouto 1963), and one interpretation of the chapter as a whole is that it teaches that deception is the root of all evil. It would seem then that custom was Eve's apple, and that it was disobedience of custom that altered the distribution of wealth and led Eve, and later others, to do both good (the creation of innovative ideas, scientific, artistic, or whatever) and evil (the commission of criminal acts). It should also be noticed that the events leading to the first crime are associated with an unexpected unequal distribution of wealth: "And the Lord had respect unto Abel and his offering: but unto Cain and his offering he had no respect" (Genesis 4:4–5). The outcome of this situation is well known. Thus Eve's and Cain's acts might be due to a single trait, one that is reflected in many other aspects of human behavior.

It is interesting to speculate that the authors and early hearers of the Genesis story may have known that inequality was both Eve's apple and Cain's motive, and that merely the vocabulary used to describe the events was different. In the more poetic language of oral societies the apple tree might have stood for inequality (or customs) and the serpent for politicians. As for God, did not Hegel once say that all philosophical contemplations serve only to eliminate the accidental? While "God" fulfilled this role for our ancestors, "randomness" and "luck" do so for some today. But is ours a different explanation, or is it merely the case that our vocabulary, borrowed from the latest scientific achievements, is just another way of describing the world, without, however, explaining it any better?

As will become evident, my aim in the first two chapters of this book is essentially to translate into modern (and, I hope, not too academic) language the narratives of Eve and the apple and, in chapter 2, of Cain's murder of Abel. In chapter 4 I shall return to the issue of semantics and the changing interpretations we give to certain events. But here let me now offer a more precise definition of creativity or "entrepreneurship" and present evidence on the way human beings think and become creative.

Joseph Schumpeter (1934) wrote that only in very rare cases can economic development be explained in terms of causal factors, such as an increase in population or supply of capital. Something more is needed, and Schumpeter identified this something more as the "creative response of history," a somewhat bombastic and empty concept, which Schumpeter interprets more modestly as "entrepreneurial activity" interacting with some features of the social environment.

But entrepreneurship and creativity are in general two of the most elusive concepts in the social sciences, in economics in particular. While economists from all schools of thought (Marx, Kirzner, Schultz, Schumpeter, Leibenstein, Friedman, Kuznetz) emphasize the role of these concepts in understanding economic development, none of them offers any testable hypothesis for their presence. It is nevertheless recognized that creativity is a vital component of economic growth.

Neglect of this factor is probably due to the fact that the formal economic theories are entrepreneurless. People's decisions are reduced to easy mathematical calculations that yield maximum satisfaction or maximum profits; individuals are viewed as passive calculators who merely adapt themselves to changes imposed on them by external developments and never attempt to enact changes.[11] It is thus not surprising that the treatment of technological innovations in economics has been peripheral as well (some exceptions being the work of Schmookler [1971], Mansfield [1971], Rosenberg [1976], and Griliches [1964]).

Kuznetz (1977) attributes this neglect to both the lack of adequate analysis and to the difficulty of measurement. He notes that while entrepreneurship and innovations represent sources of increase in productivity and production that could in principle be estimated, the inputs themselves could not be defined in meaningful economic terms. Cipolla (1976) translates these arguments to everyday language:

> Economists who try to split the product of this human vitality, arbitrarily attributing parts of it to this factor and parts to that, bring to mind a fellow who, confronted with one of Giotto's paintings, would try to measure how much of the beauty of the painting was due to the type of brush used, how much to the chemistry of the colors, and how much to the time taken by the artist. [pp. 117–18]

As a result, economists assume that innovations are either exogenous and independent of economic variables (in the Harrod-Domar type models), an assumption implying that economists do not know why these changes occur, or emerge in response to obvious demand. (For the theoretical model see Becker 1971; for empirical analyses see Hayami and Ruttan 1971, Schmookler 1971, and Griliches 1964.) However, as historians, psychologists, and even economists have noted, innovations do *not* seem to be systematically related to "obvious demand." How can one say that Beethoven's or Verdi's music was "demanded" or that people could not live without Picasso?

It is my hope that the precise definitions of the terms entrepreneurship, creativity, and thinking will lead rather to a verifiable hypothesis. One can argue that gambling is an activity that is not strictly related to games but to all noncustomary activities. Thus betting on an idea for which no empirical evidence yet exists also represents a gamble. Let us see what the precise nature of this gamble is.

Let P denote the amount invested in developing an idea, which, besides the direct costs of investment in time and other resources, also includes the resources invested in trying to guess the potential demand for the idea and its application. Let $\alpha(W > W_o)$ again represent the percentage of the relevant population above one's wealth, W_o, and let H denote the increase in wealth that one expects to gain by selling the idea. If he is unsuccessful, with a probability p, the potential innovator knows that he will lose the amount P. Translated into mathematical symbols, the conditions under which an individual will become an entrepreneur, that is, "bet" on a new idea for which no empirical evidence is available at the outset, are as follows:[12]

$$(12) \quad U(W_o, \alpha(W > W_o)) < pU(W_o - P, \alpha(W > W_o - P)) + (1 - p)$$
$$U(W_o + H, \alpha(W > W_o + H))$$

In spite of a mathematical similarity, there are significant differences between this condition and the one that defines participation in a lottery. Here the value of the "prize," H, differs among individuals: people's evaluations of the potential demand for either digital recording or of the solution to an open problem in science are subjective. Also, the probability here represents a *subjective* judgment by an individual, and there is no way to prove that he is right or wrong. This contrasts with lotteries, in which probability is defined in terms of processes that can be repeated many times and in which comparisons can be made between the probabilities facing different people.

Notwithstanding these differences, one can conclude that when one's relative position in the distribution of wealth is worsened, one will gamble more frequently on new ideas, an act that may be defined as thinking. This conclusion is thus similar to the one regarding the decision to gamble on a criminal act[13]—both decisions represent departures from customary behavior. The proof is also similar: suppose that one does not gamble on a new idea but merely follows custom and habit, so that the sign of the inequality in (12) is reversed. When one's relative wealth diminishes, one is outdone by his fellows. Taking risks one was previously reluctant to take, which are here equivalent to the creative act, can restore or even improve one's position in the wealth distribution (which may also be called one's status). To put it simply, people will change their minds when their relative position in the wealth distribution is significantly altered: for those who become poorer, either the incentive to begin thinking (that is, to gamble on new ideas) or the incentive to become "ambitious" or "motivated" increases. As Samuel Johnson put it long ago, "The mind is seldom quickened to very rigorous operations but by pain, or the dread of pain."

Thus, when the distribution of wealth changes, there will be more entrepreneurs among groups whose relative wealth has dropped. Or, if through luck a group's wealth increases, they will become lazier. Also, if inequality is *expected* to remain stable through either custom or taxation, then even if a group's relative wealth drops, one should not expect increased entrepreneurial activities, for the expectations for compensation results in the perception that the distribution of wealth will remain unaltered. All these conclusions stem from the view that people's attitudes toward risks depend on a change in their relative position in the wealth distribution and their perception of inequality. It is in this way that we may see inequality as Eve's apple, and human emotions as the creative elements of thinking.

Of course, many of the original ideas that people gamble on are proven to be false. I would suggest that when one's wealth diminishes relatively one will gamble more frequently on original ideas. Thus, if the percentage of "lucky" hits stays constant, the number of innovative ideas increases.

The view that original ideas are "lucky hits" is presented in several studies, mainly by psychologists. Koestler (1964) summarizes some of the evidence:

> Most Behaviourists . . . regard habit-formation as the essence of mental progress; original ideas, on this view, are lucky hits among random tries, retained because of their utility value. . . .
>
> A stimulating inquiry by the American chemists Platt and Barker showed that among those scientists who answered their questionnaire eighty-three per cent claimed frequent or occasional assistance from unconscious intuitions. But at the same time only seven per cent among them asserted that their intuitions were always correct; the remainder estimated the percentage of their "false intuitions" variously at ten to ninety per cent. . . . "The world little knows,"

wrote Faraday, "how many of the thoughts and theories which have passed through the mind of a scientific investigator have been crushed in silence and secrecy; that in the most successful instances not a tenth of the suggestions, the hopes, the wishes, the preliminary conclusions have been realized". Darwin, Huxley and Planck . . . made similar confessions. Einstein lost two years of hard work owing to a false inspiration. [pp. 157, 212–13]

Before turning to the first body of evidence, I would first like to contrast my views on creativity and entrepreneurship with those of economists, psychologists, sociologists, and others in order to show that their arguments are either vague or cannot be verified.

Other Social Scientists on Creativity

Entrepreneurs play a central role in Schumpeter's (1934) theories of economic development and business cycles, and, interestingly enough, also in Marx's theory. But neither Marx nor his followers were able to deal properly with such an incalculable production factor in their rigid distinction between labor and capital and their deterministic view of the world.[14]

In Schumpeter's system economic growth depends on the supply of entrepreneurs. Like Marx, Schumpeter argued that their potential supply depends on both sociological factors such as class structure, the educational system, and the social rewards that accompany business success, and on the entrepreneur's understanding of the "rules of the game." According to his view, some changes in the rules of the game have a negative effect on the flow of entrepreneurs. Changes such as the growing strength of unions, progressive income taxes, and social welfare programs that tend to limit profits and redistribute income lead to a decrease in entrepreneurial activities. Schumpeter argues that these changes were the causes of the depth and duration of the Great Depression. But his arguments are somewhat tautological and he draws no verifiable hypothesis from them. His view is that economic growth occurs when the social climate is appropriate, but the only way to test whether this climate was appropriate is to see whether or not entrepreneurs appear. The views put forward here, however, do lead to a refutable hypothesis: when the distribution of wealth is expected to become more equal, the supply of entrepreneurial activity will diminish. This means, of course, that not only will the level of innovation in business and science diminish, but the level of criminal activity will diminish as well. Whether or not Schumpteter's views of the Great Depression are correct is an open question. The views and evidence presented in this chapter and later in the book support his contention. But, in contrast to Schumpeter and maybe many people, I do not always attribute a negative connotation to the decreased supply of "creativity": recall that it is suffering that makes people creative.

Today in the economic literature the term "entrepreneurship" is very much identified with the Austrian school of thought, with Israel Kirzner as its spokesman.[15] Entrepreneurs play a central role in this "Austrian economics," but again it is not very clear where the entrepreneurs come from, what is it exactly that they are doing and why. In general, this branch of economics takes no interest in explaining some facts, its concern being mainly to present a certain philosophy and to argue that mainstream economics is not the appropriate tool for analyzing industrial structures since it neglects entrepreneurs. While their criticism is valid in some respects, how can one know that "Austrian economics" is a better approach? Unfortunately, no verifiable hypothesis can be derived from this approach, nor is evidence presented by its believers.

Weber's (1904) theory of entrepreneurship and its relationship to the Protestant Ethic is well known. He argued that the Protestant dissenters who brought about the Industrial Revolution in England were motivated not merely by a desire for profits but by an ethic that required them to work harder. Rostow (1960) criticizes this approach:

> But the known cases of economic growth which theory must seek to explain take us beyond the orbit of Protestantism. In a world where Samurai, Parsees, Jews, North Italians, Turkish, Russians, and Chinese Civil Servants (as well as Huguenots, Scotsmen and British North-countrymen) have played the role of a leading elite in economic growth, John Calvin should not be made to bear quite this weight. . . . What appears to be required for the emergence of such elites is not merely an appropriate value system but . . . [the] condition . . . [that] the new elite must feel itself denied the conventional routes to prestige and power by the traditional . . . society. . . . [p. 51]

A criticism I would make pertains to the identification of causality in Weber's hypothesis. One has to ask whether or not the groups that "gambled" on the Protestant idea had in general a greater incentive to gamble. In that case, one's willingness to adopt new ideas, whether religious or entrepreneurial, is caused by another factor—a falling to the lower end of the distribution of wealth, for example. If this was the case, as Rostow seems to suggest, one cannot state that the adoption of one idea "causes" the adoption of another; what one can say is that one's readiness to "gamble" on the two types of new ideas, in religion and business, will be positively correlated. Weber's views and the emergence of the Protestant Ethic will be discussed in chapter 3.

McClelland, a social psychologist, offers yet an additional view on entrepreneurs, claiming that they are motivated by the need for achievement and not the desire for money (see McClelland 1953; for criticism of this view see Baumol 1968, and Higgins 1968), and that the entrepreneur is not someone who chooses to bear risks but one more apt to be calculating and planning. While McClelland's views on "achievement" and success (both relative concepts) seem consistent with my approach, his distinction between "personality" and the willingness to bear risks is not very clear. I would maintain that entrepreneurs have a different "personality" in that they "gamble" more frequently than other people. However, this different personality stems from a change in their position in the distribution of wealth rather than from unexplained differences in "taste."

Bert Hoselitz's (1968) observation on the importance of culturally marginal groups in promoting economic development should also be noted. His view is that marginal individuals, because of their position from a cultural and social standpoint, are more suited to make creative adjustments and develop innovations in social behavior. Hoselitz defines marginal groups as those that have been discriminated against either socially or legally. Thus his view is another particular application of the arguments presented here, for discrimination in this regard means that the members of these groups cannot expect to be in the upper strata of the distribution of wealth unless they make greater efforts than the rest of the population.

Let us now turn to Theodore W. Schultz's (1980) views on entrepreneurship. He argues that entrepreneurship depends on economic disequilibriums. While Schultz never defines precisely either disequilibriums or entrepreneurship, I suggest that this human skill is indeed supplied when a change occurs, namely, when one's relative wealth diminishes: this change can be defined as disequilibrium. These views thus seem to give greater precision to Schultz's and can be verified as well.

But Schultz makes two additional statements that do not seem to be consistent with my hypothesis and need clarification. First, he maintains that no distinction can be made between risk and uncertainty; second, he holds, that the return on entrepreneurship cannot be viewed as a return for risk-bearing. The distinction between risk and uncertainty was first made by Knight (1921), who argued that a distinction must be made between risk, as referring to events subject to a known or knowable probability distribution, and uncertainty, as referring to events for which it was not possible to specify numerical probabilities. Further, Knight argued that economic profits arise from *uncertainty* rather than risk. Economists (Friedman, Schultz, Savage) do not believe that this is a valid distinction; if my views are correct, they are wrong. Let us try to show that such a distinction is valid, that indeed economic profits can be related to uncertainty, and that Knight was thus right, albeit without either being precise or assigning any role to the distribution of wealth in his arguments.

My definition of the entrepreneurial act enables us to perceive the difference between risk and uncertainty. When one's position in the distribution of wealth is stable one still takes risks: the orange one buys might be rotten; the car one buys might turn out to be a lemon; and one might lose $500 on a bet; yet, ex post, involvement in these acts leads to no significant changes in the distribution of wealth in the economy. Moreover, the acts represent monetary rewards and probabilities that are the same for everybody. Such situations can be defined as "risky." In contrast, when one's position in the wealth distribution changes, one is more willing to undertake an act never considered before, and no comparisons can be made between different people's perception of this act. Such a situation can be defined as "uncertain."

This distinction also enables us to comprehend the meaning of "profits" in this model. When only risky activities are undertaken in the economy, the outcomes can lead only to a redistribution of wealth. Thus if one could properly measure profits they should be equal to zero in the aggregate: one individual's gain is another's loss, since wealth is only redistributed, not created. In contrast, gambling on novel ideas involves by definition the creation of new "wealth" when a lucky hit is made. An outsider would thus measure an increase in economic profits. According to this distinction, Knight (1921) was right in stating that one should distinguish between risks and uncertainty and that only the latter results in economic profits. One must note, however, that since people are more likely to gamble on new ideas when their relative wealth diminishes, the resulting profits cannot be attributed either to "greediness" or "selfishness," or be interpreted as an increase in general welfare, for it is diminished welfare to start with that leads one to gamble on novel ideas.

Finally, we should examine what psychologists have said about creativity. Horney (1945, 1950), Sullivan (1940), and Fromm (1941) summarize the achievements of Freud's theory, and although they sometimes differ in their interpretations, there is much agreement among them. Let us turn to Freud's ideas on creativity as summarized by Fromm:

> Freud accepted the traditional belief in a basic dichotomy between man and society, as well as the traditional doctrine of the evilness of human nature. Man, to him, is fundamentally antisocial. Society must domesticate him, must allow some direct satisfaction of biological—and hence, ineradicable—drives; but for the most part society must refine and adroitly check man's basic impulses. In consequence of this suppression of natural impulses by society something miraculous happens: the suppressed drives turn into strivings that are culturally valuable and thus become the human basis for culture. Freud chose the word sublimation for this strange trans-

formation from suppression into civilized behaviour. If the amount of suppression is greater than the capacity for sublimation, individuals became neurotic. . . . Generally, however, there is a reverse relation between satisfaction of man's drives and culture; the more suppression, the more culture (and the more danger of neurotic disturbances). The relation of the individual to society in Freud's theory is essentially a static one: the individual remains virtually the same and becomes changed only in so far as society exercises greater pressure on his natural drives. . . . [pp. 24–25]

The second part of this passage is close to the approach presented here; only the vocabulary is different: the view that individuals do not change their behavior unless pressured is one of the implications of my model as well (only the word "pressure" is defined differently). For pressuring an individual may mean diminishing his wealth, his relative position in the distribution of wealth, or both. These changes, as we have seen, will affect one's behavior. When no such changes are imposed, behavior may not change; the stable structures of primitive societies are a case in point. Freud's "suppressed drive" seems similar to my definition of envy, a sentiment that can be turned into something culturally valuable under the name "ambition." Both envy and ambition arise when the distribution of wealth is unequal and people make comparisons among themselves. "Sublimation" seems to be synonymous with "incentive," and the "amount of suppression" may represent either a *change* in one's relative position in the distribution of wealth or merely one's relative position there. Then, as has been shown, the more one is "suppressed" (i.e., the lower one falls in the distribution of wealth), the greater the probability that one will either commit criminal acts (a neurotic disturbance?) or gamble on new ideas and produce more "culture." It seems then that the model Freud had in mind might be similar to mine, the difference again being one of terminology.

The term "neurotic disturbance" can be interpreted additionally in terms of my views set forth in this book. One's satisfaction depends positively on one's wealth, but negatively on one's relative position in the distribution of wealth. Thus one's satisfaction in life may become negative if one's envy, hatred, or jealousy (all sentiments that are affected by some perceived inequality in the economy) become relatively strong because of a change in the distribution of wealth. In this case one could encounter irrational or totally incoherent behavior since we do not know how people with an expected negative satisfaction in life behave.

Before presenting what other psychologists have said about creativity, it should be noted that some historians share Freud's views on the relationship between culture and pressure. Toynbee (1966) writes:

Thus there is truth in what Hume and Gibbon say—and say so eloquently—in praise of disunity and in comparative disparagement of unity. Their contention is valid as far as it goes; but, if they had probed further into their historical illustrations of their thesis, they would have seen that they must qualify this thesis by making two reservations. They should have noted that intercourse between local communities following different ways of life is stimulating only where the difference in the character and level of the local cultures is not enormous. When the difference is very great, the effect of the encounter on the party which is culturally the weaker will not be stimulating; on the contrary, it will be discouraging and perhaps even paralyzing. They should also have noted that the stimulating effect of intercourse between mutually independent local communities will be worth its inevitable cost in terms of conflict only so long as the conflict remains "temperate" to cite Gibbon's word. If and when the conflict becomes violent, its "undecisiveness" will become a curse instead of a blessing, since the only way of bringing violent warfare to an end is for one of the belligerents to win a victory that will be decisive enough to enable him to give peace to his self-tormented world by imposing political unity on it. [pp. 95–96]

The similarities between Toynbee's, Freud's, and my views on the circumstances in which "culture" is produced are clear: when a group's customs are questioned, their relative wealth diminishes, since customs protect people's position in the distribution of wealth. Also, Toynbee's criticism of Hume seems correct since Hume seemed to perceive the benefits but not the costs of "disunity," while Toynbee perceives both.

Many other psychologists besides Freud have analyzed creativity and made the observation that creative people appear in particularly large numbers during certain periods of history (see Kroeber 1944, Gray 1958, 1961, and 1966, Herbert Spencer 1873, William James 1880, and Arieti 1976). The conclusion some psychologists have derived from this evidence is that some special circumstances, rather than biology or genetics, determine the occurrence of creativity,—a view consistent with mine. Yet none of them has succeeded in giving a verifiable explanation of the phenomenon of creativity.

According to James, the occurrence of genius is determined by chance. Spencer, on the other hand, concluded that before great men can make society, society must make them. White (1949), another participant in the debate, ascribes only a passive role to the individual. The approach today, as summarized by Arieti (1976), seems to be that the potential for genius is much more frequent than its actual occurrence—the question psychologists cannot answer is just what it is exactly that activates this potential.

The approach presented here seems to provide an answer. Fluctuations in one's relative position in the distribution of wealth induce one to become creative. I would hold that the following sequence of events takes place. First, a group's relative position in the distribution of wealth diminishes (because of reasons beyond their control). Consequently, the members of the group gamble more frequently on new ideas. A fraction of the population gambles on one such idea, which is perceived as a lucky hit, and the idea comes to life. And the contrary holds as well: people will become less creative when customs crystallize and the wealth distribution is expected to be maintained stable by either customs or taxation. The meaning of "history" and the question of why the West "rose" and offered a disproportionate supply of new ideas are matters that will be addressed later in the book.

Creativity: Some Facts

Epstein's (1962) study, considered by anthropologists to be one of the best of its kind, describes the following events in India: when one of two similar Indian villages received irrigation in the 1930s, the other being passed over because it was on higher ground, during the next two decades the irrigated village experienced multiple cropping and an increase in income. The residents of the "dry" village, however, entered into a "fury of innovational activity," and by the mid-1950s the economic, social, and political structure of this village had changed as well.

On a grander scale, historians have made similar observations:

> The decline of Spain in the seventeenth century is not difficult to understand. . . . Spain, as a whole . . . became considerably richer than . . . during the sixteenth century. . . . The riches of the Americas provided Spain with purchasing power but ultimately they stimulated the development of Holland, England, France, and other European countries. . . . At the end of the sixteenth century, Spain was much richer than a century earlier, but she was not more developed—"like an heir endowed by the accident of an eccentric will." . . . In the meanwhile . . . a century of artificial prosperity has induced many to abandon the land . . . schools had multiplied, but they have served mostly to produce a half educated intellectual proletariat who scorned productive industry and manual labour and found positions in the bloated state bureaucracy which served above all to disguise unemployment. Spain in the seventeenth century lacked entrepreneurs and artisans. . . . [C. Cipolla 1976, pp. 233–35]

Toynbee, in *Change and Habit* (1966), discusses evidence that is also relevant to the views set forth in this book:

> The classical Persian poetry had been written in the course of the half-millennium between the break-up of the Abbasid empire and the political reunification of Iran in the Safavi Empire. During this period, . . . in spite of the consequent insecurity of life and destruction of wealth, a fractured Iran, like a fractured Greece and Italy, excelled in the arts. [p. 93]

I would maintain, however, that it is not in spite of diminished wealth, but rather because of it that the arts have excelled. Evidence supporting this view is also noted by McNeill (1963):

> The first notable tremor in the balance between China's commercial and landed interests occurred after the Sung emperors lost north China to Jurchen invaders (1127). Thrown back upon . . . resources of the south, China in the later Sung period saw a notable development of riverine and maritime trade. Great cities arose on the south China coast and along the Yangtze; and growing numbers of merchant vessels set sail for southeast Asia and the Indian Ocean. [p. 525]

McNeill also explains why these developments halted:

> Another dimension of Chinese social evolution during these centuries goes far to explain how old values and a fundamentally agricultural frame of society proved strong enough in Ming times to prevail so strikingly over the mercantile and urban interest. For, agriculture, too, acquired vast new resources from the eleventh century onward. Nameless peasants discovered new varieties of rice that ripened in sixty days or less, allowing two crops to be grown in a single season on the same land. Moreover these early ripening varieties required less water than others, so that terraced hillsides where irrigation was possible only during the spring run-off could now successfully be turned into paddy fields. This permitted an enormous extension of the area under intensive cultivation. . . . The result was to multiply several times over the food-producing capacity of Chinese agriculture, permitting a great growth of rural population. . . . [p. 527]

Since among rural populations a greater frequency of interactions is expected among members of any particular community, it is not surprising that this period in China saw a renewed and widespread reassertion of the Confucian principles that classified merchants as necessary evils in society and provided as well a moral code concentrating on the reciprocal obligations of family members and which envisaged the state as a huge family. (The emergence of similar ideas and their role in Europe are discussed in the following chapters.) It is clear, however, that conformity with these ideas maintains the distribution of wealth at relatively stable levels, and the supply of entrepreneurs is thus expected to diminish, as it did in China.

Let us now turn to evidence on a smaller scale: the economic and social discrimination that either legally or socially constrains some groups in their choices. If the views presented here are correct, then one would expect that groups that have been discriminated against will engage disproportionately in gambling activities, whether entrepreneurial or criminal.

The evidence on the entrepreneurial activities of groups that have been previously discriminated against is presented and referenced in Hagen (1975), Ellman (1970), Kahan (1978), Sachar (1977), Sowell (1975), Kulke (1974), Karaka (1884), and McGagg (1972). Other detailed evidence will be presented and discussed in chapter 5, along with the question why some groups are more likely to gamble on entrepreneurial acts and others on criminal acts.

In brief, the available facts are as follows. In the seventeenth and eighteenth centuries economic innovation in France was correlated with the Huguenots, who were townspeople barred from membership and close association with the king's court:

> Although the Edict of Nantes gave Protestants theoretically equal rights in government service, they were actually discriminated against and were only reluctantly, and often with difficulty, admitted to government positions. Moreover, after 1661 they were formally excluded from admission to public service. Thus the large families in the Protestant centres had no incentive to invest their capital in public posts. For this reason Protestant rather than Catholic families tended to build family businesses, to train their sons for business careers, and to expand their business interests by prudent intermarriage. Since the Huguenots formed the leading elite in French business, it can easily be understood what a terrible blow was dealt to French economic growth and to French entrepreneurship by the revocation of the Edict of Nantes and the accompanying mass emigration of French Protestants. [Hoselitz 1968, p. 101]

During the English Industrial Revolution, the Protestant dissenters, a group that had been discriminated against and that constituted only 7% of the population, later provided 43% of innovating entrepreneurs.

A detailed study of Colombia by Hagen (1975) has shown that the Antioquenos, a socially discriminated group making up 40% of the population, provided 70% of entrepreneurs at the turn of the twentieth century, when the growth in population began to accelerate, although they had less formal education and lower incomes than the rest of the population before the surge in growth began.

Detailed numerical evidence on the occupational structure and income of the Parsis, a small ethnoreligious minority of less than 100,000 people in Bombay, appears in Kulke (1974) and Karaka (1884). The Parsis left Persia 1200 years ago because of religious persecution, and after some 150 years of wandering they settled in India, where various restrictions were imposed upon them. In seventeenth-century Portuguese documents they are referred to as "Jews" because they had "mental characteristics similar to the Jews." One may glean the following facts from the first census conducted by the British authorities in 1864 in Bombay: 9% of the Parsis were doctors and 20.3% were in banking, in contrast to 0.67% and 6.9% respectively for the rest of the population. In 1931 their level of literacy was 84.5% for men and 73.4% for women, in contrast to 14.4% for Hindu men and 2.1% for Hindu women. Karaka summarizes the evidence:

> When it is remembered that the Parsees at Bombay are the descendants of a small colony which emigrated from Persia in circumstances the most miserable [sic], it is a matter of some surprise . . . that this people have [sic] simultaneously with the progress of British power in India risen into affluence and importance, while the other natives of the land, Mahomedans and Hindoos, have fallen into insignificance. [p. 243]

Hagen (1975) mentions two further examples of groups that, after being discriminated against, have provided an increased number of entrepreneurs:

> In Russia, when in 1667, for diplomatic reasons, church ritual was revised to accord with Greek practice . . . [some] "Old Believers" seceded from the church, were condemned as schismatics, and from then until the Bolshevik Revolution of 1917 were persecuted now and again with varying degrees of severity. The Old Believers were prominent in the accelerating economic growth that occurred in Russia during the last half of the 19th century. . . . George B. Sansom, a . . . historian of Japan, states that "the organization of Japan at and following the Restoration of 1868 was in a great measure the work of samurai of the lower grades." [pp. 274–5]

Sowell (1975) notes that before the seventeenth century the Scots did not take part in the leading intellectual activity of Europe, and the mass of Scottish people were "illiterate and so lacking in culture that they were regarded by many as helplessly savage." But during the eighteenth and nineteenth centuries they were concentrated in trade, had better schools, enjoyed higher rates of literacy than the English, and could boast many prominent intellectuals, among them David Hume, Adam Smith, Malthus,

Mill, and Sir Walter Scott. (Other outstanding British intellectuals at the time were Edmund Burke, an Irish convert from Catholicism and Disraeli, a converted Jew). The Scots seemed to have suffered some discrimination: Adam Smith complained to the Oxford administration for its discrimination against Scottish students, while Mill tried to conceal his Scottish origin.

Jerome Handler (1979) has analyzed the activities of entrepreneurs in eighteenth-century Barbados and notes that a group of mixed racial ancestry which was discriminated against achieved relative economic success by creatively adapting to the limited opportunities that Barbados's circumscribed social order provided. It should also be noted that the Armenians, the Ibo tribe in Africa, and Chinese refugees in Southeast Asia are also frequently mentioned as groups that have been discriminated against but have also provided a disproportionate supply of entrepreneurs, although I have been unable to find detailed numerical evidence. Barry Chiswick's (1978) evidence should also be noted: he found that in the U.S. *all* immigrant groups (not only Jews), holding schooling and labor-market experience constant, have *higher* incomes than the rest of the population. Chiswick attributes the result to "entrepreneurship," which implies, since he leaves the term undefined, that for some reason new immigrants have greater abilities than the rest of the population. This is hardly an explanation, especially considering the fact that the immigrants he considers have been among the poorest of Europe. The alternative I offer is that since these groups have been among the poor classes of Europe, they had greater incentive to gamble on the idea of migration. Then, once in the U.S., the new immigrants, at first working for lower wages than similarly skilled American-born workers (as Chiswick shows), had again greater incentive to gamble on new ideas. They thus provided an increased supply of entrepreneurial activities.

The numerical evidence on Jews is probably the most widely documented and best known, and has been summarized in the works mentioned earlier by Ellman, Kahan, Sachar, and McCagg; additional evidence appears in Kuznetz (1972), Van Den Haag (1969), and Engelman (1944), and will be discussed in chapter 5.

To conclude: even if ability was symmetrically distributed around the same average for various groups, groups that have been discriminated against in the past are expected to be disproportionately represented in entrepreneurial activities, business, science, or the arts. But while this relationship between discrimination and entrepreneurial activity seems to be fairly well documented, one still has to explain the timing of the increased supply of entrepreneurs and why some groups engage in criminal "gambling" rather than business and scientific endeavors. Both issues will be dealt with extensively in a later chapter, after an analysis of why some groups have been discriminated against to begin with.

On Revolutionary Ideas

There are additional ideas that people can gamble on, namely, revolutionary ones that advocate a redistribution of wealth. This activity represents a gamble, since there is no empirical evidence available yet that could enable one to examine these ideas scientifically. For, as already shown, the institutions that may exist under one type of wealth distribution are different from those that exist under another. Thus the effects of a system of redistribution that has never been tried before, i.e., a revolutionary system, are totally unpredictable, which is what is meant here by "nonscientific."

The conditions under which individuals will gamble on revolutionary ideas that advocate a redistribution of wealth are somewhat different from the ones that govern gambling on other novel ideas, for in this case the probability that the idea will catch fire is perceived as depending on the fraction of the population whose wealth has suddenly diminished (because of hyperinflation, for example). This contrasts with the previous cases, in which the individual has gambled in order to raise himself in the prevailing distribution of wealth by his own effort rather than by relying on either revolutions or on voting patterns. (As will be shown in chapter 5, the difference in the size of various minorities that have been discriminated against may explain in part why members of some of them have gambled on entrepreneurial acts in business, science, or the arts, while members of others have gambled on entrepreneurial acts in politics in order to achieve the same goal of changing their relative position in the wealth distribution.)

This difference aside, gambling on a revolutionary idea can be compared to gambling on other ideas. Here too probabilities represent subjective beliefs, and the advantages of alternative systems of wealth distribution can only be subjectively determined. Moreover, people may gamble on revolutionary ideas even if later they are proven to be false, since at the time of the initial gamble one does not know whether or not the revolutionary ideas are true or false. Notions of truth and falsehood are in fact undefined when the ideas to which they are being applied cannot be examined empirically. Thus people are neither stupid nor wrong when they follow false prophets for a while, at least until their falsehood is proven.

The observation that individuals who instigate revolutions tend to come from groups whose relative position has worsened has been made frequently by political scientists (including Hoffer 1951, Kornhauser 1959, and Lipset 1960). Olson (1973) summarizes their evidence:

Any adequate analysis of the relationship between economic growth and revolutionary political changes must consider the problem in terms of the individuals who bring the revolutions about. Students of the sociology of revolution often argue that . . . [these] people . . . tend to be distinguished by the relative absence of bonds that tie them to the established order. . . . Those who are *declasséf30* . . . *are more apt to support revolutionary changes. . . . It is not those who are accustomed to poverty but those whose place in the social order is changing,* who resort to revolutions. [p. 546, italics added]

The view that revolutionaries find followers when the distribution of wealth changes significantly will be examined in the following chapters within well-defined historical contexts.

It may appear that the discussion in this section is a particular application of the proverb, "Necessity is the mother of invention," or, as Robert Burton put it, "Poverty is the Muse's patrimony." In fact, the first proverb seems consistent with the broader view presented in this first chapter. Bergen Evans (1978) discusses its origins:

A basic difference between Spaniards and English is illustrated by the fact that Spaniards proverbially refer to necessity as the enemy of chastity, while the English see it as the mother of invention. That is we assume that "invention" is, somehow, virtuous. The Spaniards see a danger where we see an opportunity.

If my view of human behavior is correct, there is no contradiction between these two views. Rather, they may reflect different attitudes toward changes in the distribution of wealth: one perceives its benefits—more innovation—while the other its costs—more criminal and rebellious acts.[16] Indeed, this trade-off seems to have been noted from ancient times:

It is said to have been reported to one of the Roman emperors, as a piece of good news, that one of his subjects had invented a process for manufacturing unbreakable glass. The emperor gave orders that the inventor should be put to death and that the records of his invention should be destroyed. If the invention had been put on the market, the manufacturers of ordinary glass would have been put out of business; there would have been unemployment that would have caused political unrest, and perhaps revolution; and then the World might have been thrown back into the turmoil from which the Roman world-state had salvaged it. [Toynbee 1966, p. 124]

One may ask why I have presented evidence on minorities and on large-scale historical events rather than on individuals. The reason is that the lives of creative people whose achievements are remembered are very biased sources of evidence. Suppose one found that indeed Michelangelo, Beethoven, Verdi, Van Gogh, Singer (the inventor of the sewing machine),

Marx, Einstein, Wagner, and Callas all suddenly underwent periods of intensive suffering in their lives.[17] Could their biographies be used as convincing evidence? The answer is no, for we do not remember the names of all those who may have suffered greatly but did not become creative. I have thus been obliged to look at the facts at more aggregate levels.

Conclusions

How then, shall we interpret thinking and creativity?

The answer may at first seem surprising: thinking and creativity are equivalent to gambling on novel ideas. The act of gambling, whether criminal, artistic, or scientific, is due to the perception of inequality and to sudden unexpected changes in one's position in the distribution of wealth. Or, to paraphrase a well-known *Punch* line, "What is mind? A change in wealth. What is wealth? Never mind." For, as implied by the discussion here (and as will become clearer in the next chapter), we do not know what "wealth" is. The fact that people gamble on ideas means that the perception of what constitutes wealth changes when the distribution of wealth changes. When the distribution remains stable people's perceptions may become rigid. However, under these circumstances the questions "What is mind?" and "What is wealth?" will not be raised: habit and custom will be meekly followed.

The conclusion that one cannot measure wealth does not imply that one cannot carry out rigorous empirical analysis. Rather the contrary: since one can only examine the effects of changes in wealth, one might make comparisons between two situations even if wealth is not properly measured. It is important only to measure it consistently and hope that the changes in the distribution of wealth are perceived as minor, so that there were no drastic changes in the interpretation given to the term wealth. My use of the word "hope" in a statement defining the confidence one can give to scientific analysis should not be puzzling: we all know that at all times science is on the brink of error. In fact, my approach has showed why.

As for logic, the data in this chapter have indicated that nothing is less logical than the facts. As Herman Melville wrote, "Chance has the last featuring blow at events."

Finally, one may raise the following point: we know of primitive societies that are more egalitarian than modern societies, and that modern societies were once "primitive." What then happened? Why did the distribution of wealth in the economy change? It should be emphasized that it is crucial to my argument throughout this book that this question can be answered, for according to the views presented up to now the distribution of wealth in the economy is given and people merely react to their relative position therein. But unless I explain *why* the distribution of wealth in the economy changes and how can it become less equal, I cannot claim success in shedding light on the movement from "primitive" toward "developed" societies or make comparisons between them. This is the problem that will be addressed in the next chapter.

TABLE 1.1
Survey Evidence on Lottery Expenditures

| | Estimated 1973 expenditure per family per year: | | | | | |
| | Absolute expenditure | | | As percentage of income | | |
Annual income	(1) CT	(2) MA	(3) PA	(4) CT	(5) MA	(6) PA
$ 0–$ 5,000	$22	$28	$21	.55%	.70%	.53%
$ 5,000–$10,000	33	35	35	.41%	.44%	.44%
$10,000–$15,000	43	39	36	.37%	.33%	.30%
$15,000–$25,000	34	27	30	.17%	.14%	.15%
$25,000 or more	21	17	16	.06%	.05%	.04%

Massachusetts and Connecticut: Columns (1) and (2) are approximations based on private surveys conducted by Irwin Harrison of the Decision Research Comporation during 1973 in Connecticut and 1974 in Massachusetts.

Pennsylvania: Column (6) is derived from Spiro (1974), table 1, p. 59, which is based on a 1971 survey of Pennsylvania winners. The mean expenditure for Pennsylvania is calculated as the ratio of total state sales to the number of income-receiving households, or families plus unrelated individuals, in the state in 1970.

The income figures used for the entries of columns (4), (5) and (6) are, respectively, $4,000, $8,000, $12,000, $20,000, and $37,500, arbitrary choices intended to be representative of each group.

Source: Brinner and Clotfelter (1975), table 3, p. 400.

TABLE 1.2
Survey of Winners in the Michigan Lottery

Annual income	Expenditure	Expenditure as percentage of income
$ 0–$ 5,000	$17	.65%
$ 5,000–$10,000	$35	.45%
$10,000–$12,000	$38	.35%
$12,000–$15,000	$37	.28%
$15,000–$25,000	$30	.15%

Source: Brinner and Clotfelter (1975), table 5, p. 401.

TABLE 1.3
Lottery and Bingo Participations and Family Income

| Percentage of income bet per capita | Family income | | | | | |
	Under $5,000	$ 5,000– 10,000	$10,000– 15,000	$15,000– 20,000	$20,000– 30,000	Over $30,000
Lottery	0.3	0.23	0.13	0.06	0.06	0.02
Bingo	0.49	0.64	0.18	0.07	0.06	0.04

Source: Final Report of the Commission on the Review of the National Policy Toward Gambling [1976], pp. 156, 163.

The theory of risk-aversion is frequently used in economic analysis. Yet, as Arrow (1970) himself has admitted, there is one common observation that argues against the prevalence of risk-aversion, namely, that people gamble. Arrow, and apparently most economists, have decided that although the theory is inconsistent with the facts, they may follow the strategy of the preacher (whom Arrow quotes): "Brethren, here there is a great difficulty; let us face it firmly and pass on."

There have, however, been two attempts to reconcile the phenomenon of gambling with a general predominance of risk-aversion: (1) Friedman and Savage have shown that, with some constraints on the shape of the utility function, it is possible for an individual to show risk-aversion with respect to some risks but not with respect to others. (2) It has been argued that the gambler is one who believes the odds are more favorable to him than they really are. Gambling can thus still be consistent with risk-aversion, when the risks are understood subjectively.

Both "reconciliations" have their share of problems. Alchian (1953) and Markowitz (1952) have pointed out that Friedman and Savage's suggestions, while they can "explain" the phenomena of gambling and insurance, also lead to other predictions that are inconsistent with the facts. As to the second view, that too has been contradicted: several studies of gamblers have concluded that gamblers are as aware as nongamblers of the monetary unprofitability of gambling.

The mathematical background of the theory of risk-aversion set out by Von Neuman, Morgenstern, and Arrow has become well known by now. It is based on a set of axioms that set out the conditions according to which individuals, who only maximize the utility of their wealth, should behave when facing risky outcomes. If individuals obey these axioms, they are seen as "rational" by economists.

But what if this is not how people behave? What if people do not maximize the expected utility of their wealth, and are seen to be guided by other motives? Since this question puts in doubt not only the whole theory of risk-aversion, but much of what is being done in economics in general, maybe I should immediately point out that Friedman and Savage seemed to argue in their article that it may be not wealth alone that people are after:

> Increases in income that raise the relative position of the consumer unit in its own class but do not shift the unit out of its class yield diminishing marginal utility, while increases that shift it into a new class, that give it a new social and economic status, yield increasing marginal utility. [p. 298]

This passage implies that what might matter to individuals when they face risks is not merely their wealth, but their relative position in the distribution of wealth. However, Friedman and Savage never rigorously define this statement.

This chapter has done just that. First, the utility function has been redefined and it has been shown how one's position in the distribution of wealth affects one's behavior. It has then been shown how this utility function can explain an individual both gambling and taking out insurance. In this appendix I shall give detailed proof of the arguments and I shall also show why the outcomes of games might not be ranked consistently. The distinction one must make is whether or not the outcome of the game can change one's position in the wealth distribution. If it cannot, my views can make no prediction as to how individuals might behave. If it can, however, then my approach predicts that people's attitudes toward risk depend on their position, or on their *changing* position, in the wealth distribution. This result obtains without making either particular ad hoc assumptions about the shape of the utility function, using second-order conditions, or using any sophisticated mathematical techniques (they don't play a role in the Friedman-Savage arguments, either). In this respect, I should again quote Arrow, who warned against confusing the means and the ends:

> Like Lange, the present author regards economics as an attempt to discover uniformities in a certain part of reality and not as a drawing of logical consequences from a certain set of assumptions regardless of their relevance to actuality. Simplified theory-building is an absolute necessity for empirical analysis; but it is a means not an end. [p. 21]

We should thus recall that mathematics is merely a language into which statements can be translated: it is an instrument of proof. But it can tell us nothing about economics or human behavior.

In the second section I tried to show that the same model that explains attitudes toward gambling can also explain attitudes toward crime. Again, no ad hoc assumptions have been made concerning the individual's like or dislike of inequality, or that the dislike leads to crime. Rather, one's *becoming* relatively poor has been shown to increase the likelihood of one's committing a crime that one was previously reluctant to commit.

Two questions have thus been raised: first, since gambling merely redistributes wealth, and crimes either redistribute it or destroy it, one could conclude that the trait of human nature postulated here has no survival value. It is thus important to show that this trait *does* have benefits. In the last section it was shown that indeed, the same trait of human nature that leads us to gamble and commit crimes also leads us to "think," i.e., to "gamble" on novel ideas and become "creative," "productive," or "entrepreneurial," although, as was shown, increased creativity (i.e., more frequent gambling on ideas) is a result of increased misery. The conclusions have been simple: necessity (and not money) is the mother of invention, and, in a broad sense, there is no such thing as a free lunch. For the perception of inequality carries with it not only costs (criminal acts) but benefits as well (entrepreneurial acts).

The second question is equally important. Granted people's position in the wealth distribution has a powerful effect on human behavior. But since it is all a game, why pursue this unhappy strategy? Why should not people cooperate, gamble on customs that maintain the wealth distribution stable, and thus check the wastefulness of gambling? I will address this point in chapter 2, where I hope to show that people have done precisely that—when populations are small and people live in relatively isolated locations. Today such societies are called "primitive." But, once population increases and fluctuates, for reasons beyond human control such cooperation is no longer feasible, and the result is the increased "gambling" activity that is today a chief characteristic of what we call "civilization." Before examining this matter in detail, however, let us turn to the formal proofs for the statements in the first chapter.

Wealth Distribution and Attitudes Toward Risk

In contrast to the theory of risk-aversion one is accustomed to meeting in economics, a theory wherein attitudes toward risks depend only on some abstract conditions governing the shape of the utility function, the theory presented here shows how these attitudes depend on the shape of the wealth distribution in the economy and on the unexpected changes that might occur in one's position in the wealth distribution. However, I must immediately point out that the kind of risks my arguments deal with are those in which the outcomes can significantly change one's position in the wealth distribution. I have nothing to say about the risks of buying a rotten tomato, of parking illegally, or of losing one hour in a physician's office—risks whose outcomes are too small to affect one's position in the wealth distribution.

I assume that the utility function $U(\cdot,\cdot)$ is a function of the individual's expected wealth W_o, and the percentage of people in the economy whose wealth is greater than W_o, $\alpha(W > W_o)$,[18] given that $\alpha(\cdot)$ is his expected position in the wealth distribution:

(1) $$U = U(W_o, \alpha(W > W_o)|\alpha(\cdot))$$

Thus an individual's satisfaction is assumed to depend on both his absolute wealth and on his relative position in the distribution of wealth. As usual, I assume that if other people's wealth remains constant, utility increases when wealth increases:

(2) $$U_1 = \frac{\partial U}{\partial W_o} > 0$$

where U_1 denotes the marginal utility of wealth. I also assume that an increase in the percentage of people whose wealth is greater than one's own decreases one's utility:

(3) $$U_2 = \frac{\partial U}{\partial \alpha} < 0$$

U_2 represents the change in one's utility when one's position in the wealth distribution changes, for example, when everybody else becomes relatively richer.

The sign of U_1 represents the usual assumption of the marginal utility of wealth being positive. The second assumption implies that when one's relative wealth diminishes, even though one's absolute wealth stays constant, one's utility diminishes. This change may be understood as being the result of envy or ambition, but an even clearer interpretation is possible.

On occasion, economists have argued that inequality or some measure of wealth distribution has a direct effect on people's behavior, or that one's consumption patterns depend on one's neighbors ("keeping up with the Joneses"). Easterlin (1974) has argued for the first assumption, and presented evidence that people's happiness is not a function of absolute wealth, but of relative wealth: in spite of the fact that wealth has increased over the years, the proportion of people considering themselves happy and unhappy has remained unaltered. The relative income hypothesis is well known in the economic literature, but its implications for behavior in situations involving risk have never been examined, although, as quoted in the introduction, Friedman and Savage seemed to have argued for some type of relative income hypothesis (see also Duesenberry 1949 and Veblen 1899).

Yet it is Knight's (1921, 1935) general approach that comes closest to the one presented here. Knight argues that one can distinguish between uncertainty and risk, a distinction some economists have been skeptical of, but which is nevertheless possible according to my approach. Second, Knight argues that human consciousness is related to uncertainty—a statement that appears to be mathematically correct in the last section of this appendix. Finally, Knight seems to view most aspects of life as a game in which luck and chance are important. The game ceases to be interesting, according to Knight, if there is too great a difference in the ability or wealth of players; he thus explains why hunters who consider themselves sportsmen always give their quarry a chance. Let us turn now to the formal proofs.

Gambling on Lotteries

I shall attempt now to show that from this utility function (which is cardinal, and which represents a probability function), and the assumption that the individual seeks to maximize his expected utility, it is possible to derive testable implications on who will engage in a gamble, even if it is probabilistically unfair, without making strong assumptions on the shape of the utility function: the utility function may be linear in its two components.

Suppose that the individual possesses wealth W_o. This represents the amount one expects to own by engaging in customary behavior. The percentage of the population whose wealth is greater than one's own is $\alpha(W > W_o)$. Assume that the individual is faced with a gamble in which he has a probability p of winning a large net amount, H, and a probability $(1 - p)$ of losing a smaller amount of money, h, the price of the lottery ticket. What is meant by "large" amount of money is a sum large enough to change the individual's place in the distribution of wealth. With regard to gambles that have maximum prizes that do not achieve this goal I cannot say anything.

If the consumer wins the gamble, his utility will be $U(W_o + H, \alpha(W > W_o + H))$. If he loses, his utility will be $U(W_o - h, \alpha(W > W_o - h))$. The individual makes the gamble if his current utility is less than the expected utility he would have if he gambled. Formally this statement means:

$$(4) \quad p\,U(W_o + H, \alpha(W > W_o + H)) + (1 - p)\,U(W_o - h, \alpha(W > W_o - h))$$
$$> U(W_o, \alpha(W > W_o))$$

In order to simplify the notation, I have omitted the statement that $\alpha(\cdot)$ denotes one's expected position in the wealth distribution. Assume that $U(\cdot,\cdot)$ is linear in both of its components, that is:

(5) $$U = a\,W_o + b\,\alpha(W > W_o)$$

Then from (4) one obtains:

(6) $pa\,W_o + paH + pb\alpha(W > W_o + H) + (1-p)a\,W_o - (1-p)\,ah$

   $+\ (1-p)b\alpha(W > W_o - h) > aW_o + b\alpha\,(W > W_o)$

Assume that the gamble is fair, i.e., $pH = (1-p)h$. Then from (6) one obtains that, in order for an individual to participate in a gamble,

(7) $pb\alpha(W > W_o + H) + (1-p)\,b\alpha(W > W_o - h) > b\,\alpha(W > W_o)$

Since $b < 0$, one obtains:

(8) $p\,\alpha(W > W_o + H) + (1-p)\,\alpha(W > W_o - h) < \alpha(W > W_o)$

If h, the price of the lottery ticket, is small relative to W_o and H, so that losing it does not change one's position in the wealth distribution (a \$5 ticket could hardly do that when there are 200 million people in the economy), then $\alpha(W > W_o - h) \simeq \alpha\,(W > W_o)$, and from (8) one obtains:[19]

(9) $$\alpha(W > W_o + H) < \alpha(W > W_o)$$

which only implies that the prize H must be large enough so that the percentage of people who possess wealth greater than $W_o + H$ is less than those who possess wealth greater than W_o. This calculation gives precision to Friedman and Savage's arguments concerning individuals who move into a "higher class." But while their results were due to an abstract assumption about the shape of the utility function, here the shape of the utility function is explained as being due to an unequal distribution of wealth.

Here is a simple numerical example that illustrates this proof: suppose that in a society 50% of the population expect wealth of \$100,000, 30% expect wealth of \$300,000, 10% expect \$400,000, and 10% expect \$500,000. Suppose that everybody's utility function in the economy is

(5a) $$U = W_o - b\,\alpha(W > W_o) \qquad b < 0$$

The poorest people's utility function is then:

(5b) $$U = W - 0.5b$$

since 50% of the population is richer. Suppose that the fair gamble costs $5 and one can gain $300,000 (i.e., $(1-p) \, 300,000 = 5$). It then results that one's expected utility, EU, from participating in this gamble is

(7a) $$EU = p(W - 5 - 0.5b) + (1-p) (W - 5 + 300,000 - 0.1b)$$
$$= W - 0.5pb - 0.1(1-p)b$$

This term is greater than the utility of the poor if they do not gamble if

(8a) $$W - 0.5pb - 0.1(1-p)b > W - 0.5b$$

This inequality is fulfilled since $0.1 < 0.5$.

If the gamble is unfair, the conditions for participation are somewhat more complex: in addition to the shape of the wealth distribution, they now also depend on how unfair the gamble is, and on the magnitude of the marginal utility of wealth relative to the utility of significantly changing one's position in the wealth distribution. For an unfair gamble means that $pH < (1-p)h$. Thus from (6) one obtains:

(7b) $$pb\alpha(W > W_o + H) + (1-p)b\alpha(W > W_o - h)$$
$$- b\alpha(W > W_o) > a(1-p)h - pa \, H$$

If h is relatively small $\alpha(W > W_o - h) \simeq \alpha (W > W_o)$, and we obtain:

(7c) $$b[p\alpha(W > W_o + H) - p\alpha (W > W_o)] > a[(1-p)h - pH]$$

The term $-(\alpha(W > W_o + H) - \alpha(W > W_o))$ equals the percentage of people whose wealth is between W_o and $W_o + H$, which we will denote by $\alpha(W_o + H > W > W_o)$. Since b is negative, the sign of the left-hand term is positive. The inequality in this case depends on more than just the shape of the wealth distribution. It also depends on the relative magnitudes of a and b, which reflect respectively one's marginal utility of wealth and one's "envy" or "ambition," on how unfair the gamble is, and on how significantly the prize enables one to move above others in the wealth distribution. Yet, as will be shown later, these coefficients play no role when we compare an individual's actions at different levels of wealth.

Would people gamble if there was an equal distribution of wealth in a society, and customs or tax laws existed that were expected to maintain wealth at equal levels in spite of fluctuations in some people's wealth because of different abilities or chance? If such customs did exist in a society, then $\alpha(W > W_o) = 0$ and $U = aW_o$. Thus, as long as such customs are expected to be enforced so that any variations in some people's wealth are expected to be either redistributed or compensated for, there is no rationale for the market of gambling to exist. This market emerges, in my model, only when the wealth distribution becomes unequal.

This conclusion does not imply that in more egalitarian societies people will not play games of chance: they will. These games, however, will have entertainment value rather than value for changing one's position in the wealth distribution.

On Taking Out Insurance

I shall now try to show that individuals who gamble may also insure themselves, and for the same reason: an attempt to prevent a change in their position in the wealth distribution. Again, it must be reemphasized that my model can say nothing about insurance when small amounts are involved, as in stocking up on food at home in order to diminish the risk (and cost) of suddenly having to run to the store, or buying a number of books in case one becomes bored, and so forth. The type of insurance my model can deal with involves amounts that can significantly change one's (or one's offspring's) position in the wealth distribution, such as life insurance, home insurance, fire insurance, and so forth.

Assume that there is a small probability, p, of losing a large amount H (because of fire, for example), and a great probability $(1 - p)$ of retaining the initial sum (if fire does not occur). The consideration for taking out a fair or an unfair insurance policy at a price h, which compensates the individual if the unfortunate event occurs, is similar to the condition for the participation in a fair or unfair gamble (the "unfairness" representing now the insurance premium):

$$(10) \quad U(W_o - h, \alpha(W > W_o - h)) > pU(W_o - H, \alpha(W > W_o - H))$$
$$+ (1 - p) \, U(W_o, \alpha(W > W_o))$$

from which it follows that the same individuals who gamble also insure themselves, and do both for the same reasons: either to change or to avoid changing their relative position in the distribution of wealth.

Again, one may ask, When is it more likely that insurance markets will rise? The answer is that an unequal distribution of wealth leads to the emergence of these markets. Assume that customs exist whereby people provide one another with a wide range of assurances. In a society where such customs are expected to be enforced, insurance will simply take the form of close ties among the members of the group rather than formal markets. As will be shown in chapter 2, insurance established by customs rather than markets is more likely to succeed where the population is relatively small and stable.

Who Is More Likely to Gamble?
Who Is More Likely to Take out Insurance?

When one's relative position in the wealth distribution falls, one's incentive to gamble increases. The proof is simple: assume that when one's expected wealth was W_o one did not gamble:

(11)
$$U(W_o, \alpha(W > W_o)) > pU(W_o - h, \alpha(W > W_o - h)) +$$
$$(1-p) \, U(W_o + H, \alpha(W > W_o + H))$$

What is the necessary condition for this individual to gamble on this lottery when his wealth diminishes? Let us assume that his wealth diminishes unexpectedly, that is, $W_1 < W_o$. Then, in order to take part in the game that he was previously reluctant to play, the inequality in (11) must be reversed:

(12)
$$U(W_1, \alpha(W > W_1)|W_1 < W_o) < pU(W_1 - h, \alpha(W > W_1 - h)|W_1 < W_o) +$$
$$(1-p) \, U(W_1 + H, \alpha(W > W_1 + H)|W_1 < W_o)$$

(For the sake of simplicity, the $\alpha(\cdot)s$ were omitted from the conditional statements.) Under what conditions concerning the distribution of wealth in the economy will this "taste" for gambling emerge? For both (11) and (12) to hold true, the following inequality must also hold true (for the sake of simplicity I now omit the conditional statements):

(13)
$$U(W_o, \alpha(W > W_o)) - U(W_1, \alpha(W > W_1)) >$$
$$p[U(W_o - h, \alpha(W > W_o - h) -$$
$$U(W_1 - h, \alpha(W > W_1 - h))] + (1-p) \,]U(W_o + H, \alpha(W > W_o + H))$$
$$- U(W_1 + H, \alpha(W > W_1 + H))]$$

Let $\Delta W = W_o - W_1$ and let us continue to assume that the utility function is linear in both of its components. We then obtain:

(14)
$$a \, \Delta W + b(\alpha(W > W_o) - \alpha(W > W_1)) > p[a \, \Delta W + b(\alpha(W > W_o - h)$$
$$- \alpha(W > W_1 - h))] + (1-p) \, [a \, \Delta W + b \, (\alpha(W > W_o + H)$$
$$- \alpha(W > W_1 + H))]$$

Assuming that the gamble is fair (that is, $ph = (1-p)H$) and that h is relatively small and the population large enough, $\alpha(W > W_o) \simeq \alpha(W > W_o - h)$, we obtain:

(15) $(1-p) [\alpha(W > W_o) - \alpha(W > W_1)] < (1-p) [\alpha(W > W_o + H)$

$\qquad - \alpha(W > W_1 + H)]$

or

(16) $\alpha(W > W_1) - \alpha(W > W_o) > \alpha(W > W_1 + H) - \alpha(W > W_o + H)$

a condition which requires only that as wealth increases the fraction of people in each additional range of H diminish. In everyday terms this result means that there is a small upper class, a larger upper middle class, a still larger middle class and lower middle class, and some fraction of poor, a wealth distribution pattern that seems to characterize most countries with large populations.

Even if one drops the assumption that U_1 is constant and assumes that the marginal utility of wealth is either increasing or diminishing, the aforementioned results can be obtained, although in this case something must be assumed concerning the magnitude of changes in this marginal utility. At the same time if one assumes that U_2 changes as well (one becomes more envious when one becomes poorer), this change may offset the changes in U_1. But since both conditions are not at all interesting (if one does not know anything about utility functions, mulling over assumptions concerning the shape of such a function cannot lead to any testable implication) they are not presented.

It should be reemphasized that when one is "outdone" by one's fellows one is more likely to start gambling. This result demonstrates how in this model individuals can "change their minds," and shows as well that the change does not require any statement about changing the "utility function"—the function stays the same; only one's position in the wealth distribution is altered.

This result has one further implication. In contrast to the "risk-aversion" theory, one of whose axioms is that bets must be ranked, the model here implies that one must distinguish between two types of games and one cannot really infer from the preferences given to one type of game what the preference will be with respect to the other. One of the implications of the expected utility theorem is presented in Arrow (1970):

> If it is preferable to bet one event rather than another with given prizes for winning and losing, then the same preference should manifest itself if the prizes are altered, as long as the prize for winning is preferred to that for losing. This conclusion is an obvious impli-

cation of the Expected Utility Theorem, for a bet on E_1, with prizes c^*, c_* is preferred to a bet on E_2 with the same prizes if and only if

$$P(E_1) U(c^*) + [1 - P(E_1)] U(c_*) > P(E_2) U(c^*) + [1 - P(E_2)]U(c_*)$$

which is obviously equivalent to the statement $P(E_1) > P(E_2)$ provided $U(c^*) > U(c_*)$. Changing the prizes does not alter the ordering among bets. [p. 70]

In my model this conclusion might be incorrect. Suppose that one were faced with a gamble with a prize of $5 million and a loss $5 million, each with a probability of .5. Suppose that this gamble is preferred to the one where these two prizes would occur with probabilities .25 and .75 respectively. This preference will tell nothing about what one's attitudes might be toward gambles where the sums involved are $50 or − $50 respectively. Since these outcomes do not change one's position in the wealth distribution, the attitude toward this gamble depends only on the local characteristics of the derivative of the marginal utility of wealth (U_1). If it is increasing, people may play the .25/.75 game. To put this statement in everyday language, if one is in a "good mood" while in Las Vegas, one might play this game. Yet not even in Las Vegas will an average person (i.e., not a multimillionaire) play the previous game involving millions.

Although never stated precisely, Allais's (1979) views on how attitudes toward risk are formed, the "paradox" that he raises, should be mentioned. First, Allais argues that psychological factors should be introduced into any theory of attitude toward risk. While he never defines what exactly he means by "psychological factors," if survival, envy, and ambition are such factors then it seems that this model goes one step toward the direction Allais argues for. Moreover, the proposition that when one loses part of one's wealth one is more likely to gamble can easily be translated to "psychological" terms such as dissatisfaction with current work or current income. Indeed, several psychologists who have analyzed gambling behavior have arrived at the conclusion that gambling behavior is well correlated with a gambler's dissatisfaction at work and that dissatisfaction with current income is a strong explanation of lottery ticket buying. What the model here achieves is lending greater precision to the vague "psychological" jargon mentioned above.

Second, Allais argues that answers to questionnaires contradict the assumptions of a consistent ordering of games, which is one of the axioms of the von Neumann-Morgenstern structure. The answers were labeled "Allais's Paradox." But does this paradox exist? Allais's questionnaires did not refer to actual games. Since what people say or do in laboratories and what they do in real life are two completely different things, one must be skeptical of the interpretations given the questionnaires. (One should keep in mind the example of how differently people behave in military games as compared to wars). How people would behave if Allais's games existed is a very different matter.

Finally, it should be mentioned that the views presented here shed light on the Saint Petersburg paradox, which gave rise to the diminishing marginal utility hypothesis. The model explains in a straightforward way why finite amounts will be paid for participation in a game, without assuming declining marginal utility of wealth, since the richer one becomes the smaller one's incentives to gamble become.

Gambling on Criminal Acts

To commit a crime is risky: one might be caught and punished, or one might get away with it. The sorts of crimes analyzed here will be those against property where monetary rewards are possible or where destroying others' wealth, with a significant effect on wealth distribution, is possible.

Before presenting the predictions that can be derived from this model on the likelihood of people committing crimes, it is useful to say a few words on what the term "crime" means.

The word does not have a precise meaning. Terrorist movements frequently refer to themselves as "liberation armies." Are they criminals or are they freedom fighters? It seems that what constitutes a crime depends on whether or not people agree with the present distribution of wealth. When the majority accepts the channels by which wealth is redistributed (markets, governments, family ties, and so forth), there is agreement as to what "crime" means.

Let us assume that there is agreement in the society as to what constitutes a crime. Who are the people most likely to commit crimes in such a society? Let G be the value of punishment if one commits a crime, and let H be the "prize" if one gets away without punishment. W_o denotes one's initial wealth and p the probability of being caught. The expected satisfaction from this crime, denoted by EU, is:

$$(17) \qquad EU = pU(W_o - G, \alpha(W > W_o - G))$$
$$+ (1-p)U(W_o + H, \alpha(W > W_o + H))$$

The sum on the right-hand side shows the expected outcome: the first term of being caught and the second of being undetected. Assume that one did *not* commit this crime when one's expected position in the wealth distribution was represented by $\alpha(\cdot)$:

$$(18) \qquad U(W_o, \alpha(W > W_o)) > EU .$$

Now let us assume either that one's wealth diminishes to W_1 or one's wealth remains constant, but that everybody else who enters into the definition of $\alpha(\cdot)$ suddenly becomes richer. Then the individual who becomes relatively poorer is more likely to commit the crime that he previously was reluctant to and the inequality in (18) may be reversed (holding probabilities, punishments, and gains from stealing constant), for the condition for this change of mind is (still assuming the same linear utility function as before, and making the same calculations as in (14)):

$$(19) \qquad \alpha(W_o > W > W_1) > (1-p)\,\alpha(W_o + H > W > W_1 + H)$$
$$+ p\,\alpha(W_o - G > W > W_1 - G)$$

which requires that the fraction of people within the same difference in wealth (ΔW) diminish quickly in the range of outcomes of the contemplated crime. The meaning of this condition is clear: $\alpha(W_o > W > W_1)$ denotes the fraction of people who have suddenly outdone our individual. The term on the right-hand side denotes the fraction of people who, on average, would outdo him if he undertook the risk. If this average is smaller than $\alpha(\cdot)$, then the individual will now undertake the risk that he was previously reluctant to.

It thus follows that people who begin to commit crimes are those who have become poor. This view of criminal acts also suggests a remedy for them: if in an economy either custom or progressive tax laws exist according to which those whose wealth diminishes can expect to receive prompt compensation, then the crime rate will diminish. Or, if inequality is lessened, the crime rate can be expected to be smaller.

Unfortunately, as we shall see in the next section, there is no such thing as a free lunch, and while promises for maintaining inequality at a stable level diminish the incentive to gamble and to commit crimes, they simultaneously diminish what most of us seem to attribute virtue to: creativity.

Creativity or the Entrepreneurial Trait

In spite of the fact that the meaning given to the utility function is that of a probability of survival, until now I have shown merely that the trait of human nature postulated here is costly and has thus no survival value, for gambling and crime either redistribute or destroy wealth. Thus, in order to complete the picture and support my assertions, it must be shown that the trait postulated here is also beneficial. In this section I hope to show that this trait leads human beings to come up with novel ideas in business, science, the arts, technology, and the organization of social institutions. The supply of novel ideas increases when either a group's relative wealth diminishes or the human population's total wealth diminishes (simultaneously with a change in the distribution). This trait provides the individual's or the human race's means for survival and enables them to maintain "wealth" per capita (on average) at a stable level, although the perception of what constitutes wealth changes significantly.

It can be argued that gambling is an activity that is not related solely to games but to *all* activities in which returns depend on luck rather than on specific skills or already available information. Since this is a characteristic of gambling, betting on an idea for which no empirical evidence yet exists also represents a gamble, although I shall emphasize below the differences between this kind of gamble and the one embodied in a lottery.

Let P denote the amount invested in developing an idea, which besides the direct costs of investment in time and other resources necessary to develop it, also includes the resources invested in trying to estimate the potential demand for the idea and its applications. Let $\alpha(W > W_o)$ again represent the percentage of the relevant population above one's wealth, W_o, and let H denote the increase in wealth that one expects to gain by selling an idea. If unsuccessful, with a probability p, the potential innovator knows that he will lose the amount P (which includes losses due to diminished reputation). Translated to mathematical notation, the conditions for an individual to become an entrepreneur, that is to "bet" on a new idea for which no empirical evidence exists with which to test it when he begins working on it, is similar to the conditions that lead one to gamble on a criminal act:

$$(20) \qquad U(W_o, \alpha(W > W_o)) < pU(W_o - P, \alpha(W > W_o - P))$$
$$+ (1-p)\, U(W_o + H, \alpha(W > W_o + H))$$

Let me emphasize the significant differences between this condition and the one that defines participation in a lottery, in spite of the similarity in the mathematical formulation. Here the value of the "prize" H differs among individuals: both people's evaluations of the potential demand for home computers and the solution of open problems in science are subjective. Also, probability here represents a subjective judgment by an individual and there is no way to prove that he is right or wrong. This contrasts with lotteries, where probabilities are defined in terms of processes that can be repeated many times. In this sense one can make a distinction between uncertainty, a situation in which probabilities are subjective and no comparisons can be made among individuals, and risk, wherein comparisons can be made since every individual faces the same probability distribution.

In spite of these important differences between the two types of gambling, the following conclusion can be drawn: when one's relative wealth drops, one has a greater incentive to gamble on novel ideas. This conclusion is thus similar to the one obtained in the previous section, and the proof is exactly the same. Assume that one did *not* gamble on a novel idea, but merely followed custom and habit, so that the sign of the inequality in (20) is reversed. When one's wealth diminishes relatively, holding probabilities, costs, benefits, and the wealth distribution constant, one is more likely to contemplate an idea that one previously dismissed.

Gambling on revolutionary ideas that advocate a redistribution of wealth can be discussed separately, since the mathematical conditions governing this situation differ from the condition that defines gambling on other new ideas.

Let W_o denote one's initial wealth, when one was reluctant to contemplate gambling on a revolutionary idea:

$$(21) \quad a W_o + b\alpha(W > W_o) > pa(W_o - P) + pb\alpha(W > W_o - P)$$
$$+ (1-p) a W_R + (1-p) b\alpha(W > W_R)$$

where P denotes the punishment and costs of investing in the revolutionary act and W_R denotes the expected wealth if the revolution succeeds. By p we may denote the subjective probability given to the revolution's lack of success.

Assume now that one's wealth diminishes but that the wealth distribution in the society does not change. Then the condition one obtains for the gamble is similar to the one on gambling on any new idea. However, if a significant percentage of the population loses its wealth (because of unexpected hyperinflation, for example), the probability that many people will be ready to change their minds increases. For the change in mind to take place, the inequality in (21) must be reversed. Let $1-p_1$, denote the subjective probability given to the revolution's success, where $p_1 < p$, and we obtain:

$$(22) \quad a W_1 + b\alpha(W > W_1) < p_1 a(W_1 - P) + p_1 b\alpha(W > W_1 - P)$$
$$+ (1-p_1)a W_R + (1-p_1)b\alpha(W > W_R)$$

For both (21) and (22) to be fulfilled one obtains:

$$(23) \quad a(W_o - W_1) - b\alpha(W_o > W > W_1) >$$
$$> a(pW_o - p_1 W_1) + a(p_1 - p)P +$$
$$+ b[p\alpha(W > W_o - P) - p_1\alpha(W > W_1 - P)]$$
$$+ (p_1 - p) [a W_R + b\alpha(W > W_R)]$$

where $(p_1 - p)$ is negative. Since the last term in brackets denotes the expected satisfaction if the revolution succeeds, and $(p_1 - p)$ is negative, the whole last term is negative. Thus a revolutionary idea that advocates a redistribution of wealth in favor of the group whose relative wealth has diminished (i.e., diminished $\alpha(W > W_R)$) always has a greater appeal when a group's position is disproportionately worsened, for the probability that the inequality is reversed increases. In conclusion, when a significant group becomes *declassé*, the probability increases that ideas advocating a redistribution of wealth in its favor will gain currency.

On Dynamic Equilibrium

A few words should be said on the meaning of the dynamic equilibrium in the model. One may ask, Even if it is true that losing $5 when one buys a lottery ticket will not change one's attitude toward risks (and one is thus in "equilibrium"), what happens if one buys 100, 1,000, or more tickets? When does one stop buying them? The answer to these questions is that once an individual has lost a relatively large amount through unfair games of chance (supposing that he began playing because he unexpectedly lost part of his wealth), he will perceive that he cannot restore his position in the wealth distribution by gambling. He may thus gamble on an entrepreneurial act: either making greater efforts at work or committing a crime. These possibilities represent the dynamic equilibrium in the model.

No numerical evidence yet exists that can verify the view that when people lose relatively large amounts by gambling they change their behavior and gamble on entrepreneurial acts. However, it is interesting to note that Dostoyevski wrote *The Gambler* in order to pay for his gambling debts. If the views here are found to be convincing, perhaps data will be gathered and attempts will be made to either verify or disprove my views with precision.

Conclusions

The results obtained here have been deduced from the assumption that people do their utmost to ensure their self-preservation. In contrast to traditional economic theory, the mathematical proofs have been very simple and neither first- nor second-order conditions have been explicitly used, since infinitesimal changes and marginal conditions play no role in my model. Yet the predictions that have been derived have been clear cut and, as shown in the text, strongly supported by the evidence.

Finally, it is useful to note that Arrow (1970), commenting on Knight's distinction between uncertainty and risk, writes:

[Knight] asserts as a basic theorem that if all risks were measurable, then risk-aversion would not give rise to any profit. . . . The argument is that, in that case, the law of large numbers would permit the wiping-out of all risks through insurance or some other form of consolidation of cases. This proposition, if true, would appear to be of the greatest importance; yet, surprisingly enough, not a single writer, as far as I know, with the exception of Hicks has mentioned it, and he denies its validity. [p. 30]

A very simple proof of Knight's proposition has been given above.

2

Trust, Population, and Wealth; or, Why Did Cain Kill Abel?

We swallow lies all day long, thanks to a press which is the shame of this country. Any idea, any definition, which risks adding to this lie or to maintain it is unpardonable today, so that in defining a certain number of key words, in rendering them sufficiently clear today so that they can serve tomorrow . . . we are doing our job.

ALBERT CAMUS

In the previous chapter I suggested that an unexpected increase in population changes the distribution of wealth and is thus likely to lead to an increase in criminal, revolutionary, and innovative ideas. But where do these novel ideas lead? In this chapter I shall argue that the emergence of agriculture, of the institutions of the market, of the legal system and of literacy can be viewed as adaptations that human populations have gambled on in response to their increased numbers and the resulting changes in both incentive and in the distribution of wealth.

The mechanism behind these adaptations can be explained as follows. Suppose that the population suddenly increases. This has the effect of diminishing wealth per capita and of changing the distribution of wealth, thus increasing the incentive to gamble on novel ideas. These ideas will be implemented when one individual "hits" on an idea on which the rest of the population gambles. Here I shall argue that it is likely that when the population increases, the new ideas that people will gamble on will involve not only technological innovations but also those organizational rules and structures that substitute contracts and law for trust and customs.

Kinship plays a major role in the allocation and distribution of resources today, but in primitive societies it played an even greater role. The way in which members of primitive societies have interacted, and the implicit contracts through which they have regulated their behavior stand in contrast to today's legally binding contracts of exchanges among strangers. Little attention has been paid to *why* this transition is taking place. Instead, attempts have been made to divide human cultures into sharply delimited sets representing stages of economic development or evolution, and to define these stages on the basis of exchanges carried out in formal markets. Technology has been considered an exogenous variable, and technological changes have been envisioned as revolutionary spurts, a result of some unexplained trait of human nature. The anonymous market mechanism has at times been seen as offering such significant and obvious economic advantages to human populations that once the appropriate level of knowledge of its functioning has been achieved, it has been assumed that its acceptance would be axiomatic. Recent researchers have in part challenged this picture, and the emphasis now is on the high costs to individuals when they try to obtain information on either prices, the qualities of goods exchanged, or the trustworthiness of the partners in exchange.

Yet in spite of the systematic transition from economies in which most exchanges are carried out among kin to economies in which they are more impersonal, the question of how and why human behavior patterns are modified was not raised. What seems to be needed, then, is a theory that can account for some widespread similarities in the structure of primitive societies, for the similarities and differences that occur when these societies make the transition to a "modern" economy, and for the timing of the transition. I shall argue that the maintenance of a small population could account for the similarities in the structure of primitive societies, and that growth in population could account for the similarities in patterns of development. I hope to show that fluctuations in population could be the factor that makes it necessary for human beings to gamble on a wide range of similar ideas, such as exchange outside bonds of kinship, augmenting food supply by agricultural and industrial methods, technological innovations in general, the development of literacy, revolutionary ideas, and the introduction of institutional changes, changes that today define economic development or Westernization. The differences among primitive societies and among patterns of development can be attributed to the random mechanism called "thinking" that was outlined in the previous chapter.

Linking human behavior to changes in population (more precisely, to changes in the frequency of interactions between any two individuals) has these additional advantages: it plausibly links the incentive to invest time and resources in getting to know somebody with expectations for a stable community size; it shows how more exchanges are based on trust and honor when one expects to interact frequently with the same people; it sheds light on the structure of laws and customs of societies today labeled "primitive" and on the changes that occur in legislation when population increases; and it suggests that some of the social institutions of an economy based on anonymous exchange substitute for the trust that prevails among trading partners when the number of people with whom one expects to deal is relatively small. Indeed, the terms "impersonal" and "anonymous" only have meaning when one deals with economies with relatively large populations. The distinction between "primitive" and "developed" economies is that the structure of the first represents an adaptation to a small, relatively stable population, while the structure of the latter represents an adaptation to a fluctuating but nevertheless rising population, an adaptation that occurs through the gambling process discussed in the previous chapter.

In support of the view that the structure of primitive societies can be understood as a sucessful adaptation to a situation in which people expect to carry out most of their exchanges with a relatively small and stable population, I shall present evidence that challenges some of the traditional views of primitive societies. This evidence consists of the following points:

1. The picture of primitive societies as existing near starvation and struggling for adequate food supplies has been challenged by an increasing number of studies, the most recent one being Cohen's *Food Crisis in Prehistory* (1977), which summarizes the arguments and the very extensive evidence. He concludes that the food basis of hunting and gathering societies was both of a higher quality and a more secure one for thousands of years than the one provided by agriculture. Thus it is not ignorance but lack of incentive that explains why some relatively isolated groups did not explore agricultural technologies. Cohen presents a wide range of archeological and other evidence that suggests that it is the increase in population that leads people to gamble on agriculture as the means of producing food. He also suggests that much of what we think of as progress is actually a regaining of standards that were widely enjoyed during prehistoric times.

2. At times features of primitive societies have been explained away not only by the inaccurate assumption that they always face the risk of hunger, but by the assumption that innovation has not arisen because the private gain to be had from it is small, that these gains could not be appropriated, or that for some reason literacy has not developed. But these views seem to be contradicted by the evidence, which shows that ideas have in fact been appropriated and that "patents" have been protected by custom. Thus one has to find reasons other than lack of appropriation for the relatively smaller supply of original ideas in these societies and for their conservatism. As I stated in the previous chapter, the smaller supply of novel ideas in these societies can be attributed to the expectation that the stability of the wealth distribution will be maintained.

3. The arguments and evidence on literacy, which is a particular technological innovation, suggest that literacy becomes more valuable when population becomes larger and trade more anonymous. Thus literacy too cannot be cited as a reason why some societies remain primitive. The evidence suggests that people have a greater incentive to gamble on lit-

eracy when their numbers increase; when their numbers diminish literacy may die out. The evidence also shows that literacy is indeed a gamble: it has many unexpected costs as well as benefits.

4. Features of primitive societies have at times also been attributed to their lack of effective government. Again, the evidence in this and the next chapter shows that the shift toward a larger role for government occurs when population increases. When population either diminishes or is relatively small, governments play smaller roles: customs, religion, and family ties substitute for them. The reason for this feature is clear: when people expect to interact within relatively small and isolated communities, trust, honor, religion, or the stability of human sentiments can diminish contract uncertainty and can substitute for those institutions that today serve the same goal: insurance, laws, and police.

Before proceeding let me emphasize an important reservation concerning the analysis presented in this chapter: the causal link between population size and the features of primitive societies is my interpretation of the evidence. Were I to analyze only features of these societies, the reader would be unable to decide whether or not my interpretation carries greater weight than others that have been offered. These societies have had stable populations of different sizes as well as stable social and exchange structures for very long periods, and we really do not know how and under what circumstances they have gambled on the customs that have kept them stable. But when an outsider observes only stable features, he cannot learn anything about causality: while anthropologists have noted that the level of "economic development" (as they measure it) is higher where the mean size of the community is greater, one cannot really infer what caused what. Did the greater economic development enable the society to maintain a greater population, or did the population increase suddenly, inducing people to gamble on novel ideas, with the population then remaining stable at the higher level?

In order to distinguish between these two views and show why a greater weight is given to the latter one, I shall present evidence that where a population has suddenly changed, the changes in economic, legal, and social structures have been in the direction I have predicted. Thus my views of primitive societies should be interpreted as implying only that their structure can be understood as an adaptation to the expectation of carrying out interactions within a small community.[1]

In conclusion, the views and evidence presented in this chapter provide an explanation for the similarities of the social and legal institutions of primitive societies and of patterns of "development." The previous chapter explained why, in spite of these similarities, one should expect differences among primitive societies and in patterns of development: thinking (i.e., gambling on novel ideas) has a random, unpredictable effect on human societies. But the arguments in this chapter suggest that in spite of these unpredictable differences, one can say something about both the general direction in which such gambling will be oriented and the timing of the increased gambling.

"Primitive" Societies: What Are the Facts?

On Hunger and Patents

Let us examine the assumptions that many writers have made in analyzing the structure of primitive societies, assumptions concerning the risk of hunger, the perishability of goods, the lack of protection of innovative ideas, and the absence of effective government, so that we may see whether these views are inconsistent with the facts and are thus not very useful in explaining the features of primitive societies.

The recent anthropological literature contains many outstanding studies of hunting and gathering groups, studies that make use of quantitative data on calorie consumption and work effort. Richard Lee (1968, 1969, 1976) carried out a detailed study of the !Kung Bushmen and found that on average their calorie intake was 2140 per person per day, well in excess of the recommended daily allowance of 1975 calories. Ninety percent of their diet came from 23 of the 85 available edible plant species, and from only 54 of the 220 edible species of animals. Moreover, not all the food gathered was consumed—some was left to rot on the ground. The group was healthy and long-lived (10% of the population was over 60). Similar observations on hunting and gathering societies have been made by a great number of scholars, including Stini (1971), Woodburn (1968a), Bose (1964), Turnbull (1966), Allan (1965), and many others quoted in Cohen (1977) as well as in Sahlins (1972), who summarizes nineteenth-century sources that make the same point. These facts can be contrasted with those available from agricultural societies (which according to Cohen [1977] became agricultural in response to population pressure): in later ones the population is exposed to new parasitic diseases and suffers deficiencies in protein, vitamins, and minerals (See Barnicot 1969, Dunn 1968, Yudkin 1969, Polgar 1964 and 1975, Howell and Bourlière 1963, and Bates 1955). This, along with other very extensive evidence, has led Cohen (1977) to the conclusion that features of hunting and gathering societies cannot very well be explained by the risk of hunger; agricultural societies have faced these risks more often (see Cohen 1977 and Boserup 1981). These facts also imply that neither can the stable populations of primitive societies be explained by assuming that there have been constraints on their food production; indeed, the evidence suggests that customs have kept them stable.

If this is the case, then one cannot attribute the relatively smaller supply of innovative ideas in hunting and gathering societies to difficulty in obtaining food and the resulting lack of time that could be allocated for "thinking." Neither can one attribute the relatively smaller supply of original ideas to the assumption that gains from innovative ideas could not be appropriated. There is much evidence that they are. Sapir and Swadesh (1939) note that for the Nootka "various kinds of ceremonially recognized property [exist] . . . whose use is restricted to a given family and is subject to certain principles of ownership, inheritance, and transfer." Knowledge of family legends is transmitted like other property; names of some commodities are exclusively held and applicable at the discretion of the owner; there are rights that pertain to carving certain designs, singing certain songs, and dancing certain dances. McKern (1922) describes the specialization of "functional families" among the Patwin of California, which is based on the right to pursue specialties that are owned as property by each family. In Savaii, one finds that a certain family has a monopoly or patent right over the very crude malauli hook made from a fish bone tied at an angle to a piece of wood, that trade marks are important, and that when a chief employs different builders, one distinguishes his work from the others and advertises himself (see Herskovits 1940). In Niue, songs, charms, names, and family traditions are important elements in family wealth (see Handy 1923, Loeb 1926, and Herskovits 1940). More on the appropriation of patents and ideas can be found in Herskovits (1940).[2] One must thus attribute the traditionality of primitive societies to reasons other than the lack of expected gain from offering original ideas. As I argued in the previous chapter, customs that justify the expectation of stable patterns of wealth distribution lead to a decline in creativity.

On Literacy, Memory, and Population

A distinguishing feature of societies labeled as primitive is their illiteracy.[3] However, literacy, like agriculture or money, can be viewed as just another innovation. The question, then, is whether its absence can plausibly be linked to the facts that population in these societies is relatively small and stable and customs are founded to maintain the stability of the wealth distribution. Can it then be said that there are no incentives to gamble on the idea of literacy? The answer is yes.

Stable social and market structures ensure that there will be repeated learning as the elder generation retires and the new one starts to work. Under these circumstances one would expect specific channels of information to evolve that simplify learning. Today we are accustomed to receiving communications from the older generation either orally, in writing, or visually. However, when the population is small and stable, the benefits of literacy are relatively small since knowledge can be transmitted by face-to-face oral and visual communication. Also, the methods of exchange do not require literacy: trust substitutes for written contracts. We must now present evidence justifying the following assertions: (1) Illiteracy does not imply either lack of innovation or lack of culture; it merely means that innovation and culture take different forms in illiterate societies than in literate (and more populous) ones.[4] (2) Literacy does not seem to be useful in all circumstances. Although it is true that when population (more precisely, the number of people with whom future interactions are expected) increases, literacy represents an innovation that is useful to gamble on, when population diminishes it becomes less useful and the probability that people will become illiterate increases. (3) Literacy is not an unqualified good: as shown in chapter 4, it has substantial costs that lead to more rigid human behavior and to misunderstandings between generations.

When all knowledge is entrusted to memory, one would expect there to be several methods used to educate the young as well as innovations in speech that would later die out or be used less.[5] Indeed, anthropological studies have emphasized that methods of cooking, growing crops, and rearing children are in general transmitted in such societies by imitation (rather than by "how to" books, as today). Cooking, for example, is frequently carried out in the open, and so conformity and homogeneity of cooking methods and types of food result. Children's games are imitative of the actions and daily routine of adults, and the greater part of the training of young women is done indirectly by imitation. Children gain knowledge of the law by oral instruction and by observation: retributions for theft, adultery, and cowardice are watched by all the tribe, including the children. That formal schooling affords little benefit in a society that expects to face stable circumstances has been noted by Schultz (1975):

> Farm people who have lived for generations with essentially the same resources tend to approximate the economic equilibrium of the stationary state. When the productive arts remain virtually constant over many years, farm people know from long experience what their own effort can get out of the land and equipment. In allocating the resources at their disposal, in choosing a combination of crops, in deciding on how and when to cultivate, plant, water and harvest and what combination of tools to use with draft animals and simple field equipment—these choices and decisions all embody a fine regard for marginal costs and returns. These farm people also know from experience the value of their household production possibilities; in allocating their own time along with material goods within the domain of the household, they too are finely attuned to marginal costs and returns. Furthermore, children acquire the skills that are worthwhile from their parents as children have for generations under circumstances where formal schooling has little economic value. [pp. 831–32]

The continuation of stable circumstances results in the younger generation's having greater incentive to spend time with the older, since the elderly literally embody the existing stock of knowledge. This seems to be a common feature of all primitive societies, excluding those where the major mode of production is based on gathering.[6] This exception can be explained: relative to other methods of producing food, such as agriculture, hunting, fishing, and herding, gathering requires the least amount of knowledge that must be acquired from the older generation. Once observations are written down, however, the younger generation can acquire knowledge by other means: they can more easily detect inconsistencies in the knowledge of the older generation, and their respect for them might diminish. Indeed, the word "skeptical" is absent from the vocabulary of primitive societies, as Goody (1977) notes:

> Members of oral . . . societies find it difficult to develop a line of sceptical thinking . . . simply because a continuing critical tradition can hardly exist when sceptical thoughts are *not* written down, *not* communicated across time and space, *not* made available for men to contemplate in privacy. . . . [italics in original, p. 43]

The gap between generations may thus be due in part to the fact that, once part of the existing knowledge is transmitted in writing rather than orally, the memories and experiences of the older are no longer the sole source of information vital to the society's continued existence.[7]

As for the means, or the innovations, that facilitate the memorizing process, the drum is mentioned in anthropological studies as one of the principal instruments of primitive societies, and a rhythmic clapping of hands is mentioned as a background for songs. It is also noted that songs consist of monotonous refrains that are chanted hour after hour, until they would drive anyone but a native to absolute distraction.[8] The reason for these features is that both rhythm and repetition facilitate the remembering of rituals, songs, and so forth. Also, Goody (1977) has found that among the LoDagaa of northern Ghana, the days are reckoned according to the incidence of neighboring markets—the very word for day is the same as that for market—and the weekly cycle is a six-day revolution of the most important markets in the vicinity. These phenomena illustrate how associations facilitate acquiring a stock of knowledge and remembering it.

That speech in primitive and oral societies was different from today's has been emphasized by some anthropologists, although they do not view this difference as a useful innovation when knowledge was transmitted orally. The Homeric epics are not a unique example of the decorum of speech of what was first oral poetry: Parry (1951) has found the same thing in another oral culture in the Yugoslavian ballads. Lord (1960) also found that it is the illiteracy of the epic singers which determines the particular form their composition takes and which distinguishes them from the literary poet. In societies where writing is unknown . . . the art of narration flourishes, provided that the culture is in other respects of a sort to foster the singing of tales . . . On the other hand, when writing is introduced . . . this audience seeks its entertainment and instruction in books rather than in the living songs of men, and the older art gradually disappears. [p. 20]

Ong (1971) argues that rhetoric, which is the art of composing as well as delivering a speech, was "the art developed by a literate culture to formalize the oral communication skills which had helped determine the structure of thought and society before literacy" (p. 49). That rhetoric also meant the art of composing stems from the fact that oral transmission could hardly be exact, and the deliverer of songs or of the history of the tribe generally made adjustments that fit the circumstances. This evidence shows that illiteracy does not imply lack of culture; it implies only that culture is a relative concept.[9]

Both the stability of population size and the relative isolation of primitive societies (which can explain their lack of literacy) are reflected in their myths. Indeed, historically, the process of generation continuously lengthens the line of genealogy. But if the population is stable, the genealogy will refer, despite its increasing length, to a constant number of ancestors. Goody (1968) takes note of this genealogical shrinkage (which one could as well call a flexible history), as did Evans-Pritchard (1940), although without relating it to the stability of the population:

> Valid history ends a century ago, and tradition, generously measured takes us back only ten to twelve generations in lineage structure, and if we are right in supposing that lineage structure never grows, it follows that the distance between the beginning of the world and the present day remain unalterable. [p. 108]

Gluckman (1965) finds similar evidence among the Bedouin of Cyrenaica, where

> the genealogy is kept at a constant depth of eleven generations. . . Genealogies of 11–12 generations in depth are found in many tribes scattered through the world: Ashanti and Tallensi lineages in West Africa, the Bedouin in North Africa, the Zulu when first recorded in the 1820's, all show this depth . . . [although] there are other societies with greater and less depth. [pp. 308–10]

These differences in length can be plausibly linked to the different but stable population sizes.

Making these adjustments in a tribe's history means that "history" will differ in each generation. Goody (1977) describes how these adjustments occur:

[A] young man gets acquainted with the art of metrical singing, not by verbatim remembering but by constructing a song out of the phrases, themes and narratives that he has heard before. The singer cannot, and does not remember enough to sing a song; he must and does learn to create phrases. So phrases get adjusted; there is no rigidity in what he hears and certainly none in what he does. [p. 117]

A person appeals to a shrine and perhaps obtains relief from suffering, but then witchcraft is seen to return because children still die and people still fall ill. . . . [Then one] may switch one's attention from one aspect of a deity to another. This latter solution is adopted in many simple societies and accounts for the turnover phenomena, the circulation of certain types of shrine. The agents who introduce or invent these new shrines are often responding to the pressures from below, the demand for new ways. [pp. 29–30]

The meaning of such demands and adjustments becomes clear when we look at these examples. Goody (1968) describes how in Nigeria British administrators, being aware of the importance of genealogies, recorded them. Forty years later, the natives maintained that they were incorrect. The explanation, consistent with the hypothesis presented here, is that the knowledge stored in memory was readjusted to the existing marriage pattern, eliminating members of the tribe who left, and retaining only those who mattered for the present pattern of social relations (for insurance or other purposes). Goody also states that at the beginning of the century some myths in northern Ghana were recorded. According to the myths the founder of the state at that time had seven sons. Sixty years later the myths mentioned only five. An examination revealed that one division of the tribe had become separated by boundaries set by the British, and another had been absorbed by a neighboring tribe. This points out that for illiterate societies, history is a flexible tool serving the present rather than a rigid interpretation of data, which it tends to become once a society acquires literacy (the issue of this rigidity and its costs will be returned to in chapter 4).[10]

This observation on the meaning of history in primitive societies has been made by several anthropologists (for a summary of their views see Gluckman 1965). Fortes (1945) writes:

The Tallensi, therefore, have no history in the sense of a body of authentic records of past events. Their memories and reminiscences of the old men are part of their biographies and never contribute to the building up of a body of socially preserved history. Their myths and legends are one means of rationalizing and defining the structural relationships of group to group or the pattern of their institutions. [p. 26]

These arguments can explain why the first written documents of human history abound in inconsistencies and contradictions, dates are rarely mentioned, and the concept of time is rather blurred. These are documents that preserve the form and style of oral cultures, both their ornamented and allegorical language and their inconsistencies. In particular, it follows that if these first texts were written down in different periods when most of the population was still illiterate, one would expect to find inconsistencies among the various versions of the same historical events. For while the oral version could be adjusted according to the rules mentioned above, the written text preserves an "objective" past. Whether or not these arguments shed light on the biblical stories and their inconsistencies is an open question, but the idea seems plausible.

What happens when population starts to grow? Exchange becomes more anonymous and money and written contracts complement exchanges previously based on trust. Thus, because of the increase in either the number of participants in exchange or in their mobility, the usefulness of oral communication decreases while that of written communication increases. Historians have taken note of this transition. Toynbee (1966) writes:

> The Sumerians did do a unifying job which was impressive by contrast with the previous condition of human affairs. Never before had so large a number of human beings shared with each other an identical language, script. . . . Egyptologists . . . note that the Egyptian script . . . is constructed on Sumerian principles and they also note that the Egyptian script makes its appearance suddenly, full-blown, in contrast to the Sumerian script, whose gradual evolution out of descriptive characters that had not originally stood for words or sounds can still be traced. . . . [pp. 64–68]

The observation that the appearance of the alphabet is related to population size, that it does not represent a sudden development but either gradually develops from existing methods of communication or is adopted from other societies (as in Egypt), has been made by Goody (1968):

> The classical age of Babylonian culture, beginning under Hammurabi in the late eighteenth century B.C. appears to have coincided with a period when the reading and writing of Akkadian cuneiform was not confined to a small group or to one nation. [p. 37]

Insufficient attention has been paid to the fact that the urban revolution of the Ancient Near East produced one innovation, the invention of writing. [p. 67]

This evidence suggests that literacy does not appear randomly but might be related to changes in population size, representing an idea (or innovation) that people then had a greater incentive to gamble on.

It follows that the opposite may occur: when population diminishes people may become less literate. Evidence that this happens is presented in the next two chapters, where the issue of literacy is discussed in further detail. It may, however, be helpful to note that it seems fairly well documented that the fall of the Roman Empire and the first feudal age corresponded with a great and universal decline in population (see Bloch 1940, McNeill 1976, and North and Thomas 1973). Thompson (1939) gives a detailed account of the decline in education and literacy:

> By the fourth century, the decay of interest in learning and culture even among the elite of Roman society attracted the attention of the government. Abortive and clumsy endeavours were made to stimulate learning by establishing the Atheneum at Rome, and chairs of rhetoric and law in the important schools in the province. . . . These governmental measures soon proved ineffective in checking the tendency of the times. The decline of education is also seen in the history of private charters, which, owing both to the increase in illiteracy and the growing practice of forgery, were now required by law to be registered in provincial or municipal archives. The fate of the libraries, either neglected, or destroyed by decay and dispersion, is another symptom of intellectual decline. Already in the fourth century Ammianus Marcellinus (A.D. 378) had mournfully written: "bibliothecis sepulcrorum ritu in perpetuum clausis"—the libraries were shut forever like tombs. [pp. 1–2]

It is useful to present other interpretations that have been placed on features of primitive societies discussed in this section. Adam Smith (1762) contended that dancing and poetry were pastimes of the most primitive nations. Dancing required music, and as this developed so too did poetry:

> Thus it is that poetry is cultivated in the most rude and barbarous nations, often to considerable perfection; whereas they make no attempt towards the improvement of prose. It is the introduction of commerce . . . that first brings on the improvement of prose. . . . Prose is the style in which all the common affairs of life, all business and agreements, are made. No one ever made a bargain in verse. . . . [quoted in E. G. West 1976, pp. 71–72]

He views the transition toward literacy and prose as a sign of an evolutionary process, rather than as an adaptation to an increased human population. A more recent observer, Lévi-Strauss (1968), notes that people
in primitive societies invest much time in memorizing their kinship:

> I see no reason why mankind should have waited until recent times
> to produce minds of the caliber of a Plato or an Einstein. Already
> two or three hundred thousand years ago there were probably men
> of a similar capacity, who were of course not applying their intel-
> ligence to the solution of the same problem as these most recent
> thinkers; instead they were more interested in kinship! [p. 351]

What Lévi-Strauss fails to note is that this behavior can plausibly be linked
to the fact that insurance and exchange were based on trust among kin,
that the benefits of literacy are relatively small when population size is
small, that information can be transferred by face-to-face communication,
and that when inequality is expected to be relatively slight and maintained
at stable levels there will be no Einsteins and no Platos. Who needs them?

In conclusion, while the absence of literacy can be used in understanding some characteristics of culture in primitive societies, it cannot be used
as a causal factor in explaining their lack of economic development. That
such societies do not gamble on literacy can plausibly be linked to their
success in maintaining their population and wealth distribution stable
through custom.

Without relating the issue of literacy to fluctuations in population size
(or, more correctly, the extent of isolation of some communities), some
anthropologists have reached this same conclusion, that literacy is *not* a
causal factor in development. Kathleen Gough (1968) writes:

> Kerāla did not display the array of features that Watt and I saw as
> potential consequences of widespread literacy, which did nothing
> either to break down caste barriers or to foster a strong interest in
> history or science. Despite the failure to develop in these ways,
> literacy was of great significance. It assisted in maintaining kingdoms
> of a large size both by increasing the communication links . . . and
> by facilitating the collection and recording of taxes. . . .My discus-
> sion of literacy in traditional Kerāla thus tends to bear out conclu-
> sions reached from a general consideration of China and India.
> Literacy is for the most part an enabling factor rather than a causal
> factor. . . . [pp. 132, 153]

In *The Psychology of Literacy* (1981), Sylvia Scribner and Michael Cole
reach similar conclusions. Their in-depth analysis of the Vai people of
western Liberia, who in the nineteenth century invented and adopted a
wholly original writing system, leads them to conclude that the mere fact

of learning to read and write doesn't bring with it any important psychological development. What matters is the uses people make of literacy. As I have tried to make clear in this section, literacy can be more extensively used when population increases and exchange becomes more anonymous.[11]

Population Stability and Custom

How did primitive societies maintain stable populations for such long periods? As the evidence suggests, it was not because of lack of food. Also, the evidence (summarized in Cohen 1977) contradicts both Denham's (1974) view that frequent epidemics can explain the constancy of populations, and Sussman's (1972) view that requirements of child spacing combined with high child mortality could have been the reasons for the absence of significant population growth in primitive societies. Cohen's summary (1977, based on studies by Birdsell [1968], Divale [1972], Hayden [1972], and Polgar [1975], among others) suggests that population growth was primarily limited by cultural means. He concludes that it is fairly well documented that effective birth control mechanisms have been known to all contemporary cultures (see Devereux 1955 and 1967, Hassan 1973, Laughlin 1968, and Marshall 1962), and that even prehistoric populations unconsciously spaced births and made use of fertility-reducing mechanisms (see Scott, Wynne-Edwards, and Binford, quoted in Cohen 1977). Moreover, not only did mechanisms exist for stabilizing the population of individual tribes; such mechanisms also existed among neighboring tribes. Several studies demonstrate how this mechanism worked: Birdsell (1953) found a high correlation between rainfall and population density among the aborigines in Australia. He concluded that these groups shared a mechanism of migration in response to changes in their wealth, in this case variations in rainfall. Cohen (1977) summarizes much similar evidence on Micronesia and North America. Other studies (by Turnbull [1968], Woodburn [1968b], and Lee [1968]) emphasize that closed groups do not exist: individuals move from one group to another, and population density tends to be equalized in adjacent regions. Cohen's (1977) interpretation of this intertribal migration is that these contacts among neighboring groups are the means for avoiding conflicts and for providing protection against attacks, which seem to correspond to occasional famines but which are local in character (see Goody 1962, Gluckman 1965, and Cohen 1977).

These contacts among neighboring groups are achieved by a number of incentives and customs. Frequently the prestige of members of primitive societies is derived from their success in establishing contacts with neighboring groups. For the Kauimaipa, a man's prestige in his own group depends on his skill as an organizer of pig-exchanges and on the number of partners he has in several directions. . . . He has to be able to direct the marriages of his group's men and women so that they acquire in-laws in strategic positions. . . .

[In] the *kula* exchange . . . of New Guinea . . . a man's internal standing depended on his role in the external exchange, so that for internal prestige he had to have alliances with foreigners. . . . Blood brotherhood, enabling people to move in foreign lands, was similar in form through large regions of Central Africa. . . . Among the . . . Ibo of Nigeria a man moves to trade at a distance by going to an in-law in a neighbouring group, and is passed on, under the protection of this relative, to the protection of one of the latter's relatives yet further on, and thus he progresses across the land. [Gluckman 1965, pp. 91–92]

Also, the frequent finding that extratribal marriage involves the movement of women rather than men suggests that one function of such movement may well be to equalize population density, since part of a group's reproduction capacity is thus exported (see Cohen 1977).

I shall assume then that some societies have at one time gambled on customs that succeeded in maintaining the stability of their and their neighbor's populations, and have simultaneously developed other customs that led to expectations for maintaining their inequality at stable levels. The next question is how one would expect exchanges to be organized in such societies, and whether or not the evidence is consistent with these expectations.[12]

Contract Uncertainty, Kinship, and Population

Contract Uncertainty and Population

Let us consider the situation faced by communities of no more than 100 to 3000 people within loosely organized tribes. Trouble involving members of different local groups frequently sparks violence, which often leads to feuding. While it appears that every primitive society has developed some procedures for avoiding or stopping feuds, the data show that hunting, gathering, and herding societies have wrestled with the problem of maintaining order among members of a local group as well as among neighbouring groups. The disputes frequently revolve around matters of exchange and fulfillment of commitments (see Hoebel 1954, Gluckman 1965, Posner 1980, and Hambly 1926). The question is how relatively stable and small communities diminish the probability of such disputes occurring.

Members of such communities expect exchanges among themselves with various degrees of frequency. Participation in ceremonies, observation, gossip—activities that require spending time or other resources—enable one to get acquainted with others and to decide how much they can be trusted. The costs of establishing this rapport is an investment that facilitates future exchanges between the parties. One could call the resource produced by this investment the amount of trust people share. Parties to a contract can establish rules or norms for their relationship enabling them to share views concerning contingencies, and procedures for settling feuds and for enforcing contracts—rules that will serve them beyond a single interaction. The incentive to negotiate and establish these rules depends on the expected frequency of interaction, which is determined by the size and the mobility of the population with whom the future exchanges are expected: the smaller these factors are, the greater the incentive.

But trust means investment in other human beings. Thus it becomes virtually impossible to show how much exactly is "invested." Should a dispute arise, it would be difficult to define what the parties' obligations are exactly. In order to diminish this difficulty kin are expected to provide collateral and to adopt strict rules for enforcing contracts, since they are better acquainted with the trustworthiness of their members. Thus when the number of people with whom future exchanges are expected is relatively small and stable, the mutual protection and the enforcement of law and custom can be expected to be provided by kinship ties, which today have been replaced by the role of the government in diminishing contract uncertainty and protecting individuals in the case of feuds.[13]

The cost of establishing personal ties is an investment that lowers the costs of future exchanges between parties (in particular within a family) and of protecting property. I have called the resource produced by this investment the amount of trust people share. One cannot assume, however, that once people know one another they can be trusted without reservation; like any other resource, trust depreciates with time unless continuous "investments" are made to maintain it.

The continuous investment in trust has taken various forms. Bloch (1973) describes in detail the organization of production among the Merina in Madagascar:

> Merina kinship groups who had moved to areas where the rest of the population were not their kinsmen, formed ties of artificial kinship in order to have some reliable co-operators. . . . These ties were created between neighbours who were not genealogical kinsmen, but who . . . behaved towards each other as kinsmen. . . . How did this different evaluation between "real" and "artificial" kinsmen affect agricultural cooperation? . . . The cooperation teams . . . al-

ways included more artificial kinsmen than was necessary, while potential members of the team who were real kinsmen seemed to have been passed over. [pp. 78–79]

The natives' explanation for this phenomenon was that

they needed lots of people on whom they could call for agricultural work. 'Real' kinsmen would always come . . . 'artificial' kinsmen would only come if one kept up the typical kinship behaviour of repeated requests for help. . . . For long term planning only social relationships which are *reliable* in the long term can be used . . . , it is this reliability which assures a kind of safety net for the Merina peasant. [p. 79, italics added]

Another method for maintaining trust is to become a "blood brother"; again, repeated transactions characterize this relationship. Sahlins (1972) has noted another device by which the security of trade is enhanced: "good measure," that is, a buyer deliberately overpaying a seller in order to induce him to deal fairly with him in the future. Continuously giving gifts, according to Pitt-Rivers (1973), Herskovits (1940), and Gluckman (1965) fulfills a similar function. Also, the interpretation given to continuous participation in ceremonies is that of maintaining trust. Fortes (1945), for example, writes that

to sacrifice together is the most binding form of ritual collaboration. According to the ethical and religious ideas of the Tallensi, it is totally incompatible with a state of hostility—that is with an open breach of good relations. . . . One can sacrifice with a person whom one despises or dislikes, as long as these feelings do not lead to an infringement of the ties of mutual obligation. . . . [p. 98]

Similar observations have been made by Malinowski (1926), Thomson (1949), Evans-Pritchard (1940, 1963), and Gluckman (1965). Some of the ways by which personal ties diminish contract uncertainty may be seen in natives of various groups of the Upper Zambesi, who begin by bartering with one another and when they have bartered a few times strike a compact of friendship with general obligations of hospitality and help (see Gluckman 1965, Herskovits 1940, and Posner 1980). These obligations are important in blood brotherhood, for they enable people to trade and to move in foreign lands; this is the typical arrangement through large regions of central Africa (Gluckman 1965). Among the Ibo of Nigeria a man trades at a distance by going to an in-law in a neighboring group. He is then passed on under the protection of relatives and is thus able to move from place to place.[14] Goody (1962) illustrates what extreme contingencies general obligations of kinship can cover:

When a Trobriand canoe-crew was wrecked on the island of Dobu, all were killed save one whose kula-partner [a term for kinship] was among the party of Dobuans who found them. [p.152]

Kuznets (1979) summarizes the role kinship ties play in general, and states that one role of such ties is to substitute for many of the roles governments perform today:

Perhaps [the] most far reaching aspect of the investment in children is that of security—not merely or primarily the economic security of parents who, in their old age, have to rely on the help of surviving children, but much broader, encompassing protection against natural and social calamities, protection not provided by the government or other non-blood-related organs of society. The pressure in many preindustrialized societies . . . for larger families and a wider blood-tie group has been associated with the weakness of the government and the need to rely on family ties for security of the individual members. As long as governmental and other non-blood related organizations remain weak, an adequate increase of those related by protective blood ties will be a high priority goal. [pp. 43–44]

Morality and Custom

Trust is thus generated by both direct (gifts given to others) and indirect (time devoted to educating children) transfers of resources. Teaching one's children the Ten Commandments, or that good children take care of their parents when they are old and sick, is in part consumption (one may derive satisfaction from sharing the same beliefs with one's children, or from "good" children, with "good," of course, being defined by custom), in part investment against old age, and in part insurance against disputes. The distinguishing characteristic of these investments, in contrast to investment in one's own education or one's own physical property, is that they are made in other human beings, and that the expected returns will depend on the amount of trust the interacting partners share. In principle, this rate of return is not different from rates of return on other forms of owned resources, either property or education. In practice, however, the difference is clear: the value of the amount invested in other individuals is in the eye of the beholder. Thus the rate of return on the investment cannot be as sharply defined as other rates of return, and some flexibility in its interpretation will always exist.

Although economists are mainly concerned with rates of return on property and education and have paid no attention to rates of return "paid" on trust (since they have assumed anonymous exchanges), other social scientists have. They argue that the return on this investment is protected by custom or morality (which comes from the Latin *mos,* plural *mores,* meaning custom):

> The fact that morality carries the inevitable corollary of "long-term" means two things. First that we can, however imprecisely, estimate the amount of morality in a relationship by observing its degree of tolerance of imbalance in the reciprocal aspects of the relationship. The greater the degree of tolerance, the more the morality. . . . The second point . . . is that even if kinship is the most 'moral' social relationship there are many types of kinship, some implying shorter term commitment, some longer term commitment. . . . [To conclude,] if the effect of morality is the existence of long-term commitments, then there is no sharp break between kinship and other commitments but rather we should regard kinship as the end of a continuum consisting of commitments of different terms. [Bloch 1973, p. 77]

This passage implies that when exchange is not based on trust or personal ties, it will be instantaneous. In contrast, when exchange is based on trust one observes first the transfer of resources; the returns become evident only later. Pitt-Rivers's (1973) view of altruism is similar to Bloch's definition of morality—both represent the act of fulfilling implicit contracts based on trust:[15]

> Altruism is founded upon the concept of the unreciprocated gift, the 'free gift'. Gifts may be thought to be free, but they must nevertheless be repaid, for they are transactions which establish a moral relationship between donor and recipient. If they are not returned they change the nature of the relationship, hence Mauss subtitled his essay on that subject 'on the necessity to return presents'. We may well ask then, what is the 'free gift' free of? It would appear that it is free of any jural obligation. [p. 99]

The evidence that follows suggests that members of primitive societies are aware that each member "invests" in the others, that each individual has a debt toward the group that has invested in him, and that the group considers that it has some proprietary rights in this individual's productive powers, although the value of these debts cannot be very sharply defined. The customs and languages of primitive societies, as discussed by Gluckman (1965), reflect this view:

> Tribal people often speak . . . of one person "owning" another. . . . Father or husband may speak of himself as "owner" of the woman: but this is a shorthand for saying they have rights over her against each other, and accept duties toward her. . . . Indeed I have observed in the tribes I know that their word which we translate as "ownership" is used in all social relationships. . . . Bohannan ex-

plains that the Tiv word translated as "debt" . . . covers a wider range of phenomena and social relations than the English word "debt" usually does. You are in debt if you borrow and do not repay, if you herd stock for your kinsman, if your animal damages your neighbour's crop. . . . Leach stated that the Kachins in Burma, subsume many relations under the head of "debt." . . . There is a close correspondence between the Kachin's concept of debts and the anthropologists' concept of social structure. . . . Dr. Emrys Peters [notes] that Bedouins in Cyrenaica similarly used "debt" to cover wide ranges of social situations. This is true also of the Barotse whom I studied, and it is implied in reports of some other African peoples. [pp. 76, 242–43]

Goody (1962) has described how after a woman announces her pregnancy, members of the tribe go at night and wake up the couple with the words:

"take the fruit and give me the pips", [or as one member of the tribe explained the ritual:] "The man and the woman sleep together and do not think beyond their pleasure; by performing this ceremony we tell them to enjoy themselves but at the same time to remember that the child belongs to us all." [p. 196]

These examples illustrate the broad semantic content of "debt" in these societies.[16]

Attitudes toward death in primitive societies can be linked to this broad definition of debt and to small and stable community size. One goal of the individual's life is to provide insurance through family ties, and this is one of his "debts" toward his kin. Dying at a young age, the inability to have children, or committing suicide are acts that increase the risks of a particular group, for the population is no longer held constant. One would therefore expect these acts to be viewed as criminal. Hoebel (1954) notes that in west Greenland widows without protectors and grown men without sons are considered witches, and Goody (1962), in a study of the mortuary customs of some primitive societies, writes:

Death is treated as a social phenomenon and attributed to some conflict in the social system. . . . But there are two main exceptions, which fall at the extremes of the span of human life: a child who dies before being weaned is not regarded as a human at all, but as a being of the wild that has come to trouble the parents . . . [and] the death of the man whose sons have themselves begotten sons is also thought of in a different way. Such a person has reached the end of his allotted span. [p. 208]

From these arguments it also follows that in a relatively small group, "normal" death cannot be viewed as a private affair before an individual fulfills his debt of diminishing risks by providing new family ties. The custom of double funerals among tribal societies is, according to Goody (1962), a widespread custom, and the explanation is that

> societies regard themselves as on-going systems, and consequently the death of any member threatens their very existence. Thus, when a man dies, society loses in him much more than a unit; it is stricken in the very principle of its life. . . . Death is therefore perceived as something contra-social and in this sense unnatural. . . . Death, [Malinowski] claims, shakes the moral life of the society and public ceremonials are required to restore the cohesion of the group. [pp. 26–28]

The equilibrium is restored during the second funeral when the new relationships among the living are established. Thus the idea of immortality in primitive societies can be, because of their relatively small population size, linked to the idea that it is society, rather than any particular individual, that is immortal. Indeed, in such societies one cannot make a distinction between private and public. When one lives in a community of 900 families, everything is "public."[17]

The arguments and evidence presented above suggest that one can understand some features of primitive societies by assuming that their members are expected to carry out their future interactions within a relatively immobile and small sized population. Let us next examine how interactions among members of a society change when the frequency of these interactions among any two individuals is expected to diminish.

> *My family will always be my insurance. In your [Western] civilization, you don't have that insurance.*
> SAMBA KA, a Dakai history teacher

Contract Uncertainty, Government, and Population

When population is relatively small and expected to remain stable, people resort to what we call today noninstitutional arrangements for enforcing contracts: exchange is organized by basing it on trust and honor, and friends and kin provide the required collateral. Let us examine what happens when the population within which future exchanges are expected increases.

Assume that a certain level of diet and some specific labor costs are achieved when the population is held constant for a while. This equilibrium becomes threatened if population tends to grow. Members of the group may then gamble on several alternatives (notice that the incentive to gamble on novel strategies increases because the suddenly increased population leads to a redistribution of wealth): they can choose to limit population by either exporting individuals, by inducing some members to leave, or by infanticide and human sacrifice. Alternatively, members of the group can gamble on the idea of migration, extend the radius they exploit, search for less readily available sources of food, gamble on eating new foods,[18] or gamble on a new technology. As shown in the previous chapter, all these alternatives are costly and involve suffering; it can be assumed that a combination of them will be tried, the decisions being influenced by cultural factors.

The strategies of migration and extending territory result in neighbouring groups facing an increased risk that their way of life will be disturbed. As Gluckman notes,

> over-populous sections within a tribe might be compelled by the threat of hunger to try to gain control over the land of other sections which in their ideology were brothers to them, whom they should succour and help. . . . Necessity compels them to get more land, and if their neighbours are 'brothers' to them, they can only do so at the latter's expense. Yet it is believed that to commit this breach of fraternal obligations may bring misfortune, misfortunes defined by the cultural values of the society which stress the brotherhood of those . . . linked by patrilineal descent. It is a moral dilemma, even if in the end necessity prevails. [1965, p. 85]

This example shows why members of groups have the incentive continuously to invest resources in obtaining information on their "brothers' " intentions and why one can call the dilemma described above "moral."

Increased population, along with the increased probability of migration and an altered wealth distribution, lead to expectations of less frequent exchanges between any two individuals in the future and to increased probability of fraud. Thus the costs associated with exchange under existing arrangements (which are based on customs, kinship, and religion) increase. This means that wealth per capita diminishes further. It thus becomes profitable to gamble on an idea that could substitute for trust. The individuals who make the "lucky hit" on which the rest of the population gambles will create a new rule of organization for their society. As I shall argue below, the new ideas may come to life in the form of money, written contracts, laws and governments that substitute for trust, and customs and religion.

Let us examine in detail some elements of this transition. When population is stable and relatively small, the protection of property and the fulfillment of contracts can be based on trust, honor, and reputation. The right to property can be identified through acquaintance with its owner: when someone sells an article he is able to assure the buyer that the thing is his to sell. In contrast, when exchange becomes more anonymous (which by definition implies less frequent transactions among any two individuals), an alternative institution and another mechanism must exist that will provide both protection and information to the potential buyers— indeed, these are functions of governments. In a more anonymous system, promises to buyers may be broken through deliberate deceit; the probability of such an event occurring is smaller when repeated exchanges are expected. And when exchange is based on trust and kin provide the collateral, a dispute resulting from a misunderstanding between parties as to what is promised, or an unexpected event that prevents the seller from fulfilling his promises, may be settled without drawing formal contracts to cover these contingencies. However, once exchanges become anonymous these solutions are either no longer feasible or become rather costly. Exchange is then facilitated by general rules that define what will happen if there are obstacles to its performance as originally understood by the parties. Thus when exchange is anonymous legal institutions are required and written contracts complement exchange that was previously based on trust.

Similarly, money as a social institution can reduce the role of trust in an exchange. Its negotiability rests on the fact that its value is independent of buyers' and sellers' knowing one another; the parties need only be certain of the identity of the third party who issues the money.[19] Thus one way of viewing the rise of some institutions in an exchange economy such as money, contracts, law, police, and government—all of which concern property rights, their protection, and the provision of information—is to regard them as the means to ensure trust among trading partners when exchange has become more anonymous.

An additional change characterizes such periods of transition. As argued in the previous chapter, when wealth diminishes and its distribution changes, the incentive to innovate increases in general. Since these two changes occur when population unexpectedly increases, one would expect that new rules will be created in the organization of social institutions, and that innovations in technology, science, and the arts will become more frequent. Thus an outsider from a "developed" country will detect greater economic development in societies where either the population is increasing or the population has increased and is remaining stable at the higher level. But the outsider's view is biased: all that has happened is that people have adapted themselves to their increased numbers, and that at one time they have gambled more on novel ideas because of the change in the wealth distribution.

The observation that expectations of continuing exchange has a favorable effect on the behavior of parties plays an important role in my arguments, and has been frequently made in a number of theoretical as well as empirical studies. The theory of repeated games appears in game theory (see Luce and Raiffa 1966) and the theory of clubs in economics (see Buchanan 1965). The discipline of continuous dealings has been noted from Adam Smith onward, and has been applied to the subject of the uncertain nature of business contract in general (see Akerlof 1970, Darby and Karni 1973), and used to explain contract choice during the California Gold Rush (Umbeck 1977). In essence they all rely on Smith's (1762) observation that

> when a person makes perhaps twenty contracts in a day, he cannot gain so much by endeavouring to impose on his neighbours as the very appearance of a cheat would make him lose. When people seldom deal with one another, we find that they are somewhat disposed to cheat, because they can gain more by a smart trick than they can lose by the injury which it does their character. . . . Wherever dealings are frequent, a man does not expect to gain so much by any one contract, as by probity and punctuality in the whole, and a prudent dealer, who is sensible of his real interest, would rather choose to lose what he has a right to than give any ground for suspicion. [p. 318]

Several scholars have argued that the rise of social institutions, laws, and governments can be related to the emergence of impersonal markets. Adam Smith, in his *Lectures on Policy, Justice, Revenue and Arms* (1762), which he called "a sort of theory and history of law and government," argued that with the development of manufactures, individuals began to work not for one person but for an impersonal market, and he discusses how the probability of cheating is related to the frequency of expected transactions, although he does not mention the role population size or its potential mobility might play in the process. Hicks's (1969) theory is more explicit, and he relates the rise of the market to population growth:

> What are the kinds of disturbance which may have such effects? It is tempting to answer the question on economic lines, in terms of population pressure. This is a possible answer, but it should not be assumed that it is the only answer. The peoples who have maintained themselves in customary equilibrium for long periods must have found some way of containing population pressure; why should not others have done likewise? It can only be because they have passed through a stage in which such control was not necessary. If population increases, land requirements increase; there must therefore have been a stage in which there was ample land permitting an increase of population under a system of land usage which goes on long enough to become traditional. Even so, a point will come when

the land which is suitable for food production by traditional methods is fully occupied, so that the people of one tribe begin to encroach upon the land that is used by its neighbours. As the encroachment develops, it builds up into a real and continuing threat. That is certainly one of the ways in which the 'revolution' [the rise of markets] may come about; but we should be careful not to jump to the conclusion that it is the only way. [pp. 14–15]

One of the most rigorous theoretical and empirical treatments of the relationship between population growth and institutional changes appears in Cohen (1977), following Boserup's (1965) classic work. His main purpose is to present a theory that can account for the "invention" of agriculture and explain why it emerged when it did. He argues and presents an extremely broad range of evidence that agriculture does not represent a great conceptual break with traditional subsistence patterns, and that it is not easier than hunting or gathering and does not provide either a better or more palatable diet or more secure food base than the two other methods. He concludes that it is because of lack of demand that groups do not become agricultural. Cohen shows that

agriculture has in fact only one advantage over hunting and gathering: that of providing more calories per unit of land, per unit of time and thus of supporting denser populations: it will thus be practiced only when necessitated by population pressure. [p. 15]

The point I wish to make is similar, only it applies to trade and the rise of markets. Markets, supported by law and the police, have an advantage over trade based on personal ties by providing more information per unit of transaction, per unit of time. The idea of adopting this method of exchange will thus be offered and probably gain followers only when population becomes larger and denser, thus leading to increasingly anonymous trade. (One could add that the industrial production of food seems to have the same advantage over agriculture that agriculture had over hunting and gathering.)

Some social scientists have indeed noted that trade is the beginning of the new world and that the state is to be regarded as an organization that emerges to reduce costs arising from contract uncertainty (see Ben Porath 1980, Buchanan 1975, Gunning 1972, and Landa 1976); none of them, however, relates the process to population growth, although they all mention impersonal exchanges. Landa (1976, 1979a, 1979b), for example, raises the question of how traders cope with the problem of contract uncertainty in an environment where the legal framework is nonexistent or poorly developed. Her answer is that "ethnically homogeneous middlemen groups" can be viewed as an institutional arrangement that emerges to economize on contract-enforcement and information costs in an environment where the legal infrastructure is not well developed. She further argues that monetary exchange economizes on the middlemen's transaction costs and that at some point the state, by imposing the law of contract on all traders, economizes on decision-making costs:

> Once the state emerges to make contracts legally binding, the rational trader must weigh the benefits against the expected costs . . . of breach. The emergence of the legally binding contract, which establishes a nexus between the market economy and the polity, transforms the former into the social economy. . . . The existence of [this] social order (1) reduces unnecessary transaction costs arising from a trader's breach of contract and hence gives the middleman freedom to pursue his profits subject to a legal behavioral constraint; (2) facilitates the impersonal process of exchange by encouraging the trader to trade with "outsiders." [Landa 1976, pp. 915–16]

Finally, Maine's (1905) thesis on the transition from custom to law in *Ancient Laws* should be noted. He points out that

> the movement of the progressive societies has been uniform in one respect. Through all its courses it has been distinguished by the gradual dissolution of family dependency, and the growth of individual obligation in its place. [p. 149]

> [It is not] difficult to see what is the tie between man and man which replaces by degrees those forms of reciprocity in rights and duties which have their origin in the Family. It is contract. Starting, as from one terminus of history, from a condition of society in which all the relations of Persons are summed up in the relations of Family, we seem to have steadily moved towards a phase of social order in which all these relations rise from the free agreement of individuals. . . . If then we employ Status . . . to signify these personal conditions only . . . we may say that the movement of the progressive societies has hitherto been a movement from *Status to Contract*. [pp. 149, 150–51; italics in original]

While Maine considers this transition as part of an "evolutionary" process and does not relate it to expectations for diminished frequency of interactions among people and resulting anonymity, the observation is consistent with what I have argued, for transactions that take place within a small market are not specific single transactions involving exchange of goods and services among relative strangers: people hold property and exchange goods and services as kinfolk or affines. This behavior later finds its expression in law, and as Maine summarizes, "the separation of the Law of Persons from that of things had no meaning in the infancy of the law . . . the rules belonging to the two departments were inextricably mingled together.''

We can thus expect the transition from economies with small and stable populations to ones where the potential number of participants in exchange becomes large to be characterized by the following features: the fraction of exchanges that will be carried out in more anonymous markets increases, while that based on trust and personal ties decreases. While exchange in small economies is based on trust, exchange in more anonymous markets requires money, contracts (and thus eventually literacy), and is regulated by laws and governments. These transitions are today called ''economic development.'' Many people seem to attribute virtue to this process; however, it should be clear that the changes discussed here and in the previous chapter cannot be equated with either ''evolution'' or ''progress.'' Rather, these developments seem to be merely adaptations to our ever-increasing numbers and to unexpected changes in the wealth distribution.

Are there alternative strategies for making this adaptation? One could argue that the elimination of the increased uncertainty due to increased population can be achieved either by an adaptation of the exchange mechanism and the institutions protecting it *or* by people continuing to trust one another. Indeed, morality and religious education for general honesty could, in principle, substitute for laws, governments, and police, and contract uncertainty would not exist. But when population increases and the wealth distribution changes, more people will gamble on the idea of committing acts not in accordance with existing customs. Thus the incentives in the economy are changed and the existing customs can no longer fulfill the roles for which they have been created.

Statistical Evidence

Market structures from diverse primitive societies randomly distributed around the world are compared below. Before proceeding, it might be useful to state clearly what one can learn from these comparisons.

As argued, similar patterns of behavior characterize these societies, and because of these similarities they have been preselected by anthropologists. For long periods of time these societies have been relatively isolated, and have had stable populations as well as stable social and exchange structures. The previous arguments make it clear that I view these societies as those who have succeeded in gambling on some set of rules that are expected to maintain both their population and their wealth distribution stable. In light of the statistical examinations of these societies, one could view their features as adaptations to the expectation of being involved in frequent interactions with the same people. But it must be clear that one cannot give any ''causal'' interpretation to the evidence—

the causal interpretation can only be deduced from evidence presented in chapters 3 and 4, where the effects of sudden changes in population will be examined. Also, the fact that in the statistical examinations demographic variables are used to explain features of development does not imply that there are any simple rules of demographic determinism; they merely show correlations. As made clear in the previous chapter, one should expect both cultural differences among these societies and differences in the process of adjustment when their populations increase. The differences are due to the resulting changes in the distribution of wealth, which then lead to random gambling on novel ideas.

It is appropriate at this point to relate examinations presented below to others that have been carried out. In an extensive study, Pryor (1977) has examined whether or not the predictions of various anthropological theories are consistent with the evidence. This evidence refers to sixty societies, and my examinations refer to 41 of them, since for 19 societies I could not obtain information on the mean size of their communities, a variable that plays a central role in my arguments. The difference between Pryor's and my analysis is that Pryor, examining the implications of various anthropological theories, has always included among the explanatory variables a measure of economic development. He does so because anthropologists have always related economic development to the presence or absence of some markets, although what they mean by "development" is never made clear.

Such examinations are good for Pryor's purposes, but not for mine, for these tests do not have much meaning if one is dealing with economic development, since the variable one wants to explain (the emergence of some markets) is already included in the "independent" variable that defines economic development. The explanatory variables in my examinations are demographic ones, and the variables I try to explain are only those that can implicitly or explicitly enable us to verify the implications of the views presented in this chapter.

Anthropologists have constructed indices of economic development for the primitive economies they have analyzed. These indices were computed in order to make comparisons between their complexities. The indices reflect the number of markets, the number of professions, the extent of specialization, and other signs of "development." To some extent these measures of economic development should be highly correlated with demographic variables, the mean size of communities, and their density, for these two variables are crude estimates of the expected number of participants in future exchanges. Also, the greater these numbers the greater the probability that a greater fraction of exchanges will be organized into "formal" markets, and that an anthropologist will measure greater economic development. The statistical tests below support these views.

The first test examines what fit the information on the average size of communities, *PO,* and their density, *D,* gives to the indices of economic development of forty-eight primitive societies denoted by *M*:

$$M = 0.45 + 5.21PO + 3.78\,D$$
$$(4.31) \qquad (5.86)$$

(1) $R^2 = 0.68$

         $n = 41$

where *n* denotes the number of observations, and the numbers in parentheses denote the t-statistics. The data on the average size of communities and their density has been taken from George Murdock's *Ethnographic Atlas,* while the indices of economic development have been taken from Pryor's data. The two data sources are consistent, since Pryor's tables are based on information presented in Murdock's atlas. This test shows that once one has information on the average size and density of communities that have been stable for long periods of time, one can predict that the greater the average size or the density, the higher will be their index of economic development (the way *we* measure it).

In an economy with a greater population or a greater density, the probability that a greater fraction of exchanges will be carried out through "formal" markets (that is, by instantaneous exchange) is higher.[20] At the same time, the fraction of exchanges of goods and services that are not *immediately* observed as being compensated for should decrease when population is greater. Let us examine whether or not the evidence seems consistent with these implications of the arguments presented in the previous sections.

The dependent variables used below are qualitative.[21] If domestic trade, denoted by *DT,* which represents instantaneous exchange, accounts for more than 5% of the total production of goods used in the society, the value given to the index is 1; otherwise it is zero. Since the variable I try to explain is qualitative, only one statistical method can be used (maximum likelihood), and the following result is obtained:[22]

(2) $DT = -4.43 + 0.745\,PO + 0.45\,D$ $; PCP = 0.75, n = 41$
         $(2.57) \qquad (1.75)$

when, as previously, the number in parentheses denotes the t-statistics, and *PCP* denotes the percentage of correct predictions.[23] As we can see, when the potential number of participants in exchanges is greater, a greater fraction of exchanges will be instantaneous.

Another qualitative variable may be used as an indicator for the relative importance of intertemporal transfers of goods and services among kin and non-kin. *ST* denotes this variable and it indicates whether or not transfers of either goods or services, for which time has elapsed between the date of donation and that of compensation for them, account for more than 5% of total production. If it accounts for more, the value given to *ST* is 1; otherwise it is zero.

In addition to the mean size of communities, one would also expect these transfers to depend on the specific mode of production, for while in gathering, hunting, and fishing societies people do not control carry-overs of food, in herding and agricultural ones they do, and one may argue that these stocks can provide insurance and substitute for intertemporal exchanges among kin. *IND* indicates the major mode of production, receiving the value 1 for hunting, fishing, and gathering societies and 0 for herding and agricultural ones. This variable and the mean size of communities turn out to be significant predictors for exchanges based on personal ties in an economy, as expected, IND being positively and the population size being negatively related to it:

$$(3) \quad ST = 5.3 - 1.01\ PO + 0.3\ IND \qquad ; PCP = 0.63,\ n = 41$$
$$(-2.9) \qquad (1.5)$$

This result can be interpreted as implying that when population is larger, one can expect more frequent transfers that are immediately compensated for.

The variable *ST* includes both transfers of labor and of goods. When separate estimates are done for these two different types of transfers, *TG* indicating whether or not transfers of goods account for 5% or more of total production of goods used in the economy, and *TL* indicating whether or not transfers of labor account for 5% of total labor outside of home, the results are as follows:

$$(4) \quad TG = 2.84 - 0.76\ PO + 0.5\ IND \qquad ; PCP = 0.59,\ n = 41$$
$$(-2.53) \qquad (1.95)$$

$$(5) \qquad\qquad TL = 1.22 - 0.53\ PO - 0.3\ IND$$
$$(0.41) \qquad\quad (-0.9)$$

Although the results of labor, *TL,* are insignificant, the reversed sign for the variable indicating the major mode of production is consistent with my arguments. Because of the specific nature of production, one would expect both that intertemporal transfers of labor will occur in agriculture and herding rather than in hunting, fishing, or gathering societies, and that transfers of goods will occur in hunting, fishing, and gathering societies rather than agricultural or herding ones, since the goods in the former societies are more perishable.

Consider now the presence or absence of money in its role as a medium of exchange. If trust is a sufficient device for intertemporal transactions, goods, and services being exchanged among family and kin, the probability that money will be "invented" is small. However, when population is greater, so that transactions are also made with outsiders, money is one institution that substitutes for trust. The probability of finding this innovation in the economy is thus greater. Further, money facilitates transactions; one would therefore expect to find it in economies where animal husbandry is the major mode of production, for in contrast to other types of output, herding is less divisible. The dependent variable is qualitative: *MO* receives the value 1 for the presence of money and 0 for its absence in the economy. *PO* continues to denote the mean size of the community and *HE* is the variable receiving the value 1 if animal husbandry contributes at least 10% of all the food produced, 0 otherwise. The result is:

(6) $MO = -4.13 + 0.706\,PO + 0.753\,HE$; $PCP = 0.44$, $n = 41$
 (2.63) (1.24)

This result supports the previous arguments and is also consistent with etymology: the word "pecuniary" comes from *pecus,* which means cattle (although the t-statistic of the animal husbandry variable is significant only at the 15% level).

If already speaking of semantics, one may note that the origins of words connected with trade suggest that its malevolent aspects were evident to participants in exchange; for example, the word "barter" originates from the Middle French word *barater,* which means to cheat, and Sumner and Keller (1927) point out the similarities in German between the word *Handel* (trade) and *Händel* (quarrel), and among the words *tauschen* (to trade), *täuschen* (to deceive), and *enttäuschen* (to disappoint).[24]

One would also expect that the greater the mean size of communities where most transactions take place, the greater the probability that the phenomenon of "interest rate" is explicitly recognized by participants in exchange. This does not mean that when population is relatively small there is no return on loans—there is, only the return is in the form of the right to call upon a group for assistance in the future when it is needed. And the contrary: interest is more likely to appear formally when exchanges become instantaneous, contractual, or more impersonal.

The dependent variable, *INT,* receives the value 1 if interest rates are explicitly recognized, zero if otherwise.[25] Two independent variables appear in the test: the mean size of communities, denoted by *PO,* and the major mode of production, denoted by *IND,* also used in equations 4, 5 and 6. The result is:

(7) $INT = -1.09 + 0.32\, PO - 0.45\, IND;$ $PCP = 0.53,\ n = 41$
           (1.3)   (1.8)

The numbers in the parentheses denote the t-statistics and they are significant at a 10% level. *PCP* denotes the percentage of correct predictions, and *n* the number of observations. The signs of the two independent variables are in the expected direction: when either the mean size of the community is greater or physical property is stored by members of the community (in herding and agricultural societies), the probability that interest rates will be explicitly recognized is greater.

One of Pryor's (1977) findings should be mentioned in connection with this evidence and that on reciprocal exchange. Reciprocal exchanges are sometimes divided in two categories: balanced and unbalanced exchanges. I have avoided this distinction because insurance represents a "balanced" transaction, since one individual buys and another sells a service. And yet from an accounting viewpoint one will find imbalance, on average, between the insured and the insurer, the imbalance reflecting a risk-premium. To determine whether or not this insurance argument sheds light on the evidence, one should observe that even after excluding transfers such as dowries, inheritances, and presents at specific occasions, transactions among kin might still be unbalanced in the long run. For while the non-kin transactions represent exchange rather than insurance, transactions within the closer family might represent to a greater extent an implicit form of insurance. Pryor's (1977) evidence on the Eskimos seems to support this view: he found that transactions are generally balanced among non-kin, while between kin they are unbalanced and the distance of kinship is an explanatory variable of net transfers among groups.[26]

I shall conclude this statistical section by examining a prediction made in the previous chapter on the relationship between inequality and methods of redistributing wealth. It was argued there that levels of inequality and optimal methods of redistributing wealth may change systematically when we compare societies with stable but different community sizes. The reasoning was that the greater the number of people with whom one interacts, the more difficult is it to know whether or not customs will be enforced. One would thus expect more frequent fluctuations in one's relative position in the wealth distribution. This argument has two implications: first, the level of economic development may be greater, since people may gamble more frequently on new ideas; second, the wealth distribution may be less egalitarian than in a smaller community since unfulfillment of implicit commitments may be more frequent. We have already seen that the evidence is consistent with the first implication (although it was then analyzed from a different angle). Let us now examine the second.

SI is the dependent variable denoting socioeconomic equality. *PO* and *IND* are the explanatory variables, the first denoting the mean size of communities, the second the indicator for the major mode of production, used in the previous tests. The reason for introducing *IND* as an explanatory variable is that one would expect greater equality in the hunting, fishing, and gathering societies, since the food produced there is more perishable and there are no property rights in land or herd. Thus inheritance could have a smaller impact on the wealth distribution relatively to societies where wealth can be stored. The result of the test is:

$$SI = 0.567 + 0.354\,PO - 0.55\,IND$$
$$(5.32) \qquad (-2.61)$$

(8)

$$R^2 = 0.49$$

$$F(2/39) = 28.4$$

which implies that if the population (or the extent of market) is greater, or the output can be stored, one can expect that the inequality in the society will be greater.

But if inequality is greater, more must be spent to prevent criminal acts or to impose sanctions against people who commit such acts. However, with a greater population a redistribution of wealth by custom becomes more expensive. Thus the probability that this function and that of inflicting punishment will be taken over by some form of central authority is greater. Socioeconomic equality and the size of the central authority should then be negatively correlated. Pryor (1977) has found such a negative correlation, as have several other studies mentioned in Erickson (1977) and Posner (1980). Also, Le Vine (1960) has found a negative correlation between equality and education for political values, which is to be expected, for the profession of politician exists *because of* the unequal distribution of wealth.

Thus the statistical evidence presented here, together with the already surveyed empirical, nonstatistical evidence, seems consistent with the views presented on the relationship between economic development, markets, and demographic variables.

And therefore if a man should talk to me . . . of a free subject; a free will; or any free, but free from being hindered by opposition, I should not say he were in an error, but that his words were without meaning, that is to say absurd.

THOMAS HOBBES, *Leviathan*

What Is Development?

What do we mean today by economic development? The widely accepted view is that when wealth per capita increases, an economy is growing. But one further question must be asked: What exactly does one include in the measurement of wealth? If the views presented here are correct, then wealth in a society also depends on the amount of trust people share: trust is one resource that, by diminishing contract uncertainty, lowers the costs of exchanges in the economy. This resource is part of a nation's wealth.

When population increases exchange becomes more anonymous and people will gamble on institutions that substitute for trust, such as formal markets, money, and legal institutions. Suppose that one includes only physical property and education when estimating an economy's wealth. Then if a comparison is made between two societies, the one with the greater population will have a greater measured wealth per capita, for the output of institutions that substitute for trust is taken into account in the economy with the greater population, but the same output (of diminished contract uncertainty) is omitted from the calculation when produced by trust and a common set of beliefs. Yet the "wealth" of the two nations could be the same.[27] Why has this argument been omitted from the analysis of development? The answer may stem not only from the fact that "trust" is rarely formally discussed in economic analysis (since exchanges are assumed to be anonymous), but also from our misunderstanding of the implications of freedom and individualism.

Economists have long known that people are the important part of the wealth of nations. Yet while they have stressed that people invest in both physical property and in themselves (i.e., their own education), they did never stress the simple fact that people invest in other human beings as well. Deep-seated moral issues are probably at work: free individuals cannot be one's property or one's marketable assets. The mere thought of investment in other human beings may seem offensive. Hence the treatment of other human beings as part of one's wealth seems to run counter to deeply held values, for it seems to reduce man to something akin to property.[28] And one may raise this question: If people really invested in one another, how could these investments be protected without resorting to slavery?

I did not raise these problems earlier because of their emotional implications. However, assuming that people invest in one another leads to testable implications, and when stated properly is not offensive. Moreover, some of the works quoted show that social scientists have been aware of the fact that such investments take place and that custom and morality complemented by laws are the means by which a society protects these investments. Special attention has been paid to the fact that children constitute an investment in societies where they provide insurance against sickness, feuds, and old age. In such societies customs protect the parents' investments, the concept of "good children" being defined only by custom. Thus when population is relatively small and stable, people can enlarge the range of choice available to them by investing in other human beings. This, indeed, is one way that "free" men have enhanced their welfare. Since enforcing customs or moral behavior is more difficult when population increases, the process of adjustment to an increasing population will be characterized by continuous change of customs, weakened family ties, a diminished role of custom and family in enforcing contracts, and their replacement by law, governments, and police. This process will be characterized by investing more in one's own education or property (that is, people will become more "materialistic" and more "individualistic"). But "free"? Instead of obeying custom, they will obey laws and regulations, and physical property and governments will provide insurance instead of kin.

Many puzzles about "growing economies" might be resolved once the issues of trust and custom are made clear and their relationship to the potential number of participants in exchange is taken into account. The "rise of markets" (call it "capitalism"), the increased demand for social institutions, the adjustment of laws, the definition of property rights, increased specialization, the increased demand for literacy, and the diminished role of custom can all plausibly be linked to population growth. Thus the only meaning I can give to "economic development" is that of adaptation to an increased population, through both the gambling process outlined in the first chapter and the adjustment process discussed here.

But I should stress that in spite of the fact that the role of population in understanding these adjustments has been emphasized, I do not suggest that economic development can be linked to some simplistic form of population determinism. Quite the contrary: when population increases, wealth per capita diminishes and the distribution of wealth changes, leading to an increased supply of criminal, revolutionary, and innovative acts. Societies we today call "primitive" might be those that have succeeded at some point (we do not know how and when) in gambling on customs that hold their population and wealth distribution stable. In contrast, in societies where population fluctuates (because of reasons beyond human control), customs are frequently abandoned and there is a greater supply of novel ideas. Recall the general mechanism that occurs under these circumstances: when the wealth distribution changes, people are more likely to gamble on new ideas. Individuals who respond to this changed incentive offer new ideas, imprinting on them their own subjective beliefs, and the rest of the society gambles on them. This introduces an unpredictable element in the history of human societies. How this process unfolds is the subject of the next two chapters.

Finally, two remarks. While the relationship between population and technology has been noted in the past (Cohen 1977, Boserup 1965 and 1981), no explanation has been given as to how or why this relationship exists. The first chapter provides the missing link. Second, what I have done in this chapter is to translate a few passages of the Bible into contemporary language:

> And she again bare his brother Abel. And Abel was a keeper of sheep, but Cain was a tiller of the ground; And in the process of time it came to pass, that Cain brought of the fruit of the ground an offering unto the Lord. And Abel, he also brought of the firstlings of his flock and of the fat thereof. And the Lord had respect unto Abel and his offering; But unto Cain and his offering he had no respect. And Cain was very wroth, and his countenance fell. [Genesis 4: 2–6]

These passages may be viewed as an allegory for the analysis in this chapter: Cain's birth represents increased population; his being a "tiller of the ground" represents the shift toward agriculture due to population pressure. The slight respect paid to farmers is common to many hunting, gathering, and herding societies, and it may be related to the higher level of effort required in agriculture and the lower quality of food produced by this method.[29] Abel's murder may be an allegory for the risks associated with increased population when even sentiments of kinship are not powerful enough to prevent fratricide.[30] Perhaps the arguments presented in this chapter were well known to our ancestors, in, of course, different language.[31] The fact that new generations frequently misinterpret the documents of their ancestors and that literate societies misinterpret the language of illiterate ones will be examined in the following chapters.

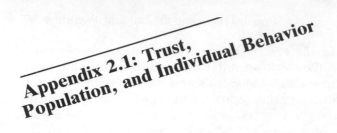

Let us assume that storing physical property is risky because of the reasons elaborated above. These risks depend on the amount of trust that exists among members of a group and on a variable that denotes the "state of nature," μ. This variable represents the existence of institutions and customs that are already adjusted to stable demographic variables, so that random variations in these demographic variables around a trend do not induce changes in them. Only when the trend changes will institutions have to be adjusted (according to the random mechanism outlined in the first chapter).

Let $U(C_1, C_2)$ be an individual's utility function. (I refer to this term as reflecting the goal of self-preservation, as explained in the first chapter. The reason I here omit one's relative position in the wealth distribution is that I assume that this position is expected to be stable.) C_1 and C_2 denote the consumption levels in two periods. I shall discuss their meaning briefly.

The model is in fact a three-period model: during the first one a new generation is born and educated, but makes no decisions, these being left to the parents. This period does not appear in the utility function, but it is at this time that tastes are formed. Only during the second period of their lives do individuals make decisions. This is what $U(C_1, C_2)$ represents, the utility function incorporating the effects of education received during the first period.

Suppose that time T is allocated in the second period for generating income and for investing in personal ties. The income foregone to generate trust represents both the fixed and the variable costs necessary to obtain and maintain such a relationship. This investment is made either directly by transfers of goods and services, or indirectly by spending time with other individuals (in ceremonial behavior, educating children, and so forth). The returns in the third period depend on the returns on the amount of "trust" that has been generated.

Without loss of generality, I assume that the transfer to other people represents an implicit or explicit form of intertemporal exchange. The qualitative results of the model are unchanged if, in part, the transfer of resources represents consumption, or altruism. The problem the individual solves is:

$$\max L = EU(c_1, c_2)$$

(1) s.t. $c_1 + i = (1 - \lambda)\, Tg_1$

$$c_2 = i\,(1 + X(\alpha\lambda, \mu)) + Tg_2$$

where L is the function maximized, subject to the two budget constraints in the two periods. $EU\,(.,.)$ denotes the expected utility, λ the fraction of time devoted to generate and maintain "trust," g_1 and g_2 the marginal and average productivities, i the amount of goods stored, and X a random variable representing the riskiness of stored goods because of the possibility of the unfulfilled contracts. The α is a function of the probability that commitments based on personal ties will be fulfilled; it depends on the frequency with which people expect to interact.

For an outsider, both λTg_1 and $X(\alpha_o\lambda_o,.)$, $\alpha_o\lambda_o$ denoting the realized values of these variables at some point of time, will look like "sharing." But Tg_1 may represent the amount of resources allowed for educating children to be "good." As a result, parents may expect children to provide insurance for old age, in which case children also enter in the definition of i. Or λTg_1 may represent the total amount of resources used when one looks for partners for insurance purposes (decreasing contract uncertainty) and maintains a stable relationship with them. The returns are protected by custom (which appears implicitly in the variable μ). But custom alone, just like police and law alone, cannot guarantee contracts; trust complements it and decreases the riskiness of implicit contracts.

The first order conditions for the problem are:

(2) $$L_{c_1} = EU_1 - EU_2\,(1 + X) = 0$$

(3) $$L_\lambda = EU_2(-Tg_1(1+X) + \alpha i X_\lambda) = 0$$

where the notation L_{c_1}, L_λ, X_λ represents the derivatives of the functions with respect to the endogenous variables, and U_1, U_2 denote the marginal utilities of consumption in the two periods. (3) can be rewritten as

(4) $$-Tg_1\, EU_2(1 + X) + E(\alpha)E(X_\lambda) + k\,\mathrm{Var}(\alpha) = 0$$

assuming X_λ to be a linear function of $\alpha\lambda$ and μ, and k is a constant number depending on λ and the parameters of X_λ. The term $Cov(\alpha,\mu)$ equals zero, for I assume that institutions, represented implicitly by μ, are adjusted to variations in α around a known trend (which for primitive societies is zero). (4) can be rewritten as

(5)
$$\frac{i\,E(X_\lambda)}{Tg_1} = \frac{EU_2(1+X)}{E(\alpha)} + \frac{k\,Var(X)}{Tg_1\,E\,(\alpha)}$$

The term on the left-hand side is a function of the expected rate of return on trust, for

$$\frac{E(X_\lambda)}{Tg_1} = \frac{E(X_{\lambda_1} - X_{\lambda_0})}{Tg_1(\lambda_1 - \lambda_0)}$$

and $Tg_1\,(\lambda_1 - \lambda_0)$ represents the costs of investing in personal ties, while $E(X_{\lambda_1} - X_{\lambda_0})$ the expected benefits.

Assume now that $E(\alpha)$ changes, but $Var(\alpha)$ stays constant. This will happen when population size changes or its mobility changes. If, for example, α decreases (i.e., anonymity becomes cheaper because of either increased migration or increased population), with a *ceteris paribus* assumption, individuals become *worse* off, since the real rate of return in the economy decreases (contract uncertainty has increased). In order to hold real income constant (the usual assumption economists make when the effects of some changes are analyzed), one must assume that there is a compensating change in the state of nature, μ, such that it holds true that the individual can still maintain the previous levels of consumption. Otherwise, for *all* values of λ, the returns would only be $X(\alpha_1\lambda,\mu)$, where α_1 is less than α. Thus with the original state of nature, μ, the real rate of return can remain constant only by investing more in either personal ties or in enforcing contracts, both of which are costly.

In order to maintain real income constant, one must therefore assume either that a "lucky hit" on an institutional change has been made (which becomes optimal because of the changed demographic variables) and the "state of nature" is adjusted by the rise of the institution that diminishes contract uncertainty, or that some technological innovation has been made. Why these innovations occur has been explained in the previous chapter. Notice that when α suddenly changes the wealth distribution is unexpectedly changed and some people's relative position in the wealth distribution is suddenly worsened.

But once the adjustments are made, the relative importance of the components of the real rate of return in the economy changes with the value of the "state of nature." Assume that in order to maintain the new institutions a fixed amount $\lambda\,g_1T$ must be paid, λ denoting the fixed amount of time one must work for maintaining them. Then the opportunity set, holding real income constant, shifts toward physical property, for even without investing anything in personal ties, a higher rate of return is now guaranteed (i.e., $X(0, \mu_o) < X(0, \mu_1)$, for all values of λ). Thus the changes in demographic variables and the adjustment of social institutions represented by μ_1 lead people to become more materialistic.

A few words on consumption and investment. The assumption that individuals maximize their utility where consumption levels appear as the endogenous variables does *not* mean that people are only interested in material goods. The terms consumption and investment are used here in order to make the distinction between activities that give pleasure only in the present and activities that are expected to give future pleasure. This distinction would lead to measurements radically different from what consumption and investment measure today, as the discussion of children, trust, and custom has implied.

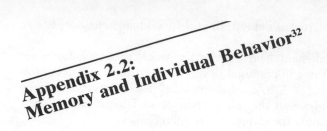

The formal model is based on Becker's (1965) model of demand for basic commodities. The consumer is subject to two constraints: one on his total income and the other on memory. More specifically, our consumer has a utility function

(1) $$U = U(Z_1, \ldots, Z_n)$$

where Z_i is a set of commodities. Each commodity Z_i is "produced" by the consumer:

(2) $$Z_i = F_i(x_i, S_i, t_i, R)$$

where x_i is the input of purchased goods into the production of Z_i, S_i is the input of memory space, t_i the input of time, and R all the other "environmental" variables involved in the production of Z_i. The reason why memory space is an input in the production of Z_i can be rationalized in the following way: when producing a commodity in the household—a meal, for instance—a housewife may either remember a recipe or look it up in a cookbook, a time-consuming and therefore costly activity, or buy a prepared meal, costlier than preparing it from scratch. Also, when buying the ingredients, she may either recall where she saw lower prices or search for them. Thus the alternatives to memory are costly whether in time or money.

The consumer maximizes (1) subject to three constraints:

(3) $$\Sigma p_i x_i = \omega t_\omega + V$$

(4) $$\Sigma t_i + t_\omega = T$$

(5) $$\Sigma S_i = S$$

where p_i = market price of x_i
ω = wage rate of the consumer
t_ω = time worked
T = time endowment of the consumer
S = memory endowment of the consumer
V = non-wage money endowment of the consumer

(3) and (4) are not independent constraints and may be combined in one constraint:

(3)′ $$\Sigma p_i x_i + \Sigma \omega t_i = \omega T + V$$

Thus the consumer's problem is to maximize (1) subject to (3)′ and (5).
The first order condition of this maximization problem takes the form:

(6) $$\frac{\partial U}{\partial Z_i} = U_i = \lambda(p_i \frac{\partial x_i}{\partial Z_i} + \omega \frac{\partial t_i}{\partial Z_i}) + \mu \frac{\partial S_i}{\partial Z_i}$$

where λ is the marginal utility of money income and μ is the marginal utility of memory. (6) can be rewritten:

(6)′ $$U_i = \lambda(p_i \frac{\partial x_i}{\partial Z_i} + \omega \frac{\partial t_i}{\partial Z_i} + \frac{\mu}{\lambda} \frac{\partial S_i}{\partial Z_i})$$

where $\frac{\mu}{\lambda}$ is the shadow price of memory. Notice that

$$\Pi_i = p_i \frac{\partial x_i}{\partial Z_i} + \omega \frac{\partial t_i}{\partial Z_i} + \frac{\mu}{\lambda} \frac{\partial S_i}{\partial Z_i}$$

is the "full price" of Z_i, which takes into consideration the cost of each factor of production.

From (6)′ we can see how an increase in wealth will affect the use of memory. First, let us consider what happens when V, the non-wage income, increases. Then, if we assume that all the Z_i are normal commodities, the demand for each Z_i will increase as all monetary income is spent. Thus both the value of goods bought and the time spent in commodity production will increase and, *ceteris paribus*, the marginal productivity of memory is raised; memory becomes more valuable. There will thus be in the household production a shift away from memory-intensive methods toward more goods- and time-intensive production methods: more books, data banks, and so forth will be used in order to economize on memory. What happens to each and every S_i depends on the relative force of the income and substitution effects.

A rise in the wage rate, ω, would essentially have the same effect, except that in this case time becomes relatively more expensive. Whether time or memory will become the relatively more expensive factor of production depends on the specific form of the production function. Production will shift toward more goods-intensive methods of production. Thus people with higher income tend to save on memory. This may explain why grandparents, who place a low value on time, told us fairy tales while our parents bought us books.

Finally, it should be noted that the biological constraint on people's memories does not imply that there is a rigid constraint on memory: diverse means such as books, computer data banks, and so forth are used as an extension of memory. But compared with the biological memory, all the mechanical and electronical extensions are costly in terms of money. Moreover, the storage of information in artificial memories is itself a memory-consuming operation: in order to retrieve information, one must remember where it was stored.

3

Usury Laws, Brotherhood, Anonymity, and the Protestant Ethic; or, Who Was Shylock?

Primum vivere, deinde philosophari.

Ideas have long lives. They seem to survive in memory, or in books (which complement human memory) long after the circumstances that lead to their development have disappeared. The idea of usury is examined in this chapter. Using the arguments presented in the previous chapters, we shall examine its appearance and decline, as well as the discussions surrounding the development of the idea.

Nelson's (1949) extensive review of the existing literature on usury draws attention to the fact that usury laws have been linked to the obligations of kinship, brotherhood, and friendship. The prohibition rests on two grounds: first, that the richer ought to help the poorer, if not by charity then at least by free loans, and second, that usury is the root of social ruin and must be outlawed. Both considerations apply only internally within a tribe, nation, or a religion; there is no obligation to help strangers, nor is public policy concerned with their well-being. The idea of usury originates in the Bible, but most discussions of it appeared during the Middle Ages and the Reformation, although usury statutes survive even in today's legislation. Some general features of the periods when these discussions took place will be described in connection with the views presented in the first two chapters; we will then be in a better position to understand the changing views on usury.

Let us briefly summarize the main arguments in the first two chapters: when people live in relatively isolated, small communities, expecting exchanges with a stable population, trust, the sharing of sentiments of brotherhood, and agreement on norms of behavior are sufficient to carry out intertemporal exchanges without written contracts, a well defined legal framework, or central authority. Trust lowers the costs of transactions and brings benefits similar to the payment of a real rate of interest, since less collateral is needed when people trust one another. Also, in these communities customs maintain a relatively stable wealth distribution and diminish the probability of criminal and rebellious acts. Thus people provide one another with a wide range of assurances, and interest rates may not be recognized as an explicit feature of contracts. In other words, in relatively small and isolated communities the return on loans takes the form of the right, protected by custom, to call upon the group for assistance in the future.

In contrast, when population increases, exchanges become more anonymous; people will gamble on social institutions such as money, literacy, and written contracts; and a central authority emerges to protect exchanges previously based on trust and custom; this authority will also redistribute wealth. Under these circumstances, interest will become an explicit feature of contracts, its payment now being protected by laws, government, and police.

These arguments shed light not only on the relationship between usury and brotherhood but also on the discussion surrounding these ideas. One would expect to encounter discussion of these subjects either when a society becomes more isolated, or when it is suddenly opened up to international trade (which results in more exchanges with strangers). As made clear in chapter 1, fluctuation rather than stability leads people to reevaluate their ideas.

When either type of fluctuation takes place, some members of a society will advocate "universal brotherhood" as the basis for exchange, while others will advocate a method of exchange protected by law and police. When communities become more isolated, more people will gamble on the idea of "universal brotherhood," on forbidding usury, and on diminishing the role of law and central authority. But when population increases, usury laws will tend to be forgotten, interest will appear as a formal aspect of contracts, and theories of "alienation" will appear.

Let us now turn to our examination of the Middle Ages.

The Middle Ages: General Trends

The early Middle Ages were characterized by *decreased* population, *increased* isolation of communities, and *decreased* role of trade. The decrease in population was due to epidemics rather than to a changed attitude toward births (see Bloch 1940, McNeill 1976, Russell 1969, and Davison and Harper 1972). This period was characterized by all the features that could have been predicted from the arguments outlined in the previous chapters.

Bloch (1940) describes some of this period's features:

The fundamental characteristic [of this age] remains the great and universal decline in population. Over the whole of Europe, the population was immeasurably smaller than it has been since the twelfth [century]. Even in the provinces formerly under Roman rule, human beings were much scarcer than they had been in the heyday of the Empire. The most important towns had no more than a few thousand inhabitants. . . . Among these sparsely scattered human groups the obstacles to communication were many. . . .Even the old Roman roads . . . went to rack and ruin for want of maintenance. . . . Added to this was the general state of insecurity increased by depopula- tion. . . . Between two inhabited centres quite close to each other the connections were much rarer, the isolation of their inhabitants . . . greater than would be the case in our day. . . . Trade . . . was not non-existent, but it was irregular in the extreme. [pp. 60–67]

Historians like North and Thomas (1973), Le Roy Ladurie (1966), and legal scholars like Vinogradoff, Maitland, and Pollock (quoted in a book edited by Lawrence Krader [1966]) emphasize the increased role of kinship in substituting for various roles of the state during this period. Essentially, they all seem to agree with Bloch's (1940) view:

The social condition we call feudalism was also marked by a real tightening of the ties of kinship. Because the times were troubled and the public authority weak, the individual gained a more lively awareness of his links with the local groups . . . to which *he could look for help*. . . . To seek a protector, or to find satisfaction in being one—these things are common to all ages. But we seldom find them giving rise to new legal institutions save in civilizations where the rest of the social framework is giving way. Such was the case in Gaul after the collapse of the Roman Empire. . . . The centuries which later witnessed the progressive breakdown of . . . authentic feudalism also experienced—with the crumbling of the large kinship groups—the early symptoms of the slow decay of family solidarities. [pp. 142–48; italics added]

The increased role of kinship during the early Middle Ages was charac- terized by features similar to those of tribal societies:

The word 'ownership' . . . would have been almost meaningless. . . . For nearly all land and a great many human beings were burdened at this time with a *multiplicity of obligations,* differing in their nature but all apparently of equal importance. [Bloch 1940, pp. 115–16; italics added]

Kinship was not necessarily based on blood relationship, and kin provided collateral before the courts: the feudal lord encouraged or even enforced these arrangements, for he considered it an advantage to hold the members of the "communal households" jointly responsible for the payment of dues.

But ties of kinship alone could not provide adequate protection. Bloch (1940) explains:

> Yet to the individual, threatened by the numerous dangers bred by an atmosphere of violence, the kinship group did not seem to offer adequate protection, even in the first feudal age. In the form in which it then existed, it was too vague and too variable in its outlines, too deeply undermined by the duality of descent by male and female lines. That is why men were obliged to seek or accept other ties. On this point history is decisive, for the only regions in which powerful agnatic groups survived—German lands on the shores of the North Sea, Celtic districts of the British Isles—knew nothing of vassalage, the fief and the manor. The tie of kinship was one of the essential elements of feudal society; its relative weakness explains why there was feudalism at all. [p. 142]

The question now is whether or not we can explain not only the similarities but also the differences between the structure of primitive and feudal societies. Historians and legal scholars have emphasized one striking difference between the organization of tribal societies and of the feudal manor, namely the pronounced role of the subordinate's link with a nearby chief. North and Thomas's (1973) interpretation is that

> two . . . basic elements entered into the manorial economy; the function of protection, and the role of labor. In the matter of protection, the fortified castle and armored knights on horseback, having specialized skills in warfare, provided local security which could never be equalled by any group of peasants ill-armed with primitive weapons and lacking military skills. Moreover, against such an enemy as roving bands of raiders . . . a local lord and castle were more immediate and comforting a safeguard than a distant king and army. [p. 19]

The specific arrangement between fiefs and lords is attributed to the increased costs of trade, viewed as a consequence of depopulation and the resulting increased costs of mobility:

> The obligation of the serf to provide labor services to his lord and protector . . . was chosen because given the constraint of high transaction costs involved in trading goods it was the most efficient. . . . The negotiation cost for sharing *inputs* (i.e. labor dues) during and prior to the tenth century would have been lower than any of the other arrangements, especially since competition between lords for labor had resulted in a rudimentary market which established at least

a range for the price of labor. [North and Thomas 1973, pp. 31–32, italics in original]

Both the similarities and the differences between European feudal structure and tribal structure in Africa have been frequently pointed out. Goody (1971), in his essay "Feudalism in Africa?", discusses this comparison and emphasizes one difference between the two structures:

> It is the thesis of the present work that the nature of the 'indigenous' African social structure, especially in its political aspects, has been partly misunderstood because of a failure to appreciate certain basic technological differences between Africa and Eurasia. It is these differences that make the application of the European concept of 'feudalism' inappropriate. But the problem is not only historical; in many areas 'traditional' African social structure exists (in a somewhat modified form) precisely because the rural economy has not greatly changed. [Preface]

Goody's explanation is consistent with the arguments and evidence presented in the previous chapters, and shows why one should expect differences between the structure of feudal and of primitive societies, for one must view European feudal structure not just as an adjustment to a smaller population, but as an adjustment to a *suddenly diminished* population. The reason one must make this distinction is that, in a society that once had a greater population one should expect to find a level of technology (in particular military technology) *different* from the level it achieved in a society that kept its population stable. As with agriculture, anonymous exchange based on written contracts, and industrial production of food, this technology appears to be merely an adaptation to increased numbers. This is why I have described it as "different" rather than "higher," which implies some form of superiority, a judgment I find inappropriate considering that "higher" military technology means only that more people can be killed more rapidly.

One should also expect differences not only between primitive and feudal societies, but also among societies in Europe depending on whether or not their population has fluctuated significantly. Historians have noted that in northern Europe the feudal manors did *not* flourish. According to Russell (1969), northern Europe was less exposed to new diseases, which resulted in smaller fluctuations in its population.

The trends involving the increased role of kinship, the diminished role of commerce, the profound weakening of the state in its protective capacity, its substitution by the feudal manor, and more extended family ties can all be plausibly linked to the large, exogenous decrease in population size. Diminished population also leads to an increased role for custom, to diminished literacy, and to relatively subjective and flexible interpretation of "history." These features also characterize the early Middle Ages.

As already shown in the previous chapter, Thompson (1939) notes the diminished demand for literacy and describes the closing down of the Roman libraries. Bloch (1940) discusses in detail both modes of feeling and thought and "folk memory":

> The truth is that the regard for accuracy, with its firmest buttress, the respect for figures, remained profoundly alien to minds even of the leading men of that age. . . . Memory was the sole guardian of tradition. Now the human memory . . . is a marvellous instrument of elimination and transformation—especially what we call collective memory. . . The plot of the Chanson de Roland is based on folklore rather than history. . . . The epic *gestes* were not . . . intended to be read . . . the epic tales . . . were the history books of the people who could not read but loved to listen. [pp. 75, 92–94, 114]

These features are similar to those described in the previous chapter; it is interesting to note, however, that historians do not relate them to diminished population, the increased isolation of communities, or the diminished benefits of literacy and arithmetic. Why does one need numbers and written contracts when people live in small communities, exchanges are based on trust, and people know each other?

As for custom, it has been noted that

> custom has become the sole living source of law, and princes, even in their legislation scarcely claimed to do more than interpret it . . . [and] each human group . . . tended to develop its own legal tradition. [Bloch 1940, pp. 111–12]

These various traditions are described by legal scholars (Krader et al. 1966) as well as by many historians, who show how extended families and custom have substituted for various functions of the state.

The repopulation of Europe began in the eighth century and continued uninterrupted until the Black Death of 1346 (see Russell 1969, McNeill 1976, Hatcher 1977, and Hollingsworth 1969). This increase transformed the face of Europe, and the process of what we today somewhat misleadingly call "economic development" occurred everywhere. Homer (1963) briefly characterizes each century:

> the tenth century has been called the century of transition . . . history records the quiet beginnings of trends and forces that can be recognized as the forces behind a new economic revival. . . . During the eleventh century, political and economic revival in western Eu-

rope became general . . . European trade with the East was . . . greatly enlarged . . . trade on the North Sea revived. . . . This was the period when the towns of northern Europe obtained power and autonomy. . . . During the twelfth century the economic development of western Europe accelerated. . . . As the population increased rapidly new free cities sprung up . . . ruled by merchants. . . . Commercial capitalism now developed rapidly. . . . [pp. 85–90]

Simultaneously,

from the twelfth century onwards, customs which were often vague were gradually replaced by a system of law more devoted to precision and clarity . . . [and] the governmental authorities through their activities as guardians of the peace contributed to the weakening of the kinship bond. [Bloch 1940, pp. 132, 139]

As shown in the previous chapters, all these changes can be seen to represent adaptations to a rising population and a changing wealth distribution.

This process of "development" was interrupted when the Black Death swept Europe, and about one-third of the total population died. In England, where scholarly study of the plague is most advanced (see Hatcher 1977 and McNeill 1976), the population seems to have declined irregularly but persistently for more than a century, and reached a low point some time between 1440 and 1480. Since then Europe's population has risen, accompanied by all the gambling and institutional adjustments that we today call the "Rise of the West."

The changing features of the early and late Middle Ages thus seem consistent with some of the broad predictions made in the earlier chapters, and can be linked to the large fluctuations in Europe's population, which were due to reasons beyond human control.

Usury and Brotherhood[1]

The first written document on usury appears in Deuteronomy:

Thou shalt not lend upon usury [*neshek*] to thy brother; usury of money, usury of victuals, usury of any thing that is lent upon usury: unto a stranger [*nochri*] thou mayest lend upon usury; but unto thy brother thou shalt not lend upon usury, that the Lord thy God may bless thee in all that thou settest thine hand to in the land whither thou goest to possess it. [23:19–20]

This different treatment accorded strangers and fellow Jews was the source of constant controversy during medieval times, until Calvin finally gave a relative interpretation to the text (an interpretation consistent with mine), namely, that one must understand the text as applying to circumstances that no longer prevailed.

While the passage above is the first *written* document on usury, we do not know for how long the ideas they capture were current or when they emerged. If one takes at least part of the Bible literally, one obtains a picture of the Hebrews as a small tribal society who together moved from Egypt to isolation in Sinai. As Moses' "biography" indicates, their legal framework was uncertain. One can then view verse 19 of the passage, dealing with the restriction of interest rates, as having been introduced when the Hebrews became an isolated tribe, thus increasing both the cohesion of the group and its stability. For, as already argued, when a group becomes more isolated, interest rates may not be formally established, but members of the group will eventually provide one another with a wide array of insurance: restriction on usury hastens this adjustment. The written document in the Bible may have preserved this idea.

From being an isolated community in Sinai, the Hebrews moved to Canaan, where the possibility of international trade existed. Now they could either trade with strangers or with members of their own group. However, international trade requires agreement on the definition of property rights and their enforcement. The absence of such agreement means that the legal framework is uncertain, and so the risks of trading are greater with strangers than with members of one's own group. Rates of interest reflect these risks, so one would expect that higher interest rates must be paid in dealings with strangers than with people who trust one another. These arguments explain verse 20 of the passage, which refers to a state of equilibrium in two types of exchange: trade with brothers and trade with strangers, which have different risks and different goals. Not only does trade with strangers bear greater risks, there is also no obligation to help strangers, nor is public policy concerned with their well-being.

Some early biblical scholars (the Amoraim)[2] reinterpreted the terms "interest" and "usury" as referring not only to the lending of four dinars for a return of five, or of one bushel of wheat for a return of two, but also to cover other arrangements (see interpretations in the Mishnah BM5:1–5:8). For instance, they argued that when two men agree to work for each other in turn, it must involve the same kind of work; otherwise the work of one might be more valuable than that of the other, and amount in fact to prohibited interest. Gifts that one man may send to another in view of a forthcoming request for a loan or in gratitude for a loan granted and returned, fall within the prohibition of interest, as do words conveying to the lender any valuable information (BM 5:10), or even greetings that otherwise would not have been exchanged (BM 75b). Whether or not the biblical laws and these new interpretations were obeyed in Canaan is another question. It seems that they were not; moreover, while some talmudic jurists extended the prohibition on interest to include transactions that were probably far removed from the loans to which the biblical prohibition referred (and which could never be enforced, like the rulings on words and greetings), others sought ways to validate transactions that clearly fell within that prohibition.

These two contrasting trends in the interpretation of the biblical prohibitions on interest appeared during the amoraic period in Babylonia, when the prohibitary laws against interest proved to be no longer compatible with the expansion of trade and the dispersion of the Jewish population, that is, increased trade with strangers. The two trends in the interpretation of the biblical laws, one practical and adjusted to the changed circumstances, the other not, is not really surprising since it does not differ from the two trends that can always be perceived among intellectuals. One trend is followed by "entrepreneurs" who break habits of thought and advocate adjustments to a changing environment; the other is followed by those for whom familiarity and habit represent verified, absolute principles.

Medieval moralists also had difficulty in interpreting the distinction in biblical law between trade among Jews and between Jews and non-Jews, and in reconciling it with the Church's general prohibition on usury and the Christian idea of universal brotherhood.

The biblical law referred to a period when international trade was increasing, that is, when people who previously did not deal with one another began to come into contact. At first they were unable to find a uniform method for enforcing contracts. In contrast, the period of the early medieval moralists was characterized by increased isolation of communities and diminished trade. Thus these moralists correctly perceived that in these circumstances the ideas of prohibiting usury and of universal brotherhood would have greater appeal. But since they still wanted to rely on the Bible as a document of absolute truth, they encountered the difficulties mentioned above.

Homer briefly summarizes the initial success and subsequent decline of the usury laws:

> These restrictions [on usury] at times seemed to approach absolute prohibition, and for many centuries they enjoyed widespread and official support. . . . During the reign of Charlemagne, circa 800, not only did the Hadriana, a collection of canons, repeat and quote these earlier prohibitions, but for the first time the state, in the Capitularies of Charlemagne, forbade usury to everyone . . . [and] it was not until the eleventh century, when European learning and trade revived, that the Church's doctrine on usury was examined in detail by scholars. . . . [p. 70]

The widespread acceptance of the usury doctrine has been analyzed in works with titles like "Usury Doctrines and Their Effect on European Credit Forms and Interest,"[3] implying either that somebody "gambled" on the idea of usury and succeeded in persuading the population to follow him in his advice, or that there was a causal relationship between usury doctrines and their effect on credit markets. I believe that the relationship between the doctrine of usury and methods of exchange is more complex: that such doctrines do not affect credit forms, but rather that, when population diminishes, forms of credit and the ideas people believe in change simultaneously. In this case the causal relationship is well defined, since fluctuations in population, which lead to a changed wealth distribution and to a greater willingness to gamble on new ideas, are unexpected.

Let us now see what predictions we can make when the reverse process occurs, that is, when population increases.

During the transition from societies characterized by exchanges based on personal ties to economies in which exchanges are more anonymous, two schools of thought will develop. One will advocate a system based on already known and practiced principles, and will posit brotherhood as a basis for society (the "old way"), while another will adapt its views to the changed circumstances and gamble on advocating formal, anonymous transactions.

One may ask why all members of a society do not instantaneously adapt to the new circumstances. There are several answers: first, there are people whose insurance is based on preserving the old way of life. Second, even if people perceive that methods of exchange and the institutions of society must change when population has permanently increased, they may perceive the rise as temporary and believe that it is not worth changing the institutions of the past since previous circumstances may return. I argued in the first chapter that one cannot really say whether it is right or wrong to hold these beliefs, for they represent a gamble on the idea that the conditions of the past might return, and no one can state with certainty that this might not turn out to be the case.

The twelfth century was characterized by increases in population, in the extent of markets, and in economic development, and by frequent appearances of Christian usurers, who camouflaged their faith and masqueraded as Jews. These developments led to renewed discussions of usury and brotherhood and to changes in the interpretations given to the biblical texts:

> All formulations of international economic policy were now seen to hinge on the adjustment of this issue. . . . [A] few of the early commentators on Gratian's *Decretum* (ca. 1140) pointed out that [demanding interest from Muslims] was a useful economic weapon in

recovering their rightful heritage as Christians from the modern Canaanites. . . . [Nelson 1949, p. 6]

Indeed, one of the new interpretations was that the religious texts in fact authorized the recovery of rightful property from enemies of Christendom, whether pagans or Jews, who were really slaves and obligated to serve Christians. Hosteinsis (d. 1271) prepared a list of exceptions to the general prohibition of usury and Henricus Bohic (d. 1350?) authorized Christians to practice usury with enemies of the Church.

As usual, the easiest and cheapest solution to the controversy was found. A new term was invented to replace the old one with its bad connotations: the term "interest" made its appearance, although what the difference was between "interest" and "usury" was never made clear:

> Already in the mid thirteenth century, advanced theological and legal circles were tending to reserve their condemnations primarily to those contracts wherein profit was openly stipulated or secretly hoped for on a mutuum. . . . After that date, moderately latitudinarian constructions steadily exempted novel arrangements, forged by developing business enterprise, from the stigma of usury. By the beginning of the fifteenth century the doctors were agreed that increments given on public loans were to be interpreted as compensation for *damna et interesse,* rather than *usura.* [Nelson 1969, p. 24]

It was only during the Reformation that for the first time in the history of Western Christianity the implications of what some came to regard as an inherited communalistic ethic were thoroughly reexamined. Some of Luther's followers insisted on the application of the Mosaic and Gospel teachings to social issues, in particular the elimination of slavery and of begging. Others continued to attack usury, among them Jakob Strauss (1480–1533), a preacher at Eisenach who hoped to make the brotherhood of men a social reality and who denounced usury as inimical to love of neighbor. Luther's (1483–1536) views fluctuated: while he argued that Christians were under no obligation to observe Mosaic injunctions, he at first condemned usury. But while some of his followers advocated a return to communal life (a gamble on the lifestyle of the past), his position changed and he later argued that interest that did not exceed four or five percent was not necessarily unjust.

The rudiments of Calvin's (1509–64) views may be found in the writings of Melanchthon, who discussed usury in several of his treatises. In the first version of *Loci theologici* (1521), he argued that the universal prohibition of usury was part of natural and divine law and that discrimination against aliens is meaningless since all are kinsmen. (Calvin later made a similar pronouncement, but by that time the statement "all are kinsmen" meant not much more than "all are strangers.") In his commentaries on the *De officiis* of Cicero (1525), Melanchthon revised his ideas and argued that the Christian injunction against usury, like the Mosaic rule, was intended only among fellow citizens:

> The Deuteronomic prohibition . . . represents an attempt on the part of Moses to guarantee the communication of good offices among fellow-citizens. One is more obligated to a fellow-citizen, than to a stranger . . . or to any enemy. Therefore, loans to fellow citizens are gratuitous. [Nelson 1949, p. 57]

This statement and the previous discussion show that borrowing and lending was viewed as one of many transactions in which members of a society engage when the population is relatively small and isolated, and that the prohibition of interest replaced alternative methods of redistributing wealth in the society. This is also the interpretation given by the Talmud to the Deuteronomic regulations, when explaining the rationale for different interest rates among brothers and strangers:[4]

> The Talmud made it clear that the prohibition of interest among brothers referred only to loans given to the needy, and not to commercial loans which entail risk of the capital. *The law was designed to strengthen the bonds of fraternity among an isolated people.* [Nelson 1949, pp. 111–12; italics added]

But one may ask why the goal of maintaining stability in a society by keeping the wealth distribution at stable levels should be achieved by restrictions on interest rates rather than by enabling the credit market to be cleared and then redistribute wealth through some well defined taxation. The answer is that the redistribution of wealth can be achieved either through custom (teaching people that they must give loans to the needy without charging interest, thus increasing the stability of the society), or through taxation by a central authority. But maintaining a central authority to define and enforce property rights is costly. Only when population increases and stays at the higher level, which renders achieving stability by teaching and enforcing customs more expensive, does it become more profitable for a society to revise its institutions and redistribute wealth through a central authority rather than through custom.

However, in periods of transition, it is not very clear what the right policy is: while custom can no longer be enforced strictly, central authorities cannot instantaneously replace it—time must elapse until the appropriate taxes can be developed and their collection can be enforced.

Zwingli (1484–1531), the Swiss reformer, pointed out that a strict prohibition against usury might not be the intent of Scripture, and that "once private property has been established in human society, it becomes theft to withhold payment of interest charges or rents." Nelson summarizes this period in the development of the idea of usury:

> Luther, Melanchthon and Zwingli do not expressly depart from the ethic of brotherhood. To do this they would have to redefine the character of the fraternal bond between men. But they did help to encourage the conviction *that the ethic of brotherhood could not be the basis of civil society.* . . . Calvin, self consciously and hesitantly, charted the path to the world of Universal Otherhood, where all became brothers in being equally "others". [Nelson 1949, pp. 67, 73; italics added]

Calvin justified the Deuteronomic double standard on the grounds that Jews had to make a living somehow,

> since otherwise a just reciprocity would not have been preserved, without which one party must needs be injured. . . . In order, therefore, that equality be preserved, He accords the same liberty to His people which the Gentiles would assume for themselves; for this is the only intercourse that can be endured, when the conditions of both parties is similar and equal. [Nelson 1949, p. 76]

With regard to usury, Calvin raises the question whether or not the fraternal union among people implies that usury should be forbidden, since this situation is similar to that of Jews. His answer is that

> there is a difference in the political union, for the situation in which God placed the Jews and many other circumstances permitted them to trade conveniently among themselves without usuries. Our union is entirely different. Therefore I do not feel that usuries were forbidden to us simply. [Nelson 1949, p. 78]

In other words, because of changed circumstances this law is no longer relevant, and another mechanism must be found to redistribute wealth in society. And redistribution of wealth was still one of Calvin's goals: he interpreted biblical rules of conduct in the light of equity, and in 1547 in Geneva he introduced several social reforms, which permitted the transfer of control of social claims to the laity and established new institutions to centralize and coordinate welfare, a process that is an expected adjustment to increased population.

While Calvin seemed to provide a relativistic explanation of usury, he did not do so when discussing the idea of friendship. He stated that to lend money only to those from whom one may expect return is simply to practice the carnal friendship of the pagan, although, according to Nelson (1949) and many others he mentions, this "carnal" friendship seems to have been equivalent to traditional notions of brotherhood. This concept seemed to imply that friends had much wider obligations to one another than today. These obligations included the sharing of goods, services, and sentiments, standing surety for a friend, and in particular exacting revenge from one's enemies:

> The man who was brought before a court found in his kinsmen his natural helpers . . . [and] it was . . . especially in the vendetta that the ties of kinship showed themselves at their strongest. . . . The Middle Ages from beginning to end, and particularly the feudal era, lived under the sign of private vengeance. . . . The solitary individual, however, could do but little. Moreover, it was most commonly a death that had to be avenged. In this case the family group went into action and the *faide* (feud) came into being. . . . No moral obligation seemed more sacred than this. [Bloch 1940, pp. 124–26]

As one would expect, the term "kin" included more than one's family and was rather indefinite: in France, one commonly referred to kinsmen as "friends" (*amis*) and in Germany, *Freunde*.

We have seen that obligations of friendship and the role of kinship may be expected to diminish with increases in population and the resulting rise of central authorities that emerge to define and protect property rights. The changing views concerning these obligations are reflected in the literature of the thirteenth to the sixteenth century. While thirteenth-century texts still state that people are required to borrow in order to pay for losses incurred in standing surety for a friend, the following three passages (in Nelson 1949) by three different writers of the sixteenth century reflect very altered views:

> Enter not into bands, no not for thy best friends, he that payeth another man's debt seeketh his own decay. . . . Lend not a penny without a pawne, for that will be a good gage to borowe.
>
> Beware of suretyship for thy best friend . . . neither borrow money of a neighbour or a friend, but of a stranger, where paying it thou shalt hear no more of it. . . .
>
> Above all things, be not made an ass to carry the burdens of other men; if any friend desire thee to be his surety, give him a part of what thou has to spare; if he press thee further, he is not thy friend at all. . . . [pp. 147–48]

Alberico Gentili (1552–1608) points out clearly both the change in the concept of friendship and the fact that laws came to replace the obligations of friendship:[5]

> We are speaking of the friendship of individuals which we see all about us, not drawing arguments from those ideal friendships which philosophy invents for our benefit, none of which we actually see. . . . We are speaking here of friendships of which our law takes cognizance; that is, those within the experience of mankind.

Nelson's (1949) summary accords with the views presented here, although, interestingly enough, he never interprets the process he describes as one of adaptation to a fluctuating population:

> When two communities merge and two sets of others become one set of brothers, a price is generally paid. The price, as this essay suggests, is an attenuation of the love which had held each set together. [p. 136]

It is now possible to explain why some have concluded that interest was the root of social ruin. Medieval scientists observed the correlation between the emergence of interest rates and both the decline of friendship and the weakening of family ties. They interpreted this correlation as a causal relationship. However, both the recognition of interest rates as an explicit feature of contracts and the weakening of customs can plausibly be linked to the large increases in population. In this case the causal relationship is well defined. In contrast, in the statement "interest was the root of social ruin" it is not, for one cannot distinguish between the view that the weakening of family ties forced people to borrow from strangers and that which holds that the ability to borrow from strangers enabled people to rely less on family. However, there is a qualification to this statement: the term "causal relationship" is used here relative to the models and evidence available today, thus my interpretation of "what caused what" will necessarily differ from medieval interpretations (more on the perception of "causal relationships" appears in the appendix to chapter 4).

Finally, one may view Shakespeare's *Merchant of Venice* as an illustration of the issues discussed here: Shylock represents the new world of legal formalities (in which all are strangers), while Antonio and Bassanio represent traditional friendship. The fact that Shakespeare selected a Jew to represent the new world may not be accidental: Jews were insecure strangers in a largely Christian medieval Europe. Because they were frequently discriminated against, they had a greater incentive to gamble on novel ideas and became entrepreneurs, thus making a quicker adjustment to changed circumstances. One of the reasons the play still speaks to us may be that we are still in the same process of transition that was going on in Shakespeare's time: as population and its mobility continue to increase, customs and family ties are weakened, and legal formalities, regulations, and social security substitute for them.

Fromm, Weber, and the Protestant Ethic

The subjects so far discussed will inevitably bring to mind the views of Fromm and Weber on medieval Europe and the emergence of the Protestant Ethic. Fromm asked, "Why do certain definite changes of man's character take place from one historical epoch to another?" (1941, p. 27), while Weber addressed himself to "the influence of those psychological sanctions, which, originating in religious belief and the practice of religion, gave a direction to practical conduct and held the individual to it" (1904, p. 97).

While Fromm seems to believe in the superiority of Western civilization, likening the Middle Ages and Reformation to the growth of a child (without explaining why the "child" retrogressed after the fall of the Roman Empire), he correctly identifies some of the features that characterized this transition:

> Ties give . . . security and a feeling of belonging and of being rooted somewhere . . . they imply a lack of individuality, but they also give security and orientation to the individual. They are ties that connect . . . the member of a primitive community with his clan and nature, or the medieval man with the Church and his social caste. . . . Once . . . the individual is free from these . . . ties, he is confronted with a new task: to orient and root himself in the world and to find security in other ways. . . . [p. 40]

> These same people had lost something: the security and feeling of belonging which the medieval social structure had offered. They were more free, but they were also more alone. . . . In the late Middle Ages . . . bewilderment and insecurity arose, but at the same time tendencies that emphasized the role of will and human effort became increasingly stronger. [pp. 64–65, 92]

While Fromm does not relate this transition to fluctuations in population and mainly emphasizes the costs associated with the transition, the similarities between his views and my analyses of primitive and medieval society and their development are clear: his "security and feeling of belonging" are similar to my concepts of family ties and customs. The "lack of individuality" may correspond to the diminished supply of "original ideas," which is a result of the wealth distribution being maintained stable by a set of customs when a community is relatively isolated. Where the population increases, customs are abandoned, family ties are weakened, and people gamble more frequently on novel ideas; thus people become more "free" and more "individualistic," although more anxious and less secure. People begin to look for new means of insurance to replace that previously provided by extended families, and they became more "materialistic" and demand social institutions that will define, enforce, and protect property rights. Thus, indeed, as Fromm states, the individual finds himself more lonely: kinship ties become weakened when the expected frequency of interaction among any two individuals diminishes and the state becomes stronger.

What ideas will be popular during the transition period from a society in which custom and family ties regulate human behavior to one in which laws and a central authority are dominant? Fromm's answer is that

> religion and nationalism, as well as any custom and any belief . . . are refuges from what man most dreads: isolation. . . . [p. 34]

> The Reformation is one root of the idea of human freedom and autonomy as it is represented in modern democracy. [p. 54]

But if this is so, how can one explain Calvin's emphasis on predestination and on the importance of human effort? Fromm's explanation is that

> the individual has to be active in order to overcome his feeling of doubt and powerlessness. This kind of effort and activity is not the result of inner strength and self-confidence; it is a desperate escape from anxiety. [p. 111]

The emphasis on human effort might have been popular for very different, but clear and pragmatic reasons. As emphasized in the previous chapters, when population unexpectedly increases people will increase their efforts, provide new ideas, specialize more, and adjust social institutions in an attempt to keep wealth constant. Unless these adjustments are made, wealth diminishes. Thus Calvin's views on human effort may have merely legitimized already existing patterns of behavior. Furthermore, this legitimization was needed in order to provide an answer to the breakdown of customs on which the redistribution of wealth was based. As Weber (1904) writes,

> The pursuit of material gain beyond personal needs must thus appear as a symptom of lack of grace, and since it can apparently only be attained at the expense of others, directly reprehensible. [p. 84]

Calvin's doctrine legitimized disobeying existing customs, and justified the new trends.

In addition to the emphasis on human effort, one would also expect that distrust of other people would have an appeal during this period and thus appear in Calvinistic doctrines. Indeed, as Fromm notes,

> In the later development of Calvinism, warnings against friendliness toward the stranger, a cruel attitude towards the poor, and a general atmosphere of suspiciousness often appeared. [p. 116]

This contrasts sharply with the Christian ideas of good works and universal brotherhood.

Briefly, when the population in Europe increased and until social institutions could be adjusted, maintaining wealth constant could only be accomplished by working harder. People changed their behavior whether or not intellectuals succeeded in explaining it. But people wanted to know *why* behavior patterns changed. Since Calvin's novel ideas provided some correct observations and some answers, although not necessarily what we would today consider "scientific" ones, people seemed ready to gamble on them.[6]

Calvin's views can thus be understood as reflecting the changed human behavior of his time. Even before Calvin articulated his views people were making greater efforts than before and trusting their neighbors less. Calvin was the "entrepreneur" who provided an insight, a "lucky hit" or doctrine, for these already existing behavior patterns.

Weber's view of the Protestant Ethic is that it had an "extraordinarily powerful psychological effect." This contrasts with my view that the psychological effects of distrust, of making greater efforts, of reduced willingness to obey custom and redistribute wealth, were already present and had only to be articulated. The ideas Weber (1904) emphasizes in Calvinistic doctrine are exactly those that could be predicted in a doctrine which exerted such wide popular appeal:

> It comes out for instance in the strikingly frequent repetition, especially in the English Puritan literature, of warnings against any trust in the aid of friendship of men. Even the amiable Baxter counsels deep distrust of even one's closest friend, and Bailey directly exhorts to trust no one and to say nothing compromising to anyone. . . .
>
> In the course of its development Calvinism added something positive to this, the idea of the necessity of proving one's faith in worldly activity. . . .
>
> Brotherly love, since it may only be practised for the glory of God and not in the service of the flesh, is expressed in the first place in

the fulfillment of the daily tasks given by the *lex naturae;* and in the process this fulfillment assumes a peculiarly objective and impersonal character, that of service in the interest of the rational organization of our social environment. [pp. 106, 121, 108–9]

As Nelson (1949) has remarked on Weber's views:

He emphasized the crucial importance of the Protestant emphasis on *impersonal service on behalf of an impersonal goal,* notably the selfless ministry in the interest of God's mastery of the world, by contrast to the *personal* . . . imitation of Christ's love, friendship, and suffering for mankind in every act oriented to any other person or object. [p. 238; italics in original]

Notice that the term "impersonal' is defined only when the frequency of interactions among any two individuals diminishes and customs are broken, which happen when population and its mobility increase. While neither Weber nor Nelson mentions Europe's fluctuating population in his arguments, their recognition that the ideas of distrust and impersonality played important roles during the Reformation is correct.

Finally, let us examine one further passage from Weber's work:

It seems . . . a mystery how the undoubted superiority of Calvinism in social organization can be connected with this tendency to tear the individual away from the closed ties with which he is bound to this world. (p. 108).

Several important points are raised here. As the evidence indicates, Calvinism did not tear the individual away from family ties; rather, the process of disintegration of kinship ties was well on its way owing to increased population and the replacement of various roles of the extended family by the state. Calvinistic doctrine legitimized this process, but had nothing to do with tearing the individual away from his family.

The "undoubted superiority" of the impersonal social organization probably reflects Weber's bias and may well be incorrect. As argued previously, there is nothing "superior" in the impersonal social organizations we are accustomed to today: societies that succeed in holding their populations stable through custom and whose social organizations are adapted to these stable structures are not "inferior" to modern structures. What one can state is that *if* societies do not succeed in finding these rules and population continuously increases, "impersonal social organization" represents one method of adjustment.

There is thus no mystery in the correlation between the weakening of family ties, the emergence of Calvinistic doctrine, and the development of impersonal social organization, nor is there any causal link. Rather, all this evidence can be linked to the extremely large fluctuations in Europe's population, which repeatedly destroyed its customs and increased the risks of trusting other people. According to this view, Calvinistic doctrine is an endogenous, although random, event, representing a gamble on ideas that justified already existing behavior patterns and so appealed to a segment of the public when the wealth distribution changed.

In contrast to this view, many historians and sociologists tend to view this doctrine, as any other sign of creativity, as something exogenous that influenced behavior, although I must admit that the contrast is not sharp. Two reservations must be stated in pointing out this contrast. First, one must distinguish between periods when novel ideas emerge and subsequent periods when they already became part of a society's customs. The arguments here have addressed only their emergence. But in subsequent periods, one can treat these ideas as exogenous, for parents educate their children by teaching them the customs they practice and believe in. The younger generation does not always question the origin of their customs. One can say that the Protestant Ethic may have had a powerful effect on them. The second reservation is that I do not claim that all of Calvin's ideas can be viewed as providing an explanation for already observed patterns of human behavior. People whose relative wealth has diminished may gamble on a doctrine because it provides some correct insights. Yet the doctrine has an unpredictable component that is due to the writer's own beliefs, which he imprints on the doctrine. In this sense one can still say that the doctrine may have an effect on human behavior: people might gamble on a "package deal" rather than on each individual idea.

Conclusions

The reader has by now probably recognized how the arguments outlined in the previous chapters can be used and how predictions about how people think in various circumstances can be made. The evidence presented here supports the view that thinking or creativity is not a random activity that springs from curiosity, or some unexplored biological trait of human nature, but is affected by changes in wealth and its distribution. The picture that emerges from this view is that history is a random process in which, in addition to fluctuations in population that at times cannot be controlled, the ideas that people have gambled on have affected the uncertain directions history has taken.

Finally, let me clarify two points: one can ask why usury laws appear in the Bible, but not in the myths of tribal societies. I would maintain that it is because the Hebrews became isolated after being part of a large economy in Egypt, and then again moved into a larger economy in Canaan, while other tribes have remained relatively isolated. As made clear in the first chapter, it is fluctuation, not stability, that leads human beings to address new questions.

As for the subject of causality that is emphasized both here and in the previous chapters, we succeed in finding a causal relationship between two phenomena in the social sciences when the one that fulfills the causal role is exogenous or totally unpredictable. Unexpected fluctuations in population play this role continuously in my analysis. How people interpret causal relationships when some information is *not* available is one of the subjects discussed in the next chapter and in its appendix.

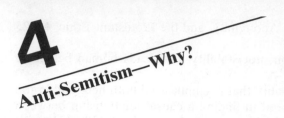

4
Anti-Semitism—Why?

Verba volant, scripta manent.

There are several possible explanations for social and ethnic discrimination: sheer irrationality (and on this social scientists have not much to say), exploitation, the desire to limit competition. A widely accepted view among economists seems to be that discrimination in the United States today can be explained by the scarcity of information on the characteristics of individuals.[1] A substitute channel of information (color, sex, race, or name) is then used to ascribe to each individual in an ethnic or religious group the characteristics of that group, and discrimination results. The term "discrimination" defines the act of attributing to an individual some of a group's characteristics without considering whether or not the individual possesses them.

But discrimination does not refer to avoiding association in employment, housing, or recreation with a group whose work habits and manners are not considered customary by the majority's standards. The reason that only attitudes toward an individual constitute discrimination, rather than attitudes toward a group, is that one can say of groups as a whole that if their members are known to have similar customs and nonformal education, they may prefer to interact more frequently with one another since they share greater trust. If one defines such preference as discrimination the word would lose any practical meaning, since even the more frequent interactions within a family would come to be labeled discriminatory.

But why are some particular groups disliked and not others? Do manifestations of discrimination fluctuate according to predictable patterns? These questions have rarely been rigorously addressed. The answer that discrimination is a matter either of "information" costs or of disliking competition is hardly convincing, for how could·one explain why the twentieth century has been characterized by the most blatant forms of discrimination (against Armenians and Jews) and by the notion of "eliminating competition" (through killing potential competitors) being taken so literally? Viewing discrimination as a matter of taste is equally unsatisfactory, since it does not admit verification.

Also, the economic literature on discrimination concentrates on minority groups (mainly blacks) who have lower incomes than the rest of the population and analyzes whether or not these lower incomes result from discrimination. There has been no attempt to reconcile this analysis with the observation that Jews, Huguenots, Parsis, and other minority groups mentioned in the first chapter have achieved *higher* monetary incomes than the rest of the population in spite of the fact that they have been discriminated against.

The purpose of this chapter is to show how the arguments presented in the first two chapters shed light on the emergence of anti-Semitic feelings and enable us to make predictions on fluctuations in its manifestations in different times and places. I hope to show that people are likely to gamble on anti-Semitic ideas when their wealth suddenly diminishes. Indirectly, this gamble will be linked with the issue of literacy and population growth.[2]

> *Literary men are a perpetual priesthood.*
> THOMAS CARLYLE, *The State of the German Literature*

Literacy, Custom, and Anti-Jewish Feeling in Antiquity

The tribal disputes described in the Bible are not interpreted as signs of anti-Semitism: as shown in the second chapter, feuds and wars are common to all tribes, in particular when they migrate or their population rises. During early biblical times Jews and Gentiles in Canaan had different occupations: the Jewish population was mainly engaged in agriculture and the non-Jewish population in commerce. The Gentiles seemed to be contemptuous of the Jewish population, whom they regarded as an isolated people refraining from contacts with the outside world; there was, however, no open hostility between the two groups.

The first manifestations of particular resentment against Jews appear during Hellenistic times. The hostility emerged when some Hellenistic rulers, beginning with Antiochus Epiphanes (175–164 B.C.), encouraged the conquered populations to adopt Hellenistic laws and beliefs. As the historical documents indicate, only Jews among all the conquered nations were reluctant to conform. Let us see whether the arguments presented in the first two chapters can shed light on the Greeks' efforts to spread their beliefs and the Jews' reluctance to oblige.

Historians have argued that the different attitudes of Jews and non-Jews toward Hellenistic influence can be attributed to religion. Other tribes were then quite willing to acknowledge both the existence and the power of their neighbors' gods, and apparently found the existence of diverse, specialized tribal deities as natural as the existence of many tribes and occupations. The Jews, however, neither recognized other deities nor permitted members of other tribes pray to their God. But to attribute this "stubbornness" to religion is not an explanation since it amounts to saying that the Jews had different tastes merely because they were Jews.

My explanation for this stubbornness is that the Jews were then the only literate tribe whose religion was based on a sacred book rather than on an oral mythology. The difference between this view and others that have been suggested is that this view can be tested: one can determine whether or not people with an oral religion displayed more or less flexible behavior than people whose religion was based on a sacred book.

The more rigid behavior of people whose religion is based on a book rather than on oral traditions has frequently been noted by anthropologists:

> In the sphere of religion it is significant that the religions of conversion, the excluding religions are all religions of the book. In the non-literate societies of Africa, at any rate, magico-religious activity is singularly eclectic in that shrines and cults move easily from place to place. The literate religions, with their fixed point of reference, their special modes of supernatural communication, are less tolerant of change. When this occurs, it tends to do so in sudden shifts, through the rise of heresies or 'movements of reform' that often take the shape of a return to the book or to its 'true interpretation.' [Goody 1968, p. 2]

Specific examples of such occurrences can be found in Goody (1968), Rattray (1913), and Marty (1922), and in the previous chapter it was shown how and when shifts in literate religions are more likely to occur. As evidence of the rigidity of literate religions, one need only recall that many people still take the Bible literally, that three literate religions still fight over Jerusalem (for the moment with words only), and legislation contradicting biblical laws still raises great controversies.

Goody (1968), in his article "Restricted Literacy in Northern Ghana," summarizes evidence on the greater religious flexibility of illiterate people:

> Throughout northern Ghana, as in the rest of western Sudan, small groups of people who could read and write Arabic, Hausa and other local languages are found scattered through a basically non-literate peasantry. Under such conditions literacy in any one place is likely to be somewhat precarious; a small Muslim community may cease altogether to have any members who can read and write, a situation that can lead to a *relapse into paganism* of the kind recorded for a

number of groups in the area. . . . The crucial factor here [i.e., of abandoning the Muslim faith] is the failure of local Muslims to observe the prohibition of marrying pagan girls. . . . In the northern Ivory Coast, even pagans sometimes send one of their sons to a Qur'anic school, taking out supernatural insurance policy with Islam. [p. 216; italics added]

In addition to the religious flexibility of illiterate people, it is also worth noting the term "supernatural insurance." The phrase aptly describes how human attitudes toward risks are formed: praying to many gods means, after all, gambling on some ideas, and having the same beliefs does lead to expectations of diminished contract uncertainty, thus providing insurance. In this sense one can say that praying to many gods provides not only "supernatural" insurance, but also very "natural" insurance.[3]

Without discussing the role of literate religion, here is how one historian views the Jews' behavior during the Hellenistic period. The contrast with the behavior of illiterate tribes is evident:

No other nation at that time denied the gods of its neighbours; on the contrary, it recognized them, identifying them with its own deities. This panreligiosity was used with considerable success by the Hellenistic ruling authorities to create a social bond between the various peoples in their domains. None of the people refrained from dining at one table with their neighbours and from partaking of the sacrifices offered to their gods except the Jews. None of the peoples refused to send gifts to its neighbours' temples, except the Jews. None of the peoples was unequivocally hostile to intermarriage, except the Jews. They characterized it as a misanthropy, a flagrant denial of the Hellenic principle of the unity of mankind. [*Encyclopedia Judaica* 1971, vol. 3, p. 88]

Today we consider the benefits of writing as so obvious that we neglect its costs, namely, the greater rigidity it introduces in cultures and behavior. How can a literate religion and literacy make such a difference in human behavior?

Before answering this question, let us point out what this more rigid behavior means. The Jews were prevented by written laws from either serving other deities or marrying and socializing outside their group. Dietary laws, in part, served the goal of protecting group identity: food directly or indirectly used in idolatrous worship was forbidden. For example, the special prohibition against pork was apparently the result of the Seleucid attempt to force the Jews to sacrifice pigs, one of the symbols of the Roman legions who fought in Palestine happening to be a pig.[4] Blood and milk, sometimes mixed, were offered up on pagan altars and were therefore forbidden for consumption. But even today many Jews continue to follow these customs. Sticking to the letter of the law was very much evident in other issues as well: Jews rejected Roman money because it bore the portraits of emperors, thus contradicting the Mosaic commandment that forbids making "any likeness of anything" and "bowing down thyself to them or serving them." All these restrictions appeared as written laws in a sacred book which served as a guideline for everyday life, fulfilling the same roles that custom and orally transmitted myths have fulfilled in nonliterate societies, namely, of maintaining the stability of the group and diminishing contract uncertainty among its members. The question is why literate people follow custom more rigidly than illiterate people.

The answer seems clear: illiterate people who have an oral religion lack an authority that can be consulted in case of doubt. Their members can therefore adjust their behavior and beliefs more quickly to a changing environment. Memory is a remarkably flexible tool. In contrast, literate people who grow up learning written laws and myths can always consult the sacred book. Skepticism toward even one of its laws or doubt about its origins and relevance can lead to abrupt abandonment of the whole set of laws, exact adherence, or to the effort to find new interpretations. The strategy of abrupt change is rather costly for it means abandoning a whole way of life and severing ties of kinship. In contrast, oral societies can adjust one of their customs without totally abandoning their traditional way of life. The latter two strategies lead either to totally unbending behavior, or to a slightly more yielding stance. But since finding new interpretations and convincing others of their validity take time, the last strategy still takes longer than changing one's mind when memory is the sole guardian of tradition. When "facts" are written down people have no choice but remember them. If circumstances change, people are obliged to seek new interpretations (or burn the books).[5]

Two recent books by psychologist Elizabeth Loftus further support this view of the way memory is formed and changed. In *Eyewitness Testimony* (1979) she makes a strong case against the reliability of the recollections of court witnesses, while in *Memory* (1976) she indicts recollection in general. Many social scientists have long believed that most early childhood memories are dreamlike reconstructions of stories told by parents and friends. Loftus makes a stronger point: she shows that the memories of adults are as unreliable as children's, so entangled are experience, desire, and suggestion. Moreover, people forget some facts and "fill in the gaps" between those they do remember accurately; they tend to adjust their memories to suit their picture of the world, and she concludes that memory is thus apt to be biased.

Thus the reason why illiterate people follow custom less rigidly than literate people is based on the arguments presented in the previous chapters, in which the relationship between history, myths, population, literacy, and the role of genealogy was discussed. The point made there was that in oral cultures "history" serves the present, facilitating a greater flexibility in human relationships. Goody (1968) summarizes the evidence in the anthropological literature:

> Genealogies often serve the same function that Malinowski claimed for myth; they act as 'charters' of present social institutions rather than as faithful historical records of times past. They can do this more consistently because they operate within an oral rather than a written tradition and thus tend to be automatically adjusted to existing social relations as they are passed by word of mouth from one member of the society to another.

> Like the Bedouin Arabs and the Hebrews of the Old Testament, the Tiv people of Nigeria give long genealogies of their forebears, which in this case stretch some twelve generations in depth back to a . . . founding ancestor. Neither these genealogies, nor the Biblical lists of the descendents of Adam, were remembered purely as feats of memory. They served as mnemonics for systems of social relations. When on his deathbed Jacob delivered prophecies about the future of his twelve sons, he spoke of them as the twelve tribes or nations of Israel. It would seem . . . that [these] genealogical tables . . . refer to contemporary groups rather than dead individuals; the tables presumably serve to regulate social relations among the twelve tribes of Israel in a manner similar to that which was analyzed in Evans-Pritchard's work (1940) on the Nuer . . . and Fortes' account (1945) of the Tallensi of northern Ghana. [pp. 33, 31–32]

This view is similar to the one Solomon Gandz (1936) presents in his article "Oral Tradition in the Bible." He shows that the Hebrew word *toledot* which originally denoted "genealogies" also assumed the meaning of "stories and accounts" about the origin of the nation, and that myths and facts are mixed in these stories. This evidence, along with that presented in the previous chapters, shows that in addition to adjusting their beliefs and customs to new circumstances, oral cultures could even adjust their *past* to fit present interests, thus revealing more flexible behavior. Once myths and genealogies are written down this flexibility, as well as religious tolerance, diminishes and written laws, religious or other, guide human behavior in part.

Not surprisingly, the religious tolerance of oral religions in antiquity went far beyond what we are accustomed to today. People not only recognized the right of others to follow their own religion but also seemed to believe that other religions were no less true than their own. As Goody notes, even today societies with nonliterate religions consider it prudent to take out "supernatural insurance" with other religions. Unless one attributes the different behavior of the Jews to their literate religion, their actions may seem absurd: a small, insignificant tribe claims that their God is the only real one while all other groups believe in false ones, and fails to make concessions to present interests, instead adhering rigidly to past beliefs. For cultures with oral religions this behavior might well have seemed intolerant and irrational. Today, most people belong to one of the religions that follows a sacred book, and thus understand the Jews' behavior; at one point or other in the past many of these groups showed extreme rigidity when forced either to abandon their sacred books or to accept new interpretations (the previous chapter has illustrated just one minor episode). But of course, our views today *are* biased: in antiquity the Jews were rightly viewed as peculiar fanatics.

Oral religions of the Hellenistic period and of African tribes did not deny the gods of their neighbors; on the contrary, these groups sacrificed to the alien deities. This behavior characterized the Jews before they came to believe in the written law: when Moses left the camp in Sinai, the Jews made sacrifices to other deities. Whether or not this particular event is myth or fact does not matter. The point is clear: when the Jews and their religion were illiterate, their behavior was similar to that of other tribes; that they were a race apart and happened to be Jews made no difference. Rather, they became different when their myths and customs were written down.

Yet at this point another question arises: Why did only the Jews write their myths down? It would be rash to pretend to solve this problem. One solution nevertheless suggests itself: if the events in Sinai as described in the Bible are an allegory for what happened there, it seems that Jews themselves were far from being a homogeneous group. One problem facing their leader was how to maintain their cohesiveness. A literate religion is one strategy a leader could gamble on; even today letters and symbols are viewed by some tribes as magical, and in antiquity this view was quite widespread.[6] This idea was of course a gamble. The fact that the leader who offered it imprinted on the written text some of his own beliefs and succeeded in finding followers can be linked to the discussion in the previous chapters of the incentive to gamble on new ideas and the emergence of adherents who gamble on it. Remember that the Jews in Sinai continually complained that they were becoming worse off. Indeed, Gandz (1936) has pointed out that writing is first mentioned in the Bible in connection with Moses; that the introduction of writing was an unheard of innovation, violating ancient customs; and that the Bible repeatedly emphasizes that the innovation was the act of God.

The evidence on Jews and on oral and literate religions in general suggests that the behavior of Jews in the Hellenistic and Roman periods was not only a matter of taste (or "religion") but can be linked to their having a literate religion when other tribes had an oral one. It may be significant that the Jews were labeled the "people of the Book" (which originally may not have been complimentary).

Let us turn to the second part of the question: Why and when would one culture tend to impose its own laws and set of beliefs on other cultures? In order to answer this question, we shall draw on the arguments presented in the previous chapters on the relationship between the expected frequency of interactions among people and the role of a central authority.

Political scientists and economists seem to agree that the basic role of government is to maintain law and order and prevent the coercion of one individual by another, to enforce contracts voluntarily entered into, and to define property rights. This is easier said than done. Consider the various forms of contract uncertainty involved in an exchange: a seller may either fail to deliver goods or deliver a product different from the one agreed upon. A buyer may refuse either to accept the goods or to pay for them. These uncertainties may lead to feuds and disputes and render the definition of property rights, their enforcement, and the maintenance of law and order expensive to a central authority. If instead of relying on a central authority buyers and sellers have similar customs or belong to the same kinship group, the problems might be solved internally: not only is there greater information on members of kinship groups or groups known to have similar customs, but sanctions against violators of rules and of implicit contracts make it more expensive for a member of a group to breach them. Having the same customs, sets of beliefs, and strengthening relationships among groups by intermarriage are expected to *lower* the cost of defining property rights and of enforcing law and order. When most of the population is illiterate a central authority will fail to fulfill these roles by any other means.

One can thus understand why both the Hellenistic and Roman authorities interpreted the isolation of a group as a refusal to recognize the authority of the state: the separation then between state, customs, and religion was somewhat blurred, and the isolation of a group could reasonably be expected to diminish the stability of the society. For nonliterate societies the Jews' claim that everybody else has false gods struck at the law itself, since a "word" bore the same burden of social cohesion and stability in an illiterate society that written contracts and laws bear in literate societies. If this intransigence were to go unpunished it could weaken social ties, for it asserted that holy names or other words and values (Hellenistic or Roman) that guaranteed contracts could be used with impunity ("freedom of speech" represents very different things for literate and nonliterate societies).[7]

Illuminating in this respect are the orders issued by the emperor Claudius soon after the restoration of peace in Alexandria, following the riots among the Greeks and Jews there. Claudius confirms the original privileges granted to the Jews allowing them to observe the laws of the Torah without any restrictions and declares: "I enjoin upon them also by these presents to avail themselves of this kindness in a more reasonable spirit, and not to set at naught the beliefs about the gods held by other peoples."[8] It may also be useful to note that the word "religion" stems from the Latin *religare*, which means to tie up, and as quoted earlier historians agree that praying to other gods and intermarriage were used with considerable success by the Hellenistic and later the Roman ruling authorities to link the various peoples in their domain. With the Jews alone it was unsuccessful.

Before analyzing the anti-Jewish feeling of the Middle Ages let us repeat the main conclusions derived from the evidence presented so far. First, it would be hard to label either the Greek or the Roman attitudes as either an irrational form of anti-Semitism, the desire to exploit or to limit competition, or tyranny. Rather, their attitude reflects part of the problem that central authorities still face today, namely, how to hold together an increasing number of people at the lowest cost. Second, the Jews' lack of realism, their obstinacy and fanaticism can be linked to the fact that they alone were literate and had a literate religion. In this sense one could say that their "mentality" *was* different. The fact that today we seem to understand the Jewish attitudes is very much the effect of our own biased views: we are all now "people of the Book" and hold in contempt newer, oral religions, labeling them as "cults." In antiquity cults were in the majority and the literate Jewish religion was a disliked anomaly.[9]

Jews in the Early Middle Ages

Contract Uncertainty or Anti-Semitism?

Even after Christianity became the official religion of the Roman Empire (A.D. 321) historians agree that until the eleventh century dislike of the Jews was mainly limited to the clergy, and this hostility might have been fed by the rivalry for converts. While the clerical anti-Jewish polemics during these centuries deplore the influence Jews exerted on the populace, they point to the existence of cordial and intimate Judeo-Christian relations. Characteristic are the epistles of the ninth-century Christian reformer Archbishop Agobard, which show that Christians did not object to praying in synagogues:

> Things have reached a stage where ignorant Christians claim that the Jews preach better than our priests . . . some Christians even celebrate the Sabbath with the Jews and violate the holy repose of Sunday. . . . Men of the people, peasants, allow themselves to be plunged into such a sea of errors that they regard the Jews as the only people of God, and consider that they combine the observance

of a pure religion and a truer faith than ours. [*Encyclopedia Judaica* 1971, vol. 3, p. 101]

Church councils continually tried to prevent these contacts. They began to succeed in the eleventh century, and the question is, Why then and not before?

Recall the features that characterized the beginning of the so-called Dark Ages: the unexpected large decline in population, the loss of skills including literacy, and the breakup of imperial administration. Bloch (1940) describes some features of this period, and relates them implicitly to the decline in literacy:

> Whether it was a question of particular transactions or of the general rules of customary law, memory was almost the sole guardian of tradition. Now the human memory . . . is a marvellous instrument of elimination and transformation—especially what we call collective memory.

> The attempts of the learned to provide the Christian mysteries with the prop of logical speculation, which had been interrupted on the extinction of ancient Christian philosophy and revived only temporarily and with difficulty during the Carolingian renaissance, were not fully resumed before the end of the eleventh century. On the other hand, it would be wrong to ascribe to these believers a rigidly uniform creed. Catholicism was still very far from having completely defined its dogmatic system, so that the strictest orthodoxy was then much more flexible than was to be the case later on. [pp. 114, 82]

Nondogmatic attitudes, the reliance on memory, and greater religious tolerance are all behavior patterns similar to those in antiquity. They can be expected to characterize nonliterate societies even if their religion happens to be based on a book, for as Bloch points out, it would be misleading to consider the societies of the early Middle Ages as sharing a literate Christian religion: the population was illiterate (in contrast to the literate Jews of antiquity) and religious life was nourished by a multitude of beliefs and practices that, whether the legacy of age-old magic or the more recent product of a civilization still extremely fertile in myths, exerted a constant influence upon official doctrine.

These observations, together with the evidence and arguments presented in the previous section, may explain the absence of any special form of anti-Jewish manifestations during this period compared with antiquity. One could add that in the Diaspora Jews probably learned to be more careful making statements about other people's beliefs.

But by the tenth century the downward trend in population was reversed, and in the eleventh it was already rapidly rising. This period should be characterized by decreased wealth per capita, greater migration, and more disputes and wars over land. At the same time, increased literacy, technological innovations in agriculture, commerce, and legislation—processes we somewhat misleadingly call "economic development"—will also characterize this period. Indeed, this is how two historians, Johnson (1979) and Bloch (1940), describe some of this epoch's features:

> What really created the crusade, however, was the almost unconscious decision, at the end of the eleventh century, to marry the Spanish idea of conquering land from the infidel with the practice of the mass, armed pilgrimage to the Holy Land. And this sprang from a third factor—the vast increase in western population in the eleventh and twelfth centuries, and the consequent land hunger. Cistercian pioneer-farming at the frontiers was one solution. Crusading was another—the first great wave of the European colonial migrations. . . . The crusades were thus to some extent a weird halfway house between the tribal movements of the fourth and fifth centuries and the mass transatlantic migration of the poor in the nineteenth. . . . After the twelfth century, the crusading idea lost its appeal in the West. Population was no longer rising at the same rate . . . and . . . in France, tended to drift instead to towns. . . . Population did not begin to expand again significantly until the sixteenth century, when emigration was resumed, but in a westerly direction. [Johnson 1979, pp. 244–48]

> Between the orderly guilds of the towns and the feudal hierarchy of the countryside there was an immense chaos teeming with the displaced, the dispossessed, the . . . beggars . . . runaway serfs. Perhaps a third of the population did not fit into official categories. . . . [Johnson 1979, p. 256]

> Society was less uneducated than it had been and was filled with a great desire for the written word. More powerful groups—above all, the towns—demanded a more precise definition of rules whose uncertainty had lent itself to so much abuse. The consolidation of societies into great states or principalities favoured not only the revival of legislation but also the extension of a unifying jurisprudence over vast territories. [Bloch 1940, p. 118]

These features are consistent with the predictions made in the previous chapters.

Another predictable feature of these times is increased hostility among "tribes," in this case Jews and Christians. As in tribal societies, the limits of morality seemed to be restricted to a relatively well-defined group. During the Dark Ages the Church institutionalized this view by elaborating on Augustine's teachings that war might always be waged by Christians when directed against those who held other religious beliefs. Pierre de

Cluny, a French abbot, wrote: "Why should we go to the end of the world, losing many men and much money, when we let live among us infidels who are one thousand times guiltier toward Christ than the Mohammedans?" and Rodolphe, a German monk, wrote: "Avenge first our enemies who live among us, then go and fight the Turks!" Decreased wealth per capita along with this form of tribal attitude might be one reason for the emergence of enmity between Jews and Christians in the eleventh and twelfth centuries, the enmity just happened to take a religious form.

Additional developments explain the increased hostility toward Jews. People have gambled on two types of social experiments in keeping human populations together when their numbers increase: the first is exemplified by migration and by the introduction of regulations to maintain tribal structure, already existing institutions, and existing methods of exchange. The second is expressed by its alternative: a slow shift toward impersonal methods of exchange and the maintenance of law and order by reliance on a central authority rather than on family ties and customs. The latter process can only take place slowly: it requires written contracts, legislation, and a literate population, conditions that may take a long time to be achieved. Until they are achieved, attempts to maintain the tribal organization will be made.

Many institutions introduced during the tenth and eleventh centuries can be understood as a means of pursuing this strategy, and thus help in identifying members of groups. During these centuries the Jews asked for and were given greater autonomy: they developed and reinterpreted their laws, and Talmudic studies flourished (this is the period of the Rashi in Troyes).[10] The dress code of Jews and heretics was regulated, and Christian and Jewish family names appeared for the first time. Before the eleventh century neither dress codes nor family names were necessary for identification: genealogies in the relatively stable, small communities were too well known for anyone to need either visual or verbal reminders.[11] Simultaneously, the Church imposed new regulations on Christians, which led to greater isolation of the Jewish and Christian communities:

> The codification of legislation against heresy took place over half a century, roughly 1180–1230. . . . Everyone from the age of fourteen . . . were [sic] required to take public oaths every two years to remain good Catholics and denounce heretics. Failure to confess or receive communion at least three times a year aroused automatic suspicion. [Johnson 1979, pp. 253–54]

These regulations can be understood as attempts to maintain already existing "tribal" structures.

Two methods were used during these centuries to deal with the problem of keeping an increasing number of people together. One was differentiation, which was achieved by a set of regulations that lowered information costs and diminished contract uncertainty. One would expect these means to be used to increase the stability of the society when the other means, such as written contracts, legal documents, and enforcement of law and order by the state are still too expensive or simply not feasible because of the population's illiteracy. But this strategy of differentiation is a gamble not without cost: it raises barriers between different groups. The fact that mainly religious organizations provided the institutional structure doubtless played a role in raising such barriers, for the Jews' and Christians' increased isolation could only help spread rumors as to the Jews' attitude toward the Christian religion. Such rumors included accusations of desecration of the Host, which like blasphemy in antiquity was viewed as striking at the heart of laws that governed human behavior, thus leading to increased isolation between religious groups.

The alternative method of dealing with the problem of keeping the increasing number of people together (still taking into account the constraint of the illiteracy of the population) was conversion to one religion, which could substitute for uniform legislation. One may thus understand why Jews were frequently encouraged to adopt the Christian religion and why those who did were spared from massacres and were favorably described in contemporary Christian writings.

Both methods can be viewed as adaptations to rising population, taking illiteracy into account, a constraint that prevents the shift toward impersonal methods of exchange.

Literacy and Anti-Semitism

Paradoxically, the continuously increasing rate of literacy since the tenth century has contributed to religious intolerance. Historians and the public in general seem to see literacy as wholly beneficial (although Bloch notes that if speech favors change, do not books always impede it?). But literacy, like any other gamble, has its costs as well as its benefits, for becoming more literate leads to less flexible human behavior. Moreover, literacy results not only in the ability to spread more information more quickly (relative to conditions in which communication is only oral), but also in the ability to spread more *misinformation* more quickly. The rediscovery and spreading of the history of antiquity as interpreted in Roman records, with their unflattering picture of the Jews, were one source of misinformation.

But there is another aspect of misinformation due to increased literacy that can explain some features of the anti-Jewish feelings of this period. While some violent anti-Jewish manifestations during the eleventh century were based on religious hostility, between 1144 and 1150 accusations of ritual murder—that is, accusations that Jews were murdering Christian children for religious purposes—first appeared. They became widespread in the thirteenth and fourteenth centuries, and led to frequent massacres of Jews. The number of incidents later declined, although one took place in Tisza-Eszlar, Hungary, in 1882, and the last well-known one in 1911 in Kiev (the Beilis case).

Before explaining how the emergence of this myth is related to literacy, it is necessary to draw a distinction between this myth, which the Church itself not only did not endorse but even fought, and the anti-Jewish clerical tradition. Very often the established lay and ecclesiastical authorities continued to protect the Jews and desired only their conversion. In 1236, after a year of frequent massacres and riots against Jews, Frederick II of Germany appointed a public committee to investigate charges of ritual murder of infants. The decision was unequivocal: there was nothing either in the Old Testament or the Talmud that allowed Jews to drink human blood; on the contrary, they forbade the use of blood in any way. There was also no evidence that the Jews ever committed such acts. In 1247 Innocent III investigated the same question and came to the same conclusion, but to no avail: the myth seemed deeply rooted. Why did this myth emerge? Did people really believe it?

Attributing ritual murder to some groups is not unique in human history. Early Christians were accused by the Romans of similar crimes. In nineteenth-century China the Christian missionaries were accused of stealing Chinese children, killing them, and using their hearts and eyes to make charms. In Indochina Chettys were blamed, and in Madagascar in 1891 the agents of the French government were accused by local tribes. All the crimes were imaginary. This uniform pattern of behavior in populations that had no contact with one another suggests that there might be a predictable mechanism behind them.

As pointed out in the first chapters, one must be careful in interpreting written documents that preserve oral traditions and cultures. The words used have different meanings and the myths of oral cultures frequently represent an allegory of events rather than facts. Myths of ritual murder appear in oral cultures when customs have been abandoned, and have been diligently written down by representatives of a written culture who happened to be on the spot, spoke the natives' language, but probably made no attempt to understand either the natives' mentality or the meaning of the words.

Some oral cultures speak of somebody who abandons the group's customs as having "died." A trace of this use of language still survives today among very religious Jews. If a family member marries outside the Jewish religion, the family sits *shiva* (the Jewish mourning ritual) and mourns this member as if he had died. In oral cultures the statement "my child

has died" or "my child was killed by Jews or Christians" may only mean
that the child has abandoned the family's tradition for Judaism or Christianity. In a sense, customs are one's heart and eyes, and it is the young
generation that usually abandons custom. The problem is that the statements of oral cultures are taken literally by literate cultures who interpret
them as accusations of ritual murder. Worse still, later generations, in part
literate and exposed only to written documents, attribute a changed meaning to the texts they read and present this meaning to the still illiterate
public. By this time, however, no one speaks the old language and can
point out this error in interpretation. One century's language becomes a
new century's superstition.

In order to demonstrate that conditions in these centuries could have
led to such misunderstandings, it must be shown that conversions to
Judaism did indeed take place until the tenth century and that the problem
of communication between generations during the Middle Ages was severe.

Conversions to Judaism might even have been frequent: the letter of
Archbishop Agobard quoted above is typical of the period. During the
eleventh century conspicuous conversions among the nobility or members
close to it occurred: the chaplain of the duke Konrad (who was a relative
of Henry II) converted to Judaism in 1005, and the duke of Sens in 1015.[12]
Since servants and serfs usually followed their masters in adopting religions, one can assume that the duke's household was no exception. This
was probably one reason the Church forbade Jews to have Christian
servants, although the rules were not always obeyed. In 1084 Ruediger,
bishop of Speyer, delivered a charter to the Jewish population stating that
their presence added to the city's reputation and allowing them to buy
land, own arms, and have Christian serfs and servants (although he probably bore in mind the increased probability of their conversion).

Let us turn now to the issue of communication. Bloch (1940) writes:

> On the one hand, the language of the educated, which was almost
> uniformly Latin; on the other, the variety of tongues in everyday
> use: such is the singular dualism which prevailed almost throughout
> the feudal era. . . . Of course, in almost every society, the modes
> of expression vary, sometimes very considerably, according to the
> use which it is desired to make of them or the class to which the
> people concerned belong. But the contrast is limited, as a rule, to
> slight variations in grammatical exactitude or quality of vocabulary.
> In feudal society it was incomparably more profound. In a great part
> of Europe, the common languages, which were connected with the
> Germanic group, belonged to quite another family from the language
> of the educated. . . . Now, with very few exceptions . . . till the

thirteenth century, [documents were] invariably drawn up in Latin. But this was not the way in which the realities they were intended to record were first expressed. [pp. 75–78]

This problem was sometimes aggravated by political events: during the ninth century some texts were translated to the *lingua theostica* (Germanic). But the dismemberment of the Carolingian empire interrupted this process and for two hundred years, until the end of the eleventh century, almost no documents were written in Germanic. Thus the origin of the "ritual murder" myth can be seen as due to this lack of communication between literate and oral cultures and the different meanings given the same words. Later generations, in part still illiterate, merely heard the words as read by a literate priest, but by then the words had already lost their initial meaning.

Crime and Anti-Semitism

There were additional reasons for the increased hostility toward Jews. As historical documents indicate, a distinction must be made between the attitude of the established lay and Church authorities toward the Jews and the attitude of the populace. During the riots following the First Crusade in 1096, both the nobility and the bishops (Adalbert in Worms, Archbishop Ruthard in Mayence, Archbishop Herman III in Cologne, the count of Mörs, etc.) tried to protect Jews, sometimes even risking their lives. It was only the very poor who took part in the massacres and looted the property of Jews. "Anti-semitism" became a cheap way of committing crimes.

Recall some of this period's features: an unexpectedly increased population; 20% or 30% of the people poor and wandering from place to place; and the Church no longer strong enough to enforce customs, but central authorities not yet strong enough to replace them, enforce law and order, and protect property. Under these circumstances one would expect increased crime rates among the relatively poor. "Anti-Semitism" becomes a pretext for theft, which is abetted to some extent by the Church's verbal hostility toward the Jewish religion. For those who become poorer it is more profitable to believe (or to act as if they believed) in the diabolical nature of the Jews. They could thus massacre the Jews and steal their property with impunity on earth (since the central authorities were weak) and without jeopardizing their souls (either because divine authority was perceived as weaker because of weakened customs or because of the Church's success in spreading hostility toward the Jews among an illiterate population).

The first documented accusation of ritual murder surfaced in England in 1144, but in this case the authorities protected the Jews. One impoverished knight, however, killed a Jew, one who had lent him money. In the thirteenth century accusations of ritual murder were already part of "organized crime": some people hid their children and then either black-mailed Jews or organized a riot, killing them and taking their property. The source for this information is a papal bull of Gregory X issued in October 1272.

> It happens sometimes that Christians lose their children and then the enemies of the Jews blame them for stealing and killing these children since they needed their heart and blood for their sacrifices. Other times the Christian enemies of the Jews hide their children and ask money from the Jews under the entirely false pretext that their children were stolen and killed by Jews . . . while in fact the Jewish laws clearly forbid sacrificing, eating or drinking blood. . . . [author's translation of Poliakov 1955, p. 78]

Earlier, in 1247, Innocent III made some similar points:

> They [some Christians] are persecuting [Jews] on the basis of myths and in sharp contrast to our instructions, against all justice, without process of law, they are taking all their goods, starve them, torture them, treating them worse than their ancestors have been treated in Egypt. [author's translation of Poliakov 1955, p. 78]

One must thus be careful in interpreting the surviving documents on the more than 100 accusations of Host desecration and the more than 150 accusations of ritual murder. These documents may tell us more about crime rates than about religious fervor. Walt Whitman wrote, that in every religious fervor there is a touch of animal heat. Again, the problem is with later generations who take accusations of ritual murder literally and who would rather believe in motivations of religious fervor than animal heat. It does sound better—this may be the power of words.

The increased hostility toward Jews in the eleventh century can then be linked indirectly to the unexpected rise in population. This resulted in temporarily decreased wealth per capita, which increased the hostility between Jews and Christians. It also resulted in attempts to hold society together through religious institutions in order to diminish contract un-certainty, which led simultaneously to greater religious intolerance. The change in language and the misinterpretation of past oral cultures could only add to this intolerance. Finally, both the weakening of Christian customs and the absence of strong authorities to enforce law and order allowed the crime rate to increase, "anti-Semitism" becoming a euphe-mism for committing crimes with impunity. We do not have sufficient information to determine which of these components played a greater role in the emergence of violent manifestations of anti-Semitism. That baptized Jews were in general favorably treated in historical documents suggests that to some extent the hostility was religious (one could also call it "tribal"), as in antiquity. At the same time there were many massacres in which Jews were not given the choice of changing their religion and in which their wealth was illegally confiscated. These manifestations of anti-Semitism would be labeled today as either crimes, terrorist acts, or acts of war. The religious context would be similar to the nationalistic, racist, or ideological contexts that still serve today as indicators of the fluctuating boundaries of moral obligations.

A man whose ax was missing suspected his neighbor's son. The boy walked like a thief, looked like a thief, and spoke like a thief. But the man found his ax while he was digging in the valley, and the next time he saw his neighbor's son, the boy walked, looked, and spoke like any other child.
    IN *Chinese Fairy Tales and Fantasies,* TRANSLATED AND EDITED
                                            BY MOSS ROBERTS

Anti-Semitism, Inequality, and the Gamble on Ideas

Anti-Semitism can reflect religious intolerance, hostility between "tribes," hostility toward groups who do not conform (and who are thus viewed as eroding the stability of the society), or crime. But there is another aspect of anti-Semitism, otherwise how could one explain the Nazi's attitude in this century? Religious intolerance did not play a major role in their theory, conformity was no longer an issue since German Jews were among the most assimilated, and while personal greed could have played a role in some individual Germans' attitudes, their anti-Semitism reflected something more than a greater willingness to commit crimes. The Germans' attitudes apparently stemmed from belief in a racist theory: gambling on racist and nationalistic ideas substituted for the tribal and religious ideas as indicators of the vague boundaries of moral behavior. Why did people gamble on these ideas during the 1920s and 1930s, when racist theories were articulated as early as 1899 by Chamberlain? By analyzing some outbursts of anti-Semitism in different times and places after the thirteenth century, I shall try to point out a similar pattern in these incidents.

Recall the scenario for the emergence and diffusion of an original idea that advocates a redistribution of wealth: when an individual's position in the wealth distribution falls, the probability that he will gamble and offer new ideas, on the redistribution of wealth in particular, increases. These ideas are more likely to find followers among people whose relative wealth has diminished; such people gamble on the ideas and thus disseminate them.

Let us first illustrate these arguments by using the Chinese tale that serves as the epigraph for this section, and then apply them to the emergence of·new expressions of anti-Semitism. The Chinese peasant's suspicion, which is a subjective gamble on the idea of whether or not the neighbor's son is a thief, rose when his wealth diminished. Once his wealth diminished and he became suspicious, his behavior changed, for he could expect to gain something by being more prudent and by avoiding the neighbor's son's company. But when the peasant's wealth was restored his suspicion disappeared, and he behaved as if the idea that the neighbor's son was a thief never entered his mind. (Although one could still say that the idea was still latent in the back of his mind; the first chapter gave the mathematical translation of how people change their minds when their wealth unexpectedly diminishes.)

Let us analyze the various ideas people have gambled on when forming their attitudes toward their Jewish neighbors. Consider some of the new images that characterize the Jews after the thirteenth century: the Wandering Jew condemned to roam from country to country, or the Jew as a poisoner of wells, a view that emerged at the beginning of the fourteenth century. Later, during the Reformation, Calvinism held a more sympathetic image of the Jews, but Lutheranism became increasingly anti-Semitic. A passage from one of Luther's pamphlets illustrates these violent feelings:

Let me give you my honest advice. First, their synagogues . . . should be set on fire. . . . Secondly, their homes should likewise be broken down and destroyed. . . . Thirdly, they should be deprived of their prayerbooks and Talmuds in which such idolatry, lies, cursing and blasphemy are taught. . . . Fifthly, passport and traveling privileges should be absolutely forbidden to the Jews. . . . Let them stay at home. Sixthly, they ought to be stopped from usury. All their cash and valuables . . . ought to be taken from them and put aside for safekeeping. This money should be used in case (and in no other) when a Jew has honestly become a Christian. . . . Seventhly, let the young and strong Jews and Jewesses be given the flail, the ax, the hoe, the spade, the distaff, and spindle, and let them earn their bread by the sweat of their noses as is enjoined upon Adam's children. . . . If however, we are afraid that they might harm us personally . . . then let us apply the same cleverness [expulsion] as the other nations, such as France, Spain, Bohemia, etc. and settle with them for that which they have extorted usuriously from us, and after having divided it up fairly let us drive them out of the country for all time. . . . To sum up, dear princes and nobles who have Jews in your domains, if this advice of mine does not suit you, then find a better one so that you and we may all be free of this insufferable devilish burden—the Jews. [*Encyclopaedia Judaica* 1971, vol. 3, p. 106]

During the Enlightenment, anti-Semitic feelings acquired a new twist: they become part of a general antireligious attitude, Judaism being viewed as a particularly antisocial religion creating division within the state and being an obstacle to secularization.

In the nineteenth century an additional trait characterizes the Jewish image: they are now identified with "capitalism" and the "capitalist" class, a pejorative image that persists today. The Jews' disproportionately high representation among the highly skilled, as well as their disproportionately low participation in crime and their lack of alcoholism are all negatively interpreted. The first trait is viewed as a plan to dominate the world: the Jews are "pushy" and "aggressive," and that explains their higher education and position as capitalists. The second trait follows: if the Jews are conspiring to do in the rest of the world, they really do not have to commit petty crimes. As for the third trait, Jews can't afford to drink since they might disclose their sinister plans for humanity—*in vino veritas*.

Today alternative, positive explanations can be given to all these traits attributed to the Jews and to the evidence on which they are based (see the next chapter). By presenting evidence on other minorities, one can show that the Jews' behavior is the outcome of the circumstances they have faced rather than a consequence of their different "tastes" or of "race." The fact that the Jews wandered from place to place during the Middle Ages comes as a small surprise once one is acquainted with the evidence presented in the previous section and in Luther's pamphlet. The fact that even after the nineteenth century they still continued to move more frequently than other people (leading to Sombart's view that nomadism is a trait of the Jewish people) is due to continuing severe discrimination in eastern Europe, their dispersed kinship ties, and their less country-specific occupations, the last two traits being consequences of their forced mobility in the past. The accusations of well-poisoning appear during the fourteenth century when the Black Death and famine struck western Europe. Apparently the Jewish death rate was lower than that of the rest of the population, a characteristic attributed by historians to the Jews' better hygiene. This was interpreted as implying that the Jews were murderers, otherwise why didn't they die at the same rate as did Christians? The capitalist image and the positive correlation between entrepreneurship and the Jews stems from several sources. In the first chapter I showed that one can expect that groups that have been discriminated against will be disproportionately represented in innovative activities, in business in particular, since they have a greater incentive to gamble on new ideas. The specifics of Jewish history facilitated this disproportionate representation, since they were forced by Christian regulations to specialize in commerce and banking (then called "usury") and to avoid agriculture. The specialization in these despised industries turned out to be to the Jews' advantage: the Christian regulators did not expect that these industries would turn out to be those that would expand when adjustments to increased population were made.

The fact that the Jewish religion required literacy, an unlucky feature in the past, and that because of the risks of expulsion and confiscation Jews had greater incentive to invest in types of property that were either more difficult to confiscate or were easier to hide (education and jewelry) added to the Jews' advantages. Many of the new occupations required literacy and education, which the Jews happened to have. Finally, their greater sobriety may be attributed to their lesser social and political security, for excess drinking frequently leads to feuds and disputes, events that are costlier for a despised minority than for the majority. It is important to realize that Jewish traits are not attributable to religion, race, or taste. Rather, the peculiar traits of the Jews can be viewed as adaptations to circumstances they have faced combined with the chance of their having a literate religion.

How can anti-Semitic theories be characterized? They are all based on a single observation: a contrasting of the traits of Jews with those of non-Jews. But any theory based on a single observation is by definition a religion, a matter of belief, a gamble. The question is under what circumstances people will be more likely to gamble on anti-Semitic beliefs and act accordingly. In other words, when will people be more likely to gamble on novel ideas in general and on anti-Semitic interpretations of some unique evidence in particular?

Historians have long argued that anti-Semitism gains currency during periods of turmoil and defeat. The views presented in the first chapters allow a more precise prediction: when the wealth distribution changes and wealth per capita diminishes (and both occur when population increases), groups whose relative wealth has diminished will be more likely to gamble on anti-Semitic ideas. That turmoil will characterize such periods is to be expected: those whose relative wealth has diminished have a greater incentive to engage in revolutionary and criminal acts and gamble on ideas that advocate redistribution of wealth in their favor. The ideas that people are gambling on are expected to increase their wealth. The question is, how can anti-Semitic ideas lead to expectations of increased wealth?

We now know that the Black Death was the consequence of importing a new disease to Europe to which the population was not immune. This was not known, however, in the fourteenth century. As a consequence, the Jews were blamed. They made good suspects: they had been portrayed as the enemies of Christians and as ritual murderers, and if historians are right, they had a lower death rate than the Christians. Traditional hostility, combined with this evidence, could be used by some local religious or lay authorities as an easy, temporary answer to the populace's question, whose wealth and welfare had unexpectedly diminished. The image of Jews as well-poisoners could have arisen thus. Once people accept this idea, changed attitudes toward the Jews follow: since they are well-poisoners and the cause of disaster, their elimination (through massacre) is expected to improve the situation. (Let me emphasize here that the use of the term "cause" is very different from the usual one in the natural and social sciences: I give this word a precise definition in appendix 2.)

The theory that big business and dynamic capitalism are Jewish creations exercised a great influence on members of groups who had become worse off. Let us analyze the emergence and dissemination of this idea within the framework of the views presented in the first chapter. Two stages can be distinguished; first a group in the economy becomes worse off; then a politician is ready at hand who gambles on an idea and attributes the failure to a Jewish conspiracy and who imprints his own beliefs on the suggested ideology. Are not Jews disproportionately represented in capitalistic ventures? Are they not richer than the rest of the population? Are they not opposed to unselfish social justice?! Do they not promote a cosmopolitan supranational spirit so that they cannot be trusted by any nation? As shown in the first chapter, a group that has become worse off is more likely to gamble on these ideas and may vote for "reasonable" restrictions on Jewish participation in economic life and on immigration. Achieving these goals leads to a redistribution of wealth from Jews to the rest of the society.

This scenario has been repeated several times in human history, as in the following episode:

The 1870s [in Germany] were . . . critical years. . . . They were years of depression in which the shopkeeper and schoolteacher were driven perilously close to loss of white-collar status. It was during this period . . . that Adolf Stöcker . . . came to prominence. . . . Stöcker loathed the industrial middle class and feared its growing power . . . [and] he was able to appreciate the bitterness of the small businessmen of his time. . . . Stöcker was determined, therefore, to provide the lower *Mittelstand* with a species of nonproletarian socialism . . . [he] was the man who first made anti-Semitism a national issue in Germany. [Sachar 1977, pp. 224–25]

With the success of German imperialism toward the end of the nineteenth century, political anti-Semitism waned only to wax again in 1924 following the German hyperinflation. Although the data are circumstantial, historians argue that hyperinflation caused a sudden redistribution of wealth: it destroyed the middle class's wealth and redistributed it to borrowers who appeared to be of the relatively wealthier class.[13] Sachar's description is typical:

> The decade following Hitler's release from prison (1923–1933) was a nightmare of inflation, then of depression, and always of corrosive, embittered nationalism . . . [the leaders of the Weimar Republic] were blissfully ignorant of the social disintegration that was everywhere at work in the German world. . . . It was during this period that Hitler's hysterical and hypnotic oratory convinced hundreds of thousands of distraught German lower *Mittelstand* white-collar workers, the class which was the principal victim of the economic crisis of the 1920's, that the Nazi party was the only dependable instrument of Germany's salvation. [1977, pp. 423–25]

The theory of racism that emerged during this period made its own contribution. But it might be useful to note that one can link the emergence of this idea to the fact that Europe's population jumped from 140 million in 1750 to 260 million in 1850 and 500 million in 1914. The idea of dividing humanity by race rather than religion can be viewed as a new elaboration of the attempt to maintain the unity of an increasing number of people. But instead of tribes and religion, state and race define the new boundaries of moral obligation, and instead of the religious fervor that justified both the crusades (which were in fact migrations) and anti-Jewish feelings, racism lends dignity and importance to both "imperialism" (the new word for migration) and anti-Semitism. The view that history "proves" that the destinies of people are governed by racial law was first elaborated by Gobineau in 1855 and later by Chamberlain in 1899—but are their views really different from those of ancient authors who believed that destinies are governed by local or more universal religions? In historical perspective, Gobineau's and Chamberlain's contributions represent only the invention of new vocabularies advocating some form of "tribal" structure. The underlying human behavior is frightfully recognizable.

The gamble on anti-Semitic ideas was repeated in many countries in this time span and the sequence of events was always the same: first a relatively large group's wealth diminished, then politicians appeared who offered the ideological background of anti-Semitism as a substitute for revolutionary or socialist gambles and which appealed to classes whose relative wealth had diminished. Frequently the gamble succeeded:

[During the 1930s] the widespread unemployment, the sullen restiveness of the men who stood for hours in bread lines, created grave concern among Romania's propertied aristocrats . . . [and] the distraught petite-bourgeoisie of the land. Each of these groups lived in constant apprehension of a peasant or worker uprising. In search of a plausible diversion, they were not unwilling to . . . exploit the backlog of Romanian Jew-hatred. . . . Effective spokesmen were not lacking for the new campaign against the Jews. . . . If one wonders how an entire nation could go berserk, completely oblivious to the economic and political inequities that were the authentic sources of national poverty, it should be remembered that the political literacy of the Romanian people had been dulled by centuries of Turkish rule. . . . [Sachar 1977, pp. 362–64]

By the Treaty of Trianon the Magyar state was deprived of two-thirds of its territory and half of its population. 1918–19 were years of unalleviated horror for the Hungarian people. The inflation and food shortages of the immediate postwar period were intensified by a relentless, and gratuitous, Allied blockade. The blockade, in turn, undermined Hungary's economy . . . thoroughly. [Sachar 1977, p. 365]

These developments led first to a Communist dictatorship (unfortunately but predictably with Jewish leaders) then to an overthrow of the regime and massacres of Jews during 1919–20. As Hungary recovered, the more overt and violent forms of anti-Semitism declined only to be renewed when the Great Depression struck in 1930.

The gamble has not always succeeded, although when the wealth distribution unexpectedly changes a fraction of people can be expected to gamble on anti-Semitic ideas:

[During] the Great Depression [in the U.S.] there appeared a substantial amount of overt American anti-Semitism. This was carried further in the 1930s under the impetus of Nazism and its American wing, the German-American Bund. Native-born American radicalism, the populist tradition with its suspicion of the big cities, the intellectuals and, above all, of the Wall Street bankers, had its own anti-Semitic component. It looked for a moment in the 1930s as if anti-Semitism might become a substantial force in the United States. . . . [*Encyclopedia Judaica* 1971, vol. 3, p. 126]

It is beyond my scope here to review the whole history of anti-Semitic manifestations, which is filled with the same sequence of events as outlined above. One of the most detailed descriptions appears in Léon Poliakov's five volumes dedicated to a detailed account, but rarely an explanation, of the many anti-Semitic outbursts in different times and places. My goal is only to illustrate one further application of the views presented in the first two chapters. They enable one to perceive the roots of human behavior that lead to anti-Semitism and the regularity in the fluctuations of such outbursts, thus rendering the occurrence of anti-Semitic outbursts more predictable, depending on significant and abrupt changes in the wealth distribution (which occur when human populations suddenly grow).[14] I do not pretend to claim that changed wealth distribution and diminished wealth per capita are the *only* reasons for a greater willingness to gamble on anti-Semitic platforms, yet these factors undeniably play significant roles.

The fact that in modern times inflationary periods seem to have led to increased anti-Semitic outbursts could have been predicted: unanticipated inflation (e.g., the hyperinflation of central Europe between the two wars) always redistributes wealth from lenders to borrowers with the result that lenders, who generally represent the middle and lower middle classes, are worse off. This should be remembered by those who for obscure reasons (a belief in algebraic, mechanistic models of the economy or in "trade-offs" between inflation and unemployment) advocate inflationary policies. The price of these beliefs may turn out to be very high, since changes in the distribution of wealth (due to unexpected inflation) might lead people to gamble more frequently on anti-Semitic or racist ideas.[15]

I do not claim that at our current level of knowledge of human behavior we can very accurately predict the nature of anti-Semitic outbursts. There is always the role of the particular politician (the "right" man at the right time) who imprints his own ideas on the ideology he offers, a factor that is always unpredictable. What should be emphasized is the fact that there seems to be a regularity in the fluctuations of anti-Semitic behavior, fluctuations that can be theoretically and empirically linked to a measurable variable, namely, changes in the distribution of wealth in a society.

Finally, let me point out the similarity between some of the processes described in this section and those in the first chapter, where the methods of maintaining the wealth distribution stable in primitive societies were discussed. Recall that accusations of witchcraft and sorcery maintained the egalitarian basis of these societies. Not only was the rich man in danger of being accused, but he also feared the malice of witches and sorcerers among his envious fellows. What we do not know is how long it took for such customs to evolve: who was the individual who offered this idea, and when did the rest of the population gamble on it? How can the wealth distribution be maintained at a stable level in a society where population has increased, customs are abandoned, people no longer believe in witches and sorcerers, and theft of property (but not of lying or ruining reputations) is punished?

If customs and family ties are weakened only the political process remains to oversee the legal redistribution of wealth. Thus accusations of exploitation that arise when one group's wealth is relatively diminished are similar to age-old accusations of witchcraft, and are made with the same expectation of redistributing wealth. The view that anti-Semitism is the socialism of the class whose relative wealth diminishes, which is in general the lower middle class, thus seems justified: anti-Semitism is their ideological gamble, and is expected to lead to a redistribution of wealth in their favor.

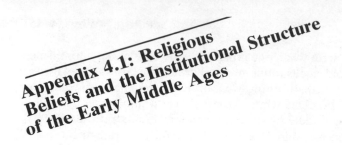

Chapters 3 and 4 have dealt with various aspects of the early Middle Ages. To add to the picture of that age, let us briefly review how historians have evaluated several of its features and how these features are consistent with the views presented in the first two chapters.

Here is how Johnson (1979) characterizes the fourth century, although he does not mention the drop in population.

> The western sector of the empire, after the closing decades of the fourth century, lacked a coordinated economic system which could be policed, and so taxed, by a central government. Unable to collect taxes, the authorities could not maintain a currency and pay the legions. There was, in effect, a vacuum of government. . . . In these circumstances, the western Church found itself the residual legatee of Roman culture and civilization and the only channel by which it could be transmitted to the new societies and institutions of Europe. . . . It had the chance to recreate the secular framework of society *ab initio,* and in its own Christian image. [p. 127]

Nothing better illustrates the fact that the Church became involved in daily aspects of human behavior than Pope Nicholas I's reply to 106 questions posed by Boris, king of Bulgaria, in 866, when he hesitated between adopting Christian rule from Rome or that of the patriarch in Constantinople. None of the 106 questions dealt with theological issues; all referred to legal questions and matters of everyday life.

In addition to being a "religion of a book" and providing answers to almost every aspect of human behavior and arrangements, McNeill (1976) also attributes the initial attractiveness of Christian doctrine during the third and later the sixth and seventh centuries to its effectiveness in coping "with the horrors . . . of unexampled epidemic. . . . By comparison, Stoic and other systems of pagan philosophy, with their emphasis on *impersonal* process and natural law, were ineffectual in explaining the apparent randomness with which death descended suddenly on old and young, rich and poor, good and bad'' (p. 109; italics added). That ideas emphasizing impersonal processes would not be successful when death rates unexpectedly increase and population diminishes is again a feature that can be linked to my hypothesis. Under these circumstances one could attribute the initial success of Christianity in part to the fact that it provided some hope of salvation by offering an idea of what happened after death, an idea on which people were willing to gamble. ''Hope'' implies a subjective gamble, and one can always gamble on a blissful afterlife. The probability that this or any new idea unsupported by evidence will find followers who gamble on it is greater when people become worse off, which was the case in this instance.

The eleventh century saw the renewal of the trends we now call ''development.'' Again, without relating these changes to the continuously increasing population, here is how Johnson (1979) characterizes this period:

In the 1050s the papal administration underwent [an] expansion. . . . The run-up to the canonical explosion took about seventy years, from 1070–1140. . . . Now, a papally-controlled legal system suddenly moved into the forefront of every individual's experience. It began to settle vast areas of ordinary life in great and expensive legal detail . . . : dress, education, ordination, status, crimes . . . charity, alms, usury, wills . . . marriage, inheritance, legitimacy. . . . The legal revolution enormously strengthened the hands of the papacy. . . . It became not so much a divine society, as a legal one. . . . As such—as a separate, rival institution—it was bound to come into conflict with the State at every level . . . they were locked in a conflict of laws. . . . The central tragedy of Christianity is the break-up of the harmonious world-order which had evolved in the Dark Ages on a Christian basis. [pp. 204–9]

Other historians seem to share these views. With regard to the legislative process, Bloch (1940) notes that between 1050 and 1250 royal justice improved and manorial courts slipped into the background.

Finally, let me add one more point on one well-known feature of the Christian religion. In this and the previous chapters I have dealt with matters of language and myth. It should thus be noted that the myth of a virgin giving birth is frequent among disparate tribes (just as the myth of the ''murdering'' of children by strangers) and is *not* a peculiar feature of the Christian religion. What could this myth represent? One interpretation is that it represents the birth of ideas which should guide human behavior, something we would today allegorically call ''divine inspiration.''[16]

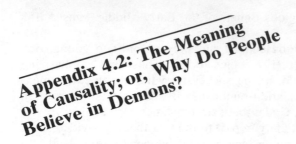

And now remains
That we find out the cause of this effect,
Or rather say, the cause of this defect,
For this effect defective comes by cause.

HAMLET, 2.2.100–103

Einstein once wrote, " 'Demons' are everywhere; maybe the belief in
their action is at the root of our concept of causality." The purpose of
the model and arguments presented in this appendix is to show that Einstein was right. I hope to show that the term "cause" can be precisely
defined in the model presented in the first chapter. It was argued there
that gambling is an activity not strictly related to games, but to *all* activities
in which returns depend on luck rather than on specific skills or already
available information. Since this is a characteristic of gambling, betting
on an idea that may explain a causal relationship, but about which there
is no information, also represents a gamble, although there are significant
differences between this "gamble" and the one represented by a lottery;
these differences have already been pointed out but they will be reemphasized below.

Gambling on the Meaning of Causal Relationships

In this section we will see that the same trait that leads human beings
to supply novel ideas in business, science, the arts, technology, or the
organization of social institutions also leads them to interpret causal relationships. An increase in both the supply of novel ideas and of interpretations given to causal relationships occurs when a group's relative
wealth diminishes or when the human population's total wealth diminishes
(simultaneously with a change in the wealth distribution). This trait provides the means of survival for the individual as well as for the entire
species, and enables us to maintain "wealth" per capita (on average)

stable, although the perception of what constitutes wealth changes significantly, and errors can be made in the interpretation of causal relationships.

Let P denote the amount invested in developing an idea, which in addition to the direct costs of investment in time and in the other resources necessary to develop it, also includes the resources invested in trying to estimate the potential demand for the idea and its applications. Let $\alpha(W > W_o)$ again represent the percentage of the relevant population above one's wealth, W_o, and let H denote the increase in wealth that one expects to gain by selling an idea. If unsuccessful, with a probability p, the potential innovator knows that he will lose the amount P (which includes losses due to diminished reputation). Translated to mathematics, the conditions for an individual to become an entrepreneur, that is, to "bet" on a new idea for which no empirical evidence is available at the outset, is similar to the conditions that lead one to gamble on a criminal act:

$$
(1) \qquad U(W_o, \alpha(W > W_o)) < pU(W_o - P, \alpha(W > W_o - P))
$$
$$
+ (1-p)\, U(W_o + H, \alpha(W > W_o + H))
$$

Let us reemphasize the significant differences between this condition and the one that defines participation in a lottery, in spite of the similarity of the mathematical formulation. Here the value of the "prize" H differs among individuals: people's evaluations of the potential demand for home computers and the solutions of open problems in science are subjectively determined. Also, probability here represents a subjective judgment by an individual, and there is no way to prove that he is right or wrong. This contrasts with lotteries, where probabilities are defined in terms of processes that can be repeated many times. In this sense one can make a distinction between uncertainty, a situation in which probabilities can be estimated only subjectively, and risk, where probabilities will be the same for everybody involved in case of nonrigged lotteries.

In spite of these important differences between the two types of gambling, the following conclusion can be drawn: when one's relative wealth drops, one has a greater incentive to gamble on novel ideas. Assume that one does *not* gamble on a novel idea, but merely follows custom and habit, so that the sign of the inequality in (1) is reversed. When one's wealth diminishes relatively, holding probabilities, costs, benefits, and the wealth distribution constant, one is more likely to contemplate an idea that one was previously reluctant to.

Gambling on revolutionary ideas that advocate a redistribution of wealth has been discussed separately, since the mathematical conditions differ somewhat from the conditions that define gambling on other new ideas. It has been show that when a significant number of people become *dé-*

classé, the probability that they will gamble on ideas advocating a redistribution of wealth in their favor increases.

Let me clarify now the meaning of "causal relationships" in this model. Suppose that initially one's wealth is W_o and that it equals the wealth one expects to achieve through existing methods of exchange. Suppose that one's wealth unexpectedly diminishes to $W_1 < W_o$. How will people interpret this event?

As shown above, when such events occur people are more likely to gamble on new ideas that are expected to increase their relative wealth. The "cause" of their diminished wealth is merely one of the ideas that people might now take up, since it is expected to increase their wealth. We may also refer to this process as the "rationalization" of events.

Before elaborating this point let us recall the Chinese tale about the man and his ax:

A man whose ax was missing suspected his neighbor's son. The boy walked like a thief, looked like a thief, and spoke like a thief. But the man found his ax while he was digging in the valley, and the next time he saw his neighbor's son, the boy walked, looked, and spoke like any other child.

The peasant's suspicion, which represents a subjective gamble on the idea of whether or not his neighbor's son is a thief, rises when his wealth unexpectedly diminishes. Once his wealth diminishes, his behavior changes: he can now expect to gain something by being more prudent and by avoiding the neighbor's son, although he may also lose something if eventually his suspicion is proven to be false. When the peasant's wealth is restored, his suspicion disappears and he behaves as if the idea that the neighbor's son was a thief never entered his mind.

I shall give two further examples in order to familiarize the reader with my arguments. Herskovits (1940) describes the following customs among tribes in the Nilgiri hills of India:

The members of this tribe were musicians and artists for the three neighbouring folk of their area, the pastoral Toda, the jungle-dwelling Kurumba, and the agricultural Badaga. Each tribe had clearly defined and ritually regulated obligations and prerogatives with respect to all the others. The Toda provided the Kota with ghee for certain ceremonies and with buffaloes for sacrifices at their funerals. The Kota furnished the Toda with the pots and knives they needed in their everyday life and made the music essential to Toda ceremonies. The Kota provided the Bagada with similar goods and services, receiving grain in return. They stood in the same exchange relationship with the forest Kurumba, but these latter, who could only provide meagre material compensation . . . were able to afford the

Kota supernatural protection, since the Kurumba were dreaded sorcerers, so feared that every Kota family must have their own Kurumba protector against the magic which others of this tribe might work against them. [p. 157]

What was the cause of the Kota's belief? How could it emerge and become a custom? The emergence of this belief can be explained in the following way: since the Kurumba were initially the relatively poor, they were the ones more likely to commit criminal acts. Realizing the threat, the Kota, in an attempt to diminish the threat, gambled on the egalitarian idea of making payments to them. The Kurumba's threat (which represents diminished wealth for the Kota) might have been the source of the custom and the cause for the emergence of the belief that the Kurumba were "dreaded sorcerers," an idea that both the Kota and the Kurumba had an incentive to gamble on.

Similar views are evident in many anthropological studies. Gluckman (1965), for example, writes:

Richards reports of the Bemba, that to find one beehive with honey in the woods is luck, to find two is very good luck, to find three is witchcraft. Generally, she concludes, for a man to do much better than his fellows is dangerous. . . . Here accusations of witchcraft and sorcery maintain the egalitarian basis of the society in two ways: not only is the prosperous man in danger of accusation, but he also fears the malice of witches and sorcerers among his envious fellows. [p. 88]

The model presented here explains the cause of these beliefs. A change in the wealth distribution has led, at some point in the history of this tribe, to increased gambling activity. One act was to gamble on the belief in "witches," which, once it became a custom, succeeded in maintaining the stability of the society by keeping the wealth distribution stable.

For us the "dreaded sorcerers" are "potential criminals." Instead of believing in custom, witches, demons, or divine authority, we put our faith in central authorities on earth, which are now expected to take over the role of redistributing wealth. This change may reflect an adaptation to our increased numbers, when customs can no longer be expected to be enforced and laws and police replace them.

The problem with the causal interpretations given to the emergence of some customs in primitive societies is that these societies have enjoyed stable conditions for very long periods of time. Thus one cannot test my views on the emergence of some ideas by examining these societies, since their social and exchange structures as well as their wealth distribution have been kept stable. In order to test my views, one must identify situations in which wealth has unexpectedly and significantly diminished and then analyze the different causal interpretations that have been given to these events.

The Plague: What Was Its "Cause"?

The Black Death struck Europe in 1346 because of rats imported to a continent whose population was not immune to the disease that the rats spread, and an estimated one-third of Europe's population died (see Cipolla [1979]). When the plague was raging, a person might have been in full health one day and have died miserably within twenty-four hours. Belief in ideologies that put great emphasis on human effort in explaining the mysteries of the world, could not accommodate such experiences. How did people in the fourteenth century interpret the cause of their diminished wealth and welfare, since they did not know that rats and their fleas were spreading the disease?

People began gambling on several ideas. Some were of a religious nature: there were those who said that the severe scourge had been sent by the Almighty, and that the persistence of the epidemic was the result of the blindness of men who thought they could remedy the pestilence solely through human care *contra consilium Altissimi*. One may ask how such an idea can lead to expectations of increased wealth. If suffering is viewed as inflicted by heaven because of sins committed by the human race, one can find comfort (or insurance) in the idea that being spared the disease might imply a blissful afterlife. And the idea of blissful afterlife is certainly a gamble, and will probably remain so.

People gambled on other religious ideas during this period. McNeill (1976) writes:

> Popular and respectable was an upsurge of mysticism, aimed at achieving encounter with God in inexplicable, unpredictable, intense and purely personal ways. Hesychasm among the Orthodox, and more variegated movements among Latin Christians—e.g., the practices of the so-called Rhineland mystics, of the Brethren of the Common life, and of heretical groups like the Lollards of England—all gave expression to the need for a more personal, antinomian access to God. . . . [p. 163]

Health officials made several shots in the dark, attributing the epidemics to "miasmas,""vapors," or the "contagiousness" of the disease. At times, by chance, they even succeeded in their policies, when they organized rapid burials and safeguarded food deliveries. As Cipolla states:

The people of the Renaissance did not fail to observe that in times of an epidemic persons who handled certain materials were more prone to catch the disease than persons who handled different materials. They recognized the dangerous nature of wool and woolens, cotton, hemp, flax, carpets, bags of grain, and the like. The observation was correct. Materials such as those just mentioned could easily harbor infected fleas. People did not, however, think in terms of microbes . . . nor did they suspect the role of fleas . . . the doctors rationalized that the venomous atoms of the miasmas would "stick" more easily to hairy and rough surfaces than to smooth and hairless ones, in the same way that perfumes and foul odors would more easily saturate a piece of cloth than a piece of marble. The people of the Renaissance also correctly recognized that the plague generally prevailed in the summer months. They failed to link the phenomenon with the life cycle of rats and fleas, but they had no difficulty reconciling it with their epidemiological theory: it was during the hottest months of the year that they smelled the foulest odors from the dirty streets, the faulty sewers. . . . Thus they correlated these facts and in the correlation found the "proof" that clearly the venomous miasmas grew out of rotting materials in the hot and humid climate of the summer. In this case, as in the previous one, a correct observation served the unfortunate purpose of strengthening a false theory. [1981, pp. 13–14]

(In certain respects, our assumptions are no better today. As shown in the first chapter, economists have for years worked on the theory of risk-aversion, neglecting the facts rather than adapting their theories to the facts as observed.) At other times the health officials were wrong: they misinterpreted the correct observation that furs, carpets, and woolens were dangerous in deducing that dogs and cats, because of their fur, and chickens and pigeons, because of their feathers, could spread the disease. Dogs and cats were therefore killed, making the rats' lives easier.

Politicians and mobs gambled on the idea that the Jews spread the pestilence by poisoning wells. Why did this emerge, and how was the causal relationship formed? Apparently the Jewish death rate was lower than that of the rest of the population, a characteristic attributed by later historians to some Jewish customs. But during the plague this observation was not made. The fact was that their mortality rate was smaller, and the question was what its cause was. The interpretation some people gambled on (which led to massacres of Jews) was that the Jews poisoned wells. They made good suspects in that they had been accused of murder in the past.

One might think that people would learn from their errors and realize that they were accusing innocents and that massacres did not prevent the epidemics. But this argument is irrelevant, since this conclusion can only be reached once people have made more than one observation. When only a single observation is available, and people's wealth suddenly diminishes, they may gamble on many kinds of ideas and interpret causal relationships in more than one way.

Causality in the Natural and Social Sciences

The concept of causality has been treated extensively in the philosophical literature, but textbooks and studies treating the methodology of economics and econometrics have relatively few things to say on the subject. I intend to show first that the definition of causality in sciences analyzing human behavior is different from that in the experimental sciences and then to show the modifications that one must introduce.

In experimental sciences the controlled variables of the experiment are called the cause variables and the observed ones are called the dependent variables. When formally expressed, this definition is reduced to a one-sided relation with a strictly exogenous variable (the controlled one) on the right-hand side. Since in the social sciences we cannot control experiments, the identification of causality (or exogeneity) requires two further conditions: one related to the theoretical definition and the other to the identification in an empirical test.

Since in the social sciences, and in economics in particular, there are no controlled variables, the view that some are exogenous and cause an event must be justified *within* a model. The model must justify the one-sided relationship, i.e., the inability of individuals acting in the model to affect the event, and purely statistical criteria cannot define causality.[17]

Two conclusions follow from these arguments: when defining a causal relationship (when dealing with human behavior), one must distinguish between the effects expected and the effects that unexpected changes in an exogenous variable have on the endogenous variables; a causal relationship can be identified only when unexpected events occur. This means that even if one says that an expected change in an exogenous variable "causes" an event, this statement can be verified only when an *unexpected* change in the exogenous variable occurs.

We can illustrate these conclusions by contrasting them with Simon's (1952) definition of the word "cause." Simon gives the following example: a is the event "it is raining" and b is the event "John is wearing a raincoat." Simon then constructs this sentence: "Rain causes John to wear his raincoat." This sentence represents a testable model: "rain" is the exogenous variable and "wearing a raincoat" the endogenous one. If this sentence is not mere word-play but has empirical, behavioral content, the coefficient of the "rain" dummy variable in the statistical test must be close to one. This sentence (or model) will be rejected in a world where rain falls unexpectedly, for in spite of the fact that it is raining one may not wear a raincoat when rain falls unexpectedly, and, contrariwise, if it unexpectedly stops raining one may still wear a raincoat. Thus in the statistical test the coefficient of the "rain" variable may be far from one. An examination that we shall probably not reject will be based on one of these two statements: "If John expects that it will rain, he will wear a raincoat" or "If rain falls unexpectedly, John will not wear his raincoat." But notice that the first statement can be verified (or falsified) only if rain either falls or does not fall unexpectedly. Otherwise, if whenever it rains John wears his raincoat, one will never be able to distinguish between these two statements: "John wears his raincoat *because* it rains" and "John *is* the rainmaker."

Consider Simon's second example: "the lighted match causes the explosion." This is again a hypothesis one can test from two different viewpoints. One can simply carry out a controlled experiment in a laboratory and see how many times when a match is lighted an explosion occurs. This is, however, a very different experiment and a very different statement from what Simon seems to have in mind, since he intends to draw implications from his definition of "cause" for actions involving human behavior.

The experiment one must carry out in order to determine whether or not Simon's definition is valid where human behavior is concerned is as follows: let people light as many matches as they like. Most of the time *no* explosions will occur, and so the statement "the lighted match causes the explosion" will be rejected. For an explosion to occur flammable gas must be present, and one can therefore test the hypothesis that the gas "causes" the explosion. Both the statements "the lighted match causes the explosion" and "the gas causes the explosion" will be rejected, for it people *know* that there is gas in the place they will not light the match and thus no explosion will occur. The statement (or model) that defines a causal relationship in which human behavior is involved, and which we shall fail to reject by an empirical test, will be: "The lighted match caused explosions when the individuals who lighted the match were unaware of the presence of the gas, or the presence of the gas was unexpected in that place."[18]

These examples point out the difference between the two definitions of causal relationships, the one that refers to human actions and the other that does not. When human actions are of no interest, one may look at some production processes and state, in the case of explosions, for example, that this process requires two inputs: a lighted match and explosive gas. Thus, for such experiments the term "cause" means only that an event cannot take place without another event occurring: the "explosion" event could not occur either without the gas or without the lighted match. But in economics and social sciences one wants to analyze human behavior. Thus if an event occurs it must be explained *within* the model *why* individuals take part in it. Consider the killing of Jews mentioned before: people gambled on the idea that they were the source of their diminished wealth. I thus tried to explain *within* the model why people gambled on the idea, and how their perception of causality was formed.

Let us illustrate by one final example why one must make a distinction between the term "cause" where one refers to a physical process concerning a controlled experiment and the very different meaning of the term when used in the context of human behavior (although one should note that physical scientists have by now abandoned the term "cause" when speaking of their experiments). The statement "fire was the cause of death" means in terms of medical language that fire destroyed some organs in the human body and it refers as well to a physical process. But in everyday language this same sentence makes a statement about human behavior and the unexpectedness of events (fire in this case).

Let me turn now to the more rigorous statistical definitions of causality suggested by Granger and Newbold (1977) in order to show the similarities and the great difference between their definition and the definition that stems from my model. In his 1969 study Granger's definition of causality is as follows:

> If $\sigma^2 (X/U) < \sigma^2 (X/U - Y)$ [where σ^2 denotes the forecasting variance of X with respect to the given information set U, or $U - Y$], we say that Y is causing X. . . . We say that Y_t is causing X_t if we are better able to predict using all available information than if the information apart from Y_t has been used. [p. 428]

This view has some elements in common with the views expressed here, for if Y_t is expected, then X_{t-1} would be already based on the information set that includes Y_t, thus the inclusion of Y_t would not decrease the forecasting variance. But if Y_t is unexpected, then inclusion of Y_t would decrease the forecasting variance. Thus in Granger's terms Y_t is causing X_t. Zellner (1979) criticizes this definition:

> First, in the previous work by Feigl, Jeffrey, Simon, Strotz, Wold, Basmann and others, *both* stochastic and non-stochastic variables are considered . . . [while] Granger and Newbold wrote: "it is sensible to discuss causality for a group of stochastic processes. It is not possible to detect causality between two deterministic processes." [p. 31, italics in original]

The arguments presented here show that on this point Zellner's criticism is not justified: while one can waste many words on causal relationships even among deterministic processes, one will never be able to *identify* them. Between deterministic processes only correlations can be identified.

Zellner's second point is that

> Granger in contrast to Feigl, Simon and Basmann includes the notion
> of temporal asymmetry in his theory of causality. . . . Granger and
> Newbold write: "The future cannot cause the past. Strict causality
> can only occur with the past causing the present or the future." [p.
> 31]

Causality, according to Granger, is defined by the inequality in forecasting errors. Since U_t includes all available information at time t, it must in particular include expectations for the future. Therefore $U_t - Y_t$ includes the expected value for Y_t but not its realized ones. Only when the future is precisely anticipated, a rather uninteresting and irrelevant case, will the information set remain unchanged. But in this case we shall never be able to detect causality; moreover, nobody will ever bother to define it. In this sense, therefore (and this is the only sense in which Granger's definition can be interpreted), the future—meaning the unexpected future—cannot cause the past. Time enters implicitly into my model since first there is an unexpected change in the wealth distribution and then there is a reaction to it.

There is one point in Zellner's criticism that is valid and should be emphasized, and which shows why, after all, Granger's definition is not applicable. As Granger (1969) recognizes,

> the only completely unreal aspect of my definition [of causality] is
> the use of the series U_t representing all available information. [p.
> 429]

This is indeed a severe restriction, in particular that the word "information" is not defined.

Consider the examples analyzed in the previous sections. When people's wealth has diminished relatively but they do not know why, they gamble on ideas and suspect that some factors maybe the cause. Suppose that social scientists want to analyze why there have been fluctuations in the presence of anti-Semitism. They observe that at some time the accusation of well-poisoning arose. And *sublata causa, tollitur effectus*, Jews were killed, and social scientists consider superstition as the "cause" of the killings. According to my hypothesis, this view of "causal relationship" would be incorrect since the basic question is why people suddenly *gambled* on this idea. Moreover, once we realize that people gamble on ideas and behave accordingly, the term "all available information" is no longer well defined.

Since Granger's definition of causality has been applied mainly in monetary theory, let us discuss briefly the way this term is used there. Sims

(1977), by trying to make Granger's definition operative, gives a rather peculiar definition of "causality":

> The ordered pair (A,B) of restrictions on [a set] S determines a causal ordering from X to Y (equivalently makes X causally prior to Y) if and only if $P_x(A \cap B) = P_x(A)$ and $P_y(A) = Y$. [p. 26]

Sims illustrates his definition:

> An example of causal ordering is a pair of linear equations in two unknowns, one of which involves only one unknown. The space S is Euclidian 2-space, X and Y are two copies of the real line; P_x projects a point in S into its first co-ordinate, and P_Y projects a point in S into its second co-ordinate. The set A is the line determined by the first equation which involves only X (a vertical line, if X is the horizontal axis) and B is the line determined by the second equation. [p. 26]

But this definition is inconsistent even with regard to the standard economic theory. Let Y be the price and X the quantity in a market. Then the example given above is one in which there is an inelastic physical supply of a good, land for example, and some usually shaped demand curve. It is unclear why, in general, one would define this, or implicitly any demand and supply process, as some form of causal ordering. First-year students in economics are taught that the Ricardian rent is demand-determined rather than, as it would follow from Sims's definition, "supply-determined," although both statements will in general be incorrect. The statement on the Ricardian rent, however, is consistent with the arguments presented previously: if one assumes that the supply of land in the short run is inelastic, then fluctuations in price will stem from unexpected changes in demand.

Sims arrives at this incorrect definition of causality with a specific model of monetary theory in mind *and* by relying on definitions of causality in experimental sciences. He writes,

> The reason it seems plausible to define a causal ordering as we have is that in a system (A,B) with a causal ordering from X to Y it is natural to contemplate varying the input A, holding B fixed, and obtaining output $P_x(AB)$ determined by A. The most interesting systems [?] are those in which the input-output relation B is one which would in fact remain if we varied A. We will call such a B "structural." . . . Definition: the set $B \subset S$ accepts X as input to Y if for any $A \subset S$ which constrains only X. . . . (A,B) makes X causally prior to Y. [p. 27]

(If the reader finds difficulties to translating Sims's definitions into terms of human behavior, he should not be blamed—they have nothing to do with one another, in spite of the fact that Sims intends to use these definitions in economic questions, which, after all, deal with human behavior.) Let B be the demand for money, or the demand for output, which has stable parameters. Let A be the aggregate output that varies systematically with unanticipated changes in the money supply. Then causality, according to Sims's definition, will stem from unanticipated changes in the money supply to changes in output. But several points should be emphasized: (1) Sims's definition of causality does not stem from an economic model, but rather from the definition of the term in experimental science; and (2) he assumes that the demand for money has stable parameters, thus neglecting the issue that is at the center of the controversy among the monetarists' and the nonmonetarists' view of the behavior of the money market.

Conclusions

The purpose of this appendix has been to present a general model that can explain how people form their interpretation of causal relationships, how the implications of this model can be tested, and why unexpected fluctuations in population are used as the causal variable in this book. The major conclusions are that the term "cause" can be defined in a model where there is uncertainty and when unexpected changes in wealth and its distribution occur. Models of simultaneous equations à la Bassman (1963), L'Esperance (1972), and Strotz and Wold (1960) cannot define causal relationships[19] nor can statistical criteria, for when human actions are involved one must always explain how human beings *arrive* at their interpretation of causal relationships.[20] Thus any model that tries to shed light on this subject must deal with the question of how ideas emerge and how people form their opinions.

5
Occupations of Minorities

In much wisdom is much grief: and he that increaseth knowledge increaseth sorrow.

ECCLESIASTES 1:18

Discrimination by law or social custom constrains members of a minority with regard to their choices. If the postulates of traditional economic theory are correct, two predictions may follow: that the costs imposed on the minority will be greater than those on the majority, and that if ability is symmetrically distributed around the same average in the two groups, the minority should have lower income and wealth.[1]

Yet while some groups that have been discriminated against have a lower average income and wealth than the rest of the population, there are many others that have higher income and wealth. How can this evidence be reconciled?

There are two lines of argument in answer to this question. The first holds that tastes differ: some groups value education and monetary wealth more than the general population, so they make greater efforts to attain these ends. At the same time other groups are lazier and exert themselves less. These statements are racist: they are merely a nice way of saying that a group is either more pushy and aggressive or else more inferior. Also, like any explanation that relies on taste, this one leads to no testable implications: it merely provides an ex-post justification for a situation. The other line of reasoning is that tastes are the same and abilities are symmetrically distributed around the same average. The different behavior of a given group is an outcome of both its position in the distribution of wealth and the altered attractiveness of some occupations *because* of past discrimination, the effects of which persist over time.

In order to distinguish between the two hypotheses I shall analyze the effects similar forms of discrimination have had on various groups' educational and occupational achievements. The observation that their behavior is similar leads to the conclusion that the differences between their incomes and occupational structure and that of the rest of the population cannot be attributed solely to systematic differences in taste. Rather, the different opportunities they face, their position in the wealth distribution, and chance all shed light on their different behavior. The changing Jewish occupational structure will be used as a benchmark against which some features of other minorities who have been discriminated against are compared.[2]

Discrimination and Entrepreneurship:
A Historical Perspective

If the analysis in chapter 1 is correct, one would expect groups that have been discriminated against to be disproportionately represented in *all* types of gambling activities, criminal *or* entrepreneurial. The arguments and the mathematical proofs were simple: when discriminatory measures are introduced against a group, this group's wealth diminishes and its relative position in the distribution of wealth changes. As a result, the group's incentives are altered: the appeal of committing criminal or revolutionary acts, or of gambling on original ideas in business, science, the arts, or the organization of social institutions, is increased. Let us examine whether or not the evidence supports this scheme.

There is no evidence of any exclusive or predominant addiction to commerce on the part of Jews in Western Europe until the rise of Islam in the seventh century. During the first centuries of the Christian era they seem to have lived sometimes in agricultural communities, and if they were blamed for anything it was for being poor and rugged. When the clergy began writing history the tone changed, and documents from the sixth century describe restrictions on Christians in socializing with Jews, eating with them, marrying them, or celebrating Passover with them. During the seventh and eighth centuries there are some references to Jewish and other merchants who speak many languages, implying that by then Jews were well represented in trade. It is not clear whether the Jews' literacy, knowledge of many languages, study of contract law in the Talmud, or slowly increasing hostility led them to this occupation. Yet there is nothing spectacular about these traits or their performance until the eleventh century.

The period from the eleventh century on, which saw massacres, expulsions, confiscations, a changing but always diabolical image of Jews, and constraints on their occupational choices (limited to usury and sometimes to collecting taxes, not the most popular of occupations), was described and analyzed in the previous chapters. The Jews of the sixteenth century in Western Europe were poor, living a miserable life, and in

Germany they were apparently disproportionately represented in criminal activity.

The evidence on the Jewish crime rate is drawn from a long series of studies, the last published in Berlin in 1842 under the title *Die Jüdischen Gauner in Deutschland* by A. F. Thiele (quoted by Poliakov 1955) and dedicated to the history of Jewish bandits in Germany. The evidence, as one would expect, is not numerical but circumstantial: it shows that in Luther's time criminal jargon was already filled with Hebrew words, that until the eighteenth century the police made special reference to Jewish bandits, and that in the nineteenth century the Jewish crime rate preoccupied social scientists. The Jewish criminals were different: they were good fathers, good husbands, and religious, and their crime was mainly theft:

> During six days, [the Jewish bandits] are not afraid of commiting sins against Divine and human laws, by stealing from others, and they would not hesitate on the seventh day if the rabbinical dogma would not forbid all commerce on Saturday. However, since their trade is stealing, from which they live, it is because of being trade rather than stealing that they don't do it on Saturdays. Before even the stars appear on the horizon, the Jewish thief stops traveling and rushes to an inn to celebrate the Sabbath. . . . [author's translation from Poliakov 1955, p. 254]

If indeed Jews were disproportionately represented in criminal activity, it could easily have been tested: the crime rate on Saturday had to be much lower than on other days. But no numerical evidence seems to have survived, perhaps because the evidence was too well known to need a statistical reminder.

It is during the eighteenth century with the rise of the states and of mercantilism that one finds reference to the Jewish entrepreneur. Recall the definition of this term: when one's relative wealth diminishes, one will gamble more frequently on novel ideas. If the percentage of lucky hits remains constant, Jews should be disproportionately represented among the successful entrepreneurs and they should acquire a reputation for "speculative thinking," which may be seen as due to circumstances rather than religion or race. This behavior pattern implies that the Jews' average monetary income may become higher than that of the rest of the population, a feature that ordinary economic theory was unable to explain. As shown in the first chapter, the Jews are not a unique example in this respect (this is what makes the hypothesis testable): many groups that have been discriminated against in the past have later provided a disproportionate supply of entrepreneurial activity (education being just one aspect of such activity) and have had higher monetary income.

It should be emphasized that, for several reasons, one cannot deduce that greater monetary wealth, a consequence of the greater frequency of gambling on novel ideas, means that these groups become wealthier. The discussion below illustrates why comparisons between the monetary wealth of two groups who face very different circumstances do not make much sense.

Feelings of insecurity caused by a lack of political insurance diminish one's wealth for several reasons: a minority whose wealth has been frequently confiscated in the past takes into account the probability of migration, which involves expenses the majority does not expect to pay (studying foreign languages, choosing less country-specific occupations, and saving for the direct outlay of eventual mobility). Expecting to pay bribes for rights that are taken for granted by majority members further diminishes the minority's wealth.

There are other subtler reasons for assuming that measured wealth is very different from wealth as minority members view it: intoxication might lead to transgression of the law or to feuds and to disputes, events that are costlier for an already disliked minority than for the rest of the population. Or, for people who fear the confiscation of their wealth, wearing nice clothing is costly because clothes reveal information about wealth. If the minorities decrease these risks by not drinking and dressing up (and these are just some strategies the groups may gamble on), the amounts spent on these devices for self-protection should be subtracted from their wealth, for the pleasures of drinking and of dressing well are opportunities foregone, and foregone opportunities are the economic definition of costs.

Thus some discriminated groups' higher monetary wealth should not be interpreted as implying either greater "wealth" or greater welfare, for it is their greater misery to start with that induces them to gamble on novel ideas, which eventually produce their greater monetary wealth. At the same time a fraction of this measured wealth should be subtracted for purposes of comparison between the majority's and the discriminated group's wealth, since the greater wealth in part merely replaces forms of insurance that the majority receives at lower costs. To put it simply, in order to possess the same level of wealth, members of a discriminated-against minority must make greater efforts and be more disciplined.

Yet even among groups that have been discriminated against and have later provided a disproportionate supply of novel ideas, the Jews are prominent. This relative success can be linked to several aspects of Jewish history, aspects that have nothing to do with "race."

The historical documents show that even when they were poor Jews were not illiterate; their learning, however, was exclusively religious. While the literacy of the Jews was the source of their suffering in antiquity, in the seventeenth and eighteenth centuries, with the increased demand for literacy, it turned out to be a valuable form of "property" from which the Jews received "rent," which could have increased their relative wealth. The liability of the past turned out to be present fortune.

Specific Christian regulations also made their contribution to increased Jewish wealth. Jews were long limited in their choice of occupations to usury and to trade in pawned articles, gold and jewelry in particular. These restrictions were the consequence of either religious restrictions or the pressure of Christian guild merchants. But growing population increased the demand for these industries: banking and retailing turned out to be the expanding industries of Western Europe, thus contributing to the Jews' increased wealth.

The restrictions on holding land and living in the countryside might also have played a role in explaining the Jews' higher level of education. The normal work options in an agricultural community that induced children to leave formal education earlier did not exist for Jewish children, and the opportunity cost of staying in school (secular or religious) was thus decreased.

Forced mobility in the past, which led to the greater dispersion of Jews, might also explain their increased wealth. In the eighteenth and nineteenth centuries this feature could have facilitated a greater flow of information among Jews relative to the rest of the population. Becoming innovating entrepreneurs and diminishing contract uncertainty across countries might thus have been cheaper for them. These dispersed ties and the resulting cheaper access to information might explain the emergence of the Jewish family firms in eighteenth-century Europe, a feature frequently noted by historians. Prominent among these firms were the Seligmans, Oppenheimers, Rothschilds, Habers, the brothers Bethmann, and the Speyer Bank, firms that originated in Frankfurt and that relied on important family branches throughout Europe. These names were the most famous, but there were many other Jewish family firms: the Warburgs in Hamburg, and the Mendelssohns and the Bleichröders in Berlin, the Oppenheimers of Cologne and Vienna, the house of Eskeles and Arnstein in Vienna, the firms of Montagu, Goldsmid, Hambro, and Sassoon in London.

It is useful to note that, like the increased supply of entrepreneurial acts, this feature too is not uniquely Jewish. During the late Middle Ages there were famous Italian merchant families, and today similar structures characterize the Chinese minorities in Singapore and West Malaysia (see Landa 1979b). The Chinese trading groups are dominated by four major clans: the Tans, the Lees, the Ngs, and the Gans. This structure might be due to either political uncertainty, the majority's (Malay) hostility toward the Chinese, or to the greater trust Chinese have in one another. Probably all these factors play a part, much as with the Jews.

There was one further regulation imposed on the Jews alone that might have contributed to their subsequent disproportionately high level of education. Toward the end of the eighteenth century one observes a large drop in Jewish birth rate in some places in Western Europe. Today all the developed countries follow this trend, and economists attribute it to the increased opportunity cost of raising children (because of higher wages, higher value of time, smaller space), to increased life expectancy, and, as argued in the previous chapters, to the protection of property being provided by states rather than kinship ties. All these lead to a greater attractiveness from the parents' viewpoint of investing in the quality of their children (education and health) rather than in their quantity.[3]

While this hypothesis could in principle be applied to explain the drop in the Jewish birth rate, the evidence suggests that the reason for the drop was much simpler and more prosaic. In 1726, fearing a large increase in the Jewish population (a fear that by itself suggests that the Jewish birth rate was in fact high), the Viennese court introduced a new regulation: only the eldest son of a Jewish family could marry; the younger boys could not. This regulation introduced into the Austrian empire, including Bohemia, Moravia, parts of Germany, and Alsace, led to the instant migration of the young Jewish generation to Eastern Europe, to Poland and Rumania (where Jewish birth rate did *not* drop). One could safely assume, however, that for the Jewish families who decided to stay in places where the regulation was enforced the law provided a radical and simple means of birth control. Adapting to the law probably led Jewish parents to have fewer children and to invest more in their education and in their health care (this is probably how the myth of the Yiddische Mame was born). Even if some parents expected to migrate in case they had two or more sons, they had an incentive to limit the number of their children since mobility is more expensive when there are more children. These parents also had an incentive to invest more in their children's quality. Moreover, the effects of these adjustments persisted over time: once the older generation had both a higher income and a higher level of education, education became cheaper for the younger generation, for it was in part transferred by interactions at home. The Yiddische Mame and the smaller number of children became Jewish customs, adopted not because they made either the mothers or their children happier, but because of an Austrian regulation. It is doubtful whether the Austrian regulators took into account these effects of their actions. Finally, it may be useful to note that the regulation might only have strengthened Jewish family ties, ties that were stronger because Jews, in contrast to people living in their own country, had to rely on stronger sentimental (or "tribal") loyalty for security. The experiences of the past taught them that they could not expect sufficient security in the countries in which they found themselves.

Since most of the regulations mentioned above were imposed only on Jews, it is difficult to estimate their separate contribution to subsequent occupational structure and behavior, in particular since the effects of regulation persist over time. In order to do this the best possible evidence on the occupational structures of groups that have faced some of the restrictions Jews have faced is presented below, and it will be shown that the direction of the adjustments these groups made were similar to those made by Jews.

The evidence on the disproportionate participation in entrepreneurial activities by members of groups that have been discriminated against was presented in the first chapter. This increased supply appeared when the extent of markets increased (either because of increased population or more extensive international trade), and the probability that central authorities could reasonably be expected to enforce law and order increased.

In addition to these groups, the other candidates for comparison are groups who have suffered loss of statehood and have been dispersed: the Armenians, the Parsis, and the Palestinians.

Although Jews and Armenians have been compared frequently, the evidence is descriptive rather than numerical.[4] Like the Jews, they have tended to live in cities, to specialize in trade, and to establish communal organizations. In the Ukraine both Jews and Armenians were accused of having destroyed the livelihood of indigenous merchants and artisans by the communal solidarity they manifested against competition, an accusation which suggests that the Armenians had established structures similar to Jewish and Chinese family firms. The observation that Armenians today are disproportionately represented in trade and music has also been made, but I have been unable to find corroborating numerical evidence. Numerical evidence on Parsis and Palestinians *is* available, however.

The tiny Parsi community (100,000) of Bombay is characterized by its involvement in trade.[5] The Parsis originated in Persia, which they were forced to leave 1200 years ago because of religious persecution. They first sought refuge in the remote region of Khurasan. One hundred years later, after the fall of the Sassanian Empire, they moved to the Persian Gulf area. Fifteen years later they arrived in India, where they waited an additional nineteen years before they were granted asylum. Restrictions similar to those imposed on Jews were imposed on them during the twelfth century, although with less severity: they had to follow a dress code and abandon their language in public places. Toward the seventeenth century they are mentioned in reports of European travelers as traders who had "mental characteristics" similar to those of Jews. Evidence from the seventeenth and eighteenth centuries shows that Parsis served as brokers in all the Portuguese, French, Dutch, and English factories. Detailed numerical evidence from 1860 on reveals a strong similarity with Jewish occupational structure: 89% of the men and 73% of the women were literate, in contrast to the averages for the rest of the population of 15% and 2% respectively. They also had a higher level of education: an 1864 survey reveals that 20.3% of Parsis were in banking and real estate, in contrast to 6.9% for the rest of the population; and 18% were either professionals or in the British government service, in contrast to 6.37% for the rest. Also, while 9% of Parsi professionals were doctors, 13% teachers, 19% clerks, and 19% watchmakers, the respective numbers for non-Parsis were 0.67%, 0.37%, 4.4%, and 0.11%. In addition to banking and medicine, they were also concentrated in law, textiles, and the press, occupations that characterized the Jews of Western Europe in the nineteenth century. In 1898, forty-six out of 100 qualified Indian advocates, and forty out of seventy-three Indian attorneys in Bombay were Parsis. Of the thirteen cotton mills established in Bombay between 1854 and 1870, nine belonged to Parsi entrepreneurs, and the initial stages of the native press in western India were almost exclusively dominated by Parsi journalism. As for more recent data, until 1959 the Parsis controlled 18% of company ownership in Maharashtra, the state in which Bombay is located, while they represented much less than 2% of the population. In companies founded between 1955 and 1962 this proportion decreased to 7.7%. It also seems that there was some sense of uncertainty as to the future of the Parsi community: in 1892 the Englishman General Dashwood described the Parsis as foreigners in India who would immediately be extirpated if England were to leave India. During 1905–7, the proposal that the entire community should emigrate to a new separate Parsi colony (in Beluchistan or East Africa) was popular because of fears about the Parsis' future in an independent Hindu India. Detailed numerical evidence on the similarities between Parsis and Jews appears in tables 5.1–5.4.

Information on the educational pattern of Palestinians is scarce.[6] Although detailed data on schooling at the elementary, preparatory, and secondary levels of Palestinians living in camps registered by the U.N. exist, this population constitutes only half of the Palestinians, and they arc not necessarily representative of the population. The professionals and highly skilled workers, whose numbers interest us, either left the camps immediately after 1948 for countries along the Persian Gulf, Europe, the U.S., or, in the case of Christian Palestinians who were relatively more educated in 1948, received Lebanese citizenship in 1948 and no longer appeared in the statistics on Palestinians. However, these exclusions make the development of the education of refugees registered by the U.N. seem all the more striking: in 1948 the percentage of elementary and secondary students in Palestine was 9%, a rate fairly constant since the 1930s (see table 5.5). This percentage is roughly the same as the one that prevailed in the neighboring Arab countries at the same time: 8.6% in Egypt and 8.61% in Syria. After 1948 when the U.N. organized the schooling system of the Palestinian refugees, the frequency of elementary and secondary students increased steadily from 10% in 1953 to 15% in the early 1960s, 18% in the late 1960s and early 1970s, and to 21.8% in 1977. These numbers are composed from two series: four-fifths of the students received education in UNRWA schools, while one-fifth were educated by the local governments in the countries where they found refuge. This evidence is suggestive considering the fact that the same numbers for Egypt and Syria are respectively 10% and 14%.

The educational pattern in Jordan since the 1950s can be used as an additional approximation to show the changes in the education of Palestinians. Since after 1948 more than half of Jordan's population was of Palestinian origin, the higher level of education there relative to that of the neighboring countries may in part reflect the Palestinians' changed attitude toward education. Jordan was the only Arab country that offered citizenship to all the refugees in 1948 regardless of religion, and the change in the eductional structure in Jordan since then may serve as a downward biased estimate for the educational choice of Palestinians. Since in Jordan the Palestinians had the opportunity to continue their main previous occupation, agriculture—a choice that was not available in either Egypt or Lebanon—the jump in the level of education can be attributed to the choice the Palestinians made when facing the new circumstances. In a recent survey of education in the Arab states Qubain (1966) writes:

> After the second World War, a tidal wave of desire for learning began. . . . There are several reasons for this development. The influx of Palestinian refugees into Jordan demonstrated clearly that knowledge is not a luxury, but a valuable capital, which one can take with him wherever he goes. [p. 306]

Tables 5.5 and 5.6 along with the evidence of this passage allow us to infer that the education of Arabs in Palestine was fairly similar to that of Arabs in Egypt, Jordan, and Syria until 1948. But between 1948 and 1970 the educational level of Palestinians became significantly different from that of the Arabs in these host countries.

Information on the changes in the occupational distribution of Palestinians does not exist. However, there are data on the professions chosen by Palestinian students at different universities which can be taken as a rough indicator of the distribution of professions. When these data are compared with the professions chosen by Egyptian, Syrian, and other Arab students, a clear difference emerges. Palestinian students do not study agriculture, humanities, or law: their choices concentrate in the sciences, medicine, and engineering—occupations that are less country-specific.

The data in tables 5.7 and 5.8 show the secular change in the professions Palestinians study and the differences in the fields they and the rest of the Arab students undertake. While between 35% and 60% of Lebanese students at the University of St. Joseph and Syrians at the University of Damascus chose law or political sciences, only 12% of the Palestinians did so. At the same time, while 9% of the Syrians and Egyptian students studied medicine, 56% of the Palestinians chose this field in the 1960s. Also, Palestinians elected engineering and the sciences more often than the arts than did the rest of the population. These trends can be attributed either to the easier transferability of some professions if further mobility is taken into account, or to discrimination in the host countries resulting in a choice of occupation in which self-employment is more feasible.

The data on agriculture are worth considering in more detail. While Palestinians ceased to study agriculture, the fraction of Egyptian students who chose this subject increased during the same years. The first UNRWA report in 1951 still mentions that "agriculture classes are perhaps the most important, as over half of the refugees used to earn their living from the land in Palestine, and will probably have to do so in countries where they settle" (p. 271), and that 696 out of 2232 students received technical instruction in agriculture. However, in reports since 1956 in which the number of students in each field is given, agricultural training no longer appears. Instead we find students pursuing metals, electrical, building, technical, commercial, and paramedical trades. Table 5.9 shows the latest distribution: only 1.5% of Palestinians chose to study agriculture.

Patterns of discrimination against Jews as reflected in restrictions on buying land, expulsions, and *numerus nullus* or *numerus clausus* are well known. Further support for the comparison between the Jewish and Palestinian occupational structures stems from the observation that Palestinians have faced patterns of discrimination similar to those faced by Jews in the past, patterns that could have lead to migration from one country to another. The UNRWA report of 1952 states:

> The refugees are people apart, lacking for the most part status, homes, land, assets. . . . In Lebanon they cannot be issued working permits, and by law cannot hold jobs. In Egypt, they cannot receive agency relief and assistance unless they are physically located in the 5–25 miles of the Gaza Strip. In Syria, although they are permitted to work, they have not been offered citizenship; in Jordan, although possessing the full rights of Jordanians they have concentrated in such vast number in areas of such meager economic opportunity that in the four year period (1948–52) only an insignificant handful have managed to become self-supporting. [p. 3]

In a recent issue of the pro-Palestinian *Journal of Palestine Studies,* one finds statements showing that the picture given in 1952 has hardly changed:

> Their movements in [Syria] were restricted. The laissez-passer which the Palestinians in all of Syria, Lebanon and Gaza were granted as travel documents became one of the instruments of their control. In Gaza all the Palestinians were severely restricted by the military authorities, etc. [Hagopian and Zahlan 1974, p. 58]

Markham (1978) mentions these regulations:

> In Kuwait, where [the Palestinians] are 25% of the poulation, there is a 'numerus clausus' giving them 10% of the places in the universities, although out of the top 50 high school science students, 48 are Palestinians. [*New York Times,* 19 February 1978]

Moreover, Palestinians are not allowed to buy shares in Kuwaiti companies, purchase property, open stores without a Kuwaiti partner, or vote in Kuwaiti unions. According to Ben Porath (1968), there were also signs of discrimination in employment on the part of the Jordanian government. These restrictions could reasonably result in a positive probability of migration from one country to another, leading Palestinians to choose less country-specific occupations.

The evidence on the higher level of education of Palestinians, Parsis, and Armenians, their choice of occupations, which tends to be less country-specific, and their concentration in trade and forsaking of agriculture are all consistent with the general predictions made in the previous chapters as well as with those on the effects a change in one's relative position in the wealth distribution might have on one's behavior. These choices represent the increased incentive to gamble on various forms of entrepreneurial acts relative to the rest of the population. Current events provide further evidence on this relationship:

> The Turkish invasion has drastically changed the Cypriot way of life. The shock of losing all their material possessions has instilled in the Greek Cypriot refugees an almost fanatic thirst for education "because that's the only thing they can't take away from you," as one refugee put it. [Gage, *New York Times,* 23 April 1978]

It is useful to add a clarifying note on literacy: both in the first chapter and above it has been argued that groups that have been discriminated against gamble more frequently on novel ideas, become disproportionately highly skilled, and, in particular, attain higher levels of literacy. Yet one can argue that the Jews were already literate in antiquity before they were discriminated against. But here once more one must draw a line between what we mean by literacy today and what literacy meant not only in antiquity but even later for some societies. As argued earlier, letters represented magical symbols for long periods of time. Thus one could become literate for religious purposes without relating literacy to education (as we interpret this term today). Indeed, "literacy" is just another example of a word whose content has changed. In comparing the changing structure of discriminated minorities I referred to literacy as we understand the term today, namely, as part of the concept of entrepreneurship.

Crime, Terrorism, and Discrimination

Let us turn now to the other type of entrepreneurship: the touchy subject of crime. Can one consider the Palestinian terrorists criminals? There is an old clause in the laws of the Ine of Wessex (see Cipolla 1976, p. 24): if fewer than seven men attack private property they are thieves, if between seven and thirty-five, they are a gang, if more than thirty-five, they are a military expedition (these numbers were relevant when populations were much smaller).

How can one interpret this law? How do we make the distinction between crime, terrorism, and the struggle for freedom? The answer seems straightforward: if the majority agrees through its laws and customs with the allocation of property rights, an attack against the allocated property will be viewed as a criminal act. But what if there is no agreement on the allocation of property rights (i.e., to whom does Palestine belong?). It will then be unclear whether an act is considered a crime or an act of liberation. When no such agreement exists people will play with words and swords.

The Israeli borders of 1967 are recognized by international law, as was the private property of the Germans by the German laws of the sixteenth and seventeenth centuries. If one then calls the Jewish thieves of those centuries criminals, then for the sake of consistency and comparison one must also call the Palestinian terrorists up to 1967 criminals and include them in the evidence on the relationship between discrimination and the subsequent increase in crime rates. As for the term "crime," it should be reemphasized that I am using it with reference to laws and customs that are adopted by the majority rather than in reference to the very popular but very vague notion of "justice."

That neither the Jews of the sixteenth and seventeenth centuries nor the Palestinians saw themselves as criminals is to be expected; their wealth was either directly or indirectly confiscated and redistributed without their consent. That Palestinian terrorists were mainly viewed by the rest of the world as criminals until 1967, but that since then they have been viewed more as "freedom fighters" is one prediction of these arguments. For while until 1967 Israel's borders were recognized by international law, its new borders after 1967 are not (i.e., no agreement has been reached on the new allocation of property rights). Thus the same acts that were previously viewed as criminal are thus now viewed in a different light.

It seems then that we do not quite agree as to what constitutes theft or murder. This is what I mean by saying that when there is no agreement on the allocation of property rights people can play with "words" and "swords." Recent events seem to support these views: the acts of the I.R.A. in Northern Ireland and of the Basques in Spain are viewed by the Catholics and the Basques as acts of freedom fighters (these groups considering themselves as being discriminated against) while the same acts are viewed by the English and Spanish as criminal.

The Jews of the sixteenth and seventeenth centuries and the Palestinians of the twentieth century are not the only oppressed groups who at one point have been disproportionately represented in crimes. In the U.S. much has been written on the leading role Italian immigrants played in crime during the 1930s, on the role of the children of Eastern European Jews in organized crime twenty years earlier, and on the prominence of individuals of Irish descent in crimes in an even earlier period.[7] Today Puerto Ricans and blacks seem to be disproportionately represented in criminal acts. This increased participation in crime is consistent with the views presented in the first chapter.

Yet one may say that in the U.S. there is no *legal* discrimination; it is thus useful to note that the effects of discrimination through social custom might not be different from those that are the consequence of discrimination by law. Consider the arguments presented in the previous chapters: in a world of contract uncertainty, customs and trust replace or complement written contracts and diminish uncertainty. In such a world there is no distinction between the effects of "social" and "market" discrimination: both lower the minority's wealth, for while market or legal discrimination prevents entry to some professions, social discrimination prevents developing ties among some groups constraining their chance of participating in markets in which trust still complements written contracts. This seems to have been the argument behind the Supreme Court's decision in Sweatt vs. Painter, which held that blacks must be admitted to state law schools. The court observed that in segregated schools blacks would have no opportunity to develop contacts with the students who were likely to occupy important positions on the bench and in the bar after graduation. According to the views presented in chapter 2, this observation was accurate.

Finally, a difficult question arises: Why did some groups that have been discriminated against turn away from crime and gamble on novel ideas in business, science, or the arts while others have remained for longer periods on the lower levels of the wealth distribution? Recall the prediction that groups discriminated against will either gamble on ideas or on crime. In addition to the differences between these two conditions, namely, that the specific circumstances of the past are expected to play a role here, there is at least one more factor that can shed light on the issue. As argued, there are various methods a group can use to change its relative position in the distribution of wealth. Wealth can be redistributed either by crimes or taxation; the latter can be carried out when a group expects to have political power. Relative position in the wealth distribution can also be changed by individual effort: gambling more frequently on novel ideas in business, science, or the arts. What variables might affect the choice between these strategies? As shown in chapter 1, there is at least one factor that influences oppressed people's choices between these two strategies for increasing their relative wealth, namely, the size of the discriminated group: Their number represents their potential political power and thus their ability to redistribute wealth by gambling on the political process.

All the minorities mentioned here and in chapter 1 (Jews, Parsis, Huguenots, etc.) who have provided an increased supply of entrepreneurial activity have one more trait in common: not only did they become more creative, but they could *not expect* a redistribution of wealth through the political market either because of their relatively small number or because of the prevailing political structure. In this case the incentive to gamble on novel ideas to increase one's relative wealth was greater than the incentive to gamble on the political strategy to achieve this goal. The contrary may also hold true: if the minority gambles on a political strategy to achieve its goal, the relative attractiveness of gambling on an entrepreneurial strategy diminishes.

Without providing any theoretical foundation for his arguments, Sowell (1975) seems to attribute the differences in income and occupational structure of some ethnic groups in the U.S. (that of the Irish and the blacks) in part to the fact that some ethnic groups have been able to use the political mechanism for increasing their relative wealth to a greater extent than other ethnic groups, such as the Japanese and the Jews. Thus, while the two latter groups gambled on the entrepreneurial strategy to increase their relative wealth (and the wealth of the society), other minorities gambled on the political mechanisms and some egalitarian ideas in order to increase their relative wealth (a strategy that only redistributes but does not increase the wealth of the society). The adoption of such a strategy and such ideas is consistent with the model outlined in the first chapter.

Recent Jewish Occupational Structure

Reference has been made several times to the well-known evidence on the disproportionate level of Jewish entrepreneurship. In order to round off the discussion, let me briefly present and discuss the evidence.

Entrepreneurship means gambling on novel ideas. Because of the circumstances they faced Jews engaged in this type of gambling more frequently. Thus, unsurprisingly, they have been disproportionately represented among Nobel Prize winners.[8] By 1939 they contributed eleven out of thirty-eight German prize winners, three out of six Austrian winners (twenty-nine times their "proportionate share" compared to the non-Jewish population), while in the U.S. between 1901 and 1965, 27% of the winners were Jewish, while they constitute about 3% of the population. Turning to less spectacular data, in the U.S. today Jews are overrepresented by 230% in medicine, 480% in psychiatry, 300% in dentistry, 265% in law, 240% in mathematics, and 70% in architecture, but not at all in engineering (although with regard to the "inventions" produced by engineers they are overrepresented by 110%). Similar evidence characterizes the Jewish communities of Western Europe from the turn of the nineteenth century (see Sachar 1977).

These phenomena have been frequently analyzed by sociologists and psychologists who attribute it to greater "ambition" or "motivation," as well as economists (see Kuznetz 1972, Veblen 1948, Marshall 1910, Alchian and Kessel 1962, and Kahan 1964), who mainly consider them as a puzzle, for economic theory has nothing to say about creativity.

As shown in the first chapter, there is no disagreement between the sociologists' and psychologists' interpretations and mine. I have, however, attempted to give greater precision to their terms, present a uniform approach toward understanding the underlying human behavior, and avoid making arbitrary and unclear distinctions between economic, psychological, or sociological factors—after all, they all deal with the same human behavior.

Let us turn now to even less glamorous evidence.[9] Data from four national surveys in the U.S. are presented below: the 1957 Government Religious Census, two nation-wide surveys (one from 1957–58, the other from 1973 by the University of Michigan), and a survey done in 1955 by NORC. The samples in the latter three surveys are much smaller than the one used by the Census in 1957. Data from Community Surveys in big and small cities are also presented.

The labor force participation of Jews and non-Jews in the 1957 Census is given in table 5.10. Table 5.11 gives an education distribution in 1973 for Jews and non-Jews. The occupational distribution from a number of sources and years is given in tables 5.12–5.13. The information derived from these data is as follows: the labor force participation for Jews below the age of twenty-four is very low in comparison to that of non-Jews, and can be explained by higher participation in high schools and universities (as subsequently reflected in the 1973 data). This picture is by no means a sudden development; already in 1901 a report of the U.S. Industrial Commission found that Jewish women had a lower labor force participation than women in the rest of the population (keeping income constant), and conjectured that the reason was the differential education given at home, and as early as 1908 the proportion of Jews who were students was 8.5%, while the corresponding figure for the rest of the population was only 2%. This is in spite of the fact that the income of Jews was then *lower* than that of the rest of the population. Tables 5.10–5.13 and the aforementioned data thus show that Jews invested and continue to invest more in education than the rest of the population.

The occupational distribution of Jews is consistently different from that of the non-Jewish population: there is persistently a much higher percentage of professionals, managers, and proprietors, and a much lower percentage of blue-collar workers than in the rest of the population. This evidence reflects two facts: Jews attain a higher general level of education, and a greater percentage of Jews are self-employed. Since being self-employed means in general that one has to make decisions more frequently, these data suggest that Jews continue to "gamble" on novel ideas more frequently than the rest of the population.

A detailed occupational classification, including the categories of professionals and nonprofessionals, is presented in tables 5.12 and 5.13. The results of four Gallup polls taken between 1963–65 that make the same classification also appear in the tables. The information one can draw from all the data is the same: the percentage of professionals and semiprofessionals among Jews is twice as great as among non-Jews.

These data enable one to infer that Jews have a higher level of education than the rest of the population in the U.S. and continue to invest more in their education relative to the rest of the population. The difference between Jews and non-Jews in the percentage of managers can be attributed either to employers' continuing discrimination or to customary behavior. These data thus imply that Jews continue to gamble more frequently on various forms of entrepreneurial acts relative to the rest of the population in the U.S. Whether or not this behavior is due to persisting feelings of insecurity, discrimination, or the by now unconscious "Jewish Mother" syndrome I cannot say.

Conclusions

The discussion and evidence presented in this chapter have several general implications:

1. They show the relationship between legal and social status and the choices individuals make, that is, how people adapt their behavior to changes in the circumstances they face.

2. They show why one would expect higher crime rates in societies where some groups consider themselves to be discriminated against, that is, when they do not agree with the present allocation of property rights. At times the minority that considers itself as being discriminated against fights back not only with swords (in criminal and terrorist acts) but with words: some of these groups refer to part of the United Kingdom as "Northern Ireland", to all of Israel as "Palestine," and to part of Canada as "Québec libre." Unfortunately, one can go on and on with such examples.

3. The discussion and evidence both here and in the previous chapters imply that when members of an oppressed group perceive that they can

choose between gambling on the redistribution of wealth through the political process and gambling on individual effort, then the greater the size of the minority and its potential political power, the greater the probability that the first strategy will be chosen. In other words, expectations for redistributing wealth through the political process lower the supply of other entrepreneurial acts.

Table 5.1
Representation of Different Communities in Bombay's Educational Institutions, 1860, 1909

	Hindus		Muslims		Parsis		Christians	
	Boys	Girls	Boys	Girls	Boys	Girls	Boys	Girls
1860								
College	82	—	3	—	66	—	—	—
High school	239	—	15	—	615	—	441	150
Middle school	214	—	19	—	585	—	—	—
Primary school	478	—	66	—	59	485	—	—
Special school	76	—	26	—	16	—	—	—
1909								
College	1287	11	39	1	505	34	186	23
High school	5077	47	786	24	3217	819	1136	645
Middle school	977	205	268	6	226	80	927	782
Primary school	10891	3662	3448	1241	2451	321	321	146
Special school	804	1	132	—	16	104	104	10

Source: Kulke (1974), p. 86.

Table 5.2
Occupational Distribution in Bombay, 1864

	Parsis	Non-Parsis
Banking, money changers, auctioneers, real estate, priests	20.3	6.9
Government service, professionals	18	6.37
Services	14.4	7.92
Small-scale business	14.4	6.36
Retail trade	11.6	9.53
Transport	4.4	6.02
Navigation (sailors, fishermen)	0.2	6.84
Agriculture, handicrafts	2.6	10.36
Workers (iron, textile)	4	26.73
Low and "unclean" occupations	0.2	5.96

Source: 1864 Census. Numbers represent the percentage of the Parsi community and of the total population of Bombay in the various occupations.

Table 5.3
Professionals in Bombay, 1864: A Selected Sample

	Parsis	Non-Parsis
Doctors	9	0.67
Teachers	13	0.37
Clerks, bookkeepers	19	4.44
Printers, bookbinders	12.8	0.55
Watchmakers	19	0.11
Photographers	6.9	0.09
Toy producers	12.1	0.21

Source: 1864 Census. Numbers represent percentage of the respective groups within a broader definition of occupation used in the Census.

Table 5.4
Representation of Different Communities in High Income Groups (1905/6)

Income class (annual)	Hindus	Europeans	Parsis	Muslims
Rs. 20,000–30,000	72	20	23	29
Rs. 30,000–40,000	36	10	11	15
Rs. 40,000–50,000	8	4	9	2
Rs. 50,000–100,000	15	12	13	9
Rs. 100,000 or more	7	not given	6	4

Source: Kulke (1974), p. 58.

Table 5.5
Palestinians' General Level of Education before 1948

Year	Population (thousands)	Students (elementary and secondary)
1934	916	67,300
1935	941	76,760
1936	970	78,140
1937	993	87,500
1938	1,011	88,189
1939	1,043	94,123
1940	1,067	96,809
1941	1,098	96,928
1942	1,122	98,800
1943	1,160	105,368

Source: Statistical Abstract of Palestine, 1944–45 (Jerusalem: Office of Statistics, 1946), pp. 185–86.

Table 5.6
A. General Education of Palestinians (1960, 1970) and Syrians (1970)

	Palestinians		Syrians
	1960	1970	1970
Illiterates	46.24	33.43	54.17
Literates	36.68	28.59	25.38
Primary	11.41	21.65	12.91
Secondary	6.25	14.69	6.8
University	.46	1.62	.7
Undetermined	.96	.02	.4

B. General Education of Palestinians, Egyptians, and Syrians (1969–70)

1969–70	Palestine	Egypt	Syria
Elementary	14.4	11.3	13.6
Secondary	5.6	3	3.8
University	1.1	.57	.57

Sources: A, I. Abu Lughod, "Educating a Community in Exile: The Palestinian Experience," *Journal of Palestine Studies* 2 (1973); B, *Arab World File* (1977).
Note: Numbers represent percentage of group population.

Table 5.7

Distribution of Professions Studied at Universities in the Arab World by Palestinian Students Sponsored by UNRWA

	1954–55	1955–56	1959–60	1960–61	1962–63	1963–64	1970–71	1972–73	1973–74	1974–75	1975–76	1976–77
Agriculture	4	5	4	1.5	1.7	4	1.95	.4	.2	.3	.3	.3
Arts	22.7	20.6	11.6	0*	0*	0*	10.6	6.4	.2	0	.3	.9
Commerce and economics	4.7	4	2.0	1.5	.9	.6	5	2.4	.8	.9	...	...
Dentistry	.3	.5	.5	1.4	1.5	1.2	1.2	2.2	1.7	.5	...	...
Education	1.3	2.3	...	...	.3	...	...	...	...	...	...	...
Engineering	11.7	19.4	24.2	28.6	32.3	32.6	24.2	25	20	18.1	19.5	25.7
Law	4	2	...	...	...	...	...	...	...	...	...	...
Medicine	21	19.7	26.4	28.1	29.3	29.5	35.8	43.9	54.8	56.7	62.4	59.5
Pharmacy	1.3	.5	2.7	3.7	3.4	4.2	5.5	4.6	4	4	2.7	1.9
Science	15.6	13.7	21	21.2*	28.2*	25.4*	13.3	13.8	13.5	16	10.2	7

Source: UNRWA Annual Reports.

Note: Numbers are percentage of all students in the various fields.

* Arts and sciences are combined.

Table 5.8
Fields of Study

A. By Nationality*

Field	Lebanese	Jordanians and Palestinians†	Syrians	Others
	American University at Beirut, 1961–62			
Arts and science	62.9	67.7	63.1	58.4
Medicine	9.1	12.7	9.4	6.8
Science	...	...	...	...
Engineering	18.5	11.1	12.3	5.2
Agriculture	1.4	3	3.6	14.7
	University of St. Joseph, 1961–62			
Medicine	14.8	56	29.3	6.8
Law and political science	61.4	12	54.3	34.1
Engineering	8.2	10	5.2	2.2
Oriental arts	6.6	2	7.3	14.8

B. University of Damascus‡

Field	1955–56	1956–57	1957–58	1958–59	1961–62	1962–63
Medicine	9.3	8.7	8.3	7.8	6.1	3.13
Law	33.6	31.6	35.6	32.7	38.3	37
Arts	22.95	26.1	29	26	28.8	31.9

C. Egypt‡

Field	1959–60	1964–65
Arts	19.1	14
Law	18	14
Commerce	23.8	22.1
Science	5	8.4
Engineering	11.4	15.3
Medicine	9.7	11.3
Agriculture	6.6	10.6

Sources: A and C, Jean-Jacques Waardenburg, Les Universités dans le monde arabe actuel (Paris: Mouton, 1966); Education in the Arab States (New York: Arab Information Center, 1966).

* Numbers represent percentages of students at each university in the various fields.

† Two-thirds of this group were Palestinians.

‡ Numbers represent percentages of students in the various fields.

Table 5.9
Vocational and Technical Education of Refugee Graduates from UNRWA/Unesco and Non-UNRWA Centres, 1952–1973

Course	Graduates from UNRWA/ Unesco Centres	Graduates from Non-UNRWA Centres	Totals
Metal trades	5,068	341	5,409
Electrical trades	2,258	7	2,265
Building trades	2,253	38	2,291
Technical courses (including instructors)	1,653	88	1,741
Business, commerce, and secretarial	1,333	1,435	2,768
Paramedical, nursing, and midwifery	408	691	1,099
Agriculture	220	70	290
Dressmaking, clothing production, home management, and hairdressing	665	162	827
Infant leaders	170	...	170
Others	...	56	56
Total	14,028	2,888	16,916

Source: UNRWA Report (1973).

Table 5.10
Labor Force Participation in the United States, 1957

		Non-Jews	
Age	Jews	White Protestants (urban)	Catholics (urban)
14–17	0	33	25
18–24	51.7	76.5	79.3
65 +	48	35.9	31.6

Source: Census (1957).
Note: 55.1% of the Jewish population and 58.1% of the non-Jewish population were labor force participants.

Table 5.11
Education in the United States, 1973

	Non-Jews	Jews
Cannot read or write	2.17	1.05
Grades 0–5	3.17	1.05
Grades 6–8	13.14	6.32
Grades 9–11	19.05	6.32
Grade 12	24.93	10.53
Grade 12 plus nonacademic training	7.99	7.37
Some college	15.84	23.16
B.A.	7.70	29.47
B.A. plus advanced degree	3.36	11.58
N.A.	2.11	3.16

Source: Michigan Panel Study of Income Dynamics (1973).
Note: Numbers represent percentage of group population.

Table 5.12
Occupational Distribution in the United States (%)

A. Jews

Occupation	1935 Detroit	1955 NORC*	1956 Detroit	1956 Greater Washington	1957 Census*	1958 Michigan*	1959 Los Angeles	1963 Greater Providence*	1963 Detroit	1964 Milwaukee*	1964 Canada County	1965 Boston	1966 Los Angeles
Professional	7	17.6	16	37.8	20.3	19	24.9	20.7	23	22	34	32	35.6
Managers and proprietors	31	36	49	24.5	35.1	32	30.5	40.7	54	36	31	27	23.5
Clerical and sales	32	...	14	20.8	23†	...	24.2	25.4	13	27	22	31	20.8
Blue collar	30	...	21	9.7	...	...	...	11	10	10	11	10	...

B. Non-Jews‡

Occupation	1940 Detroit	1950 Detroit	1956 Greater Washington	1960 Detroit	1963 Greater Providence	1964 Camden	1964 Milwaukee	1965 Boston
Professional	5	8	22	12	9.2	13	12	15
Managers and Proprietors	9	10	15	10	10.5	18	8	8
Clerical and Sales	17	15	17	16	15.5	17	26	27
Blue collar	69	67	40	62	45.8	47	54	50

Sources: NORC survey (1955); Michigan survey (1957); local surveys from the respective Jewish community reports (see Yisrael Ellman, "The Economic Characteristics of American Jewry," in *Dispersion and Unity*, ed. Yehuda Adin [Jerusalem: World Zionist Organization, 1970], vol. 7).

* Survey distinguishes professions by other categories.

† Estimated.

‡ The data for non-Jews in the national surveys of NORC and the University of Michigan are the same as the ones in the 1957 census.

Table 5.13
Occupational Distribution in the United States, 1957 and 1973

	Jews 1957	Non-Jews 1957	Jews 1973	Non-Jews 1973
Professional, technical	20.3	9.9	24.21	11.41
Managers, officials, proprietors, self-employed businessmen*	35.1	13.3	31.52	10.77
Clerical	8	6.9	8.42	9.26
Craftsmen, foremen	8.9	20	11.58	19.95
Operatives	10.1	20.9	7.37	19.25
Laborers, service†	2.4	13.8	3.16	13.87
Farmers	.8	2.5	1.05	2.29

Sources: Michigan Panel Study of Income Dynamics (1973) and census (1957).

 * In the Michigan panel study a distinction was made between "self-employed business-men" and "managers and proprietors." The sum of these two numbers appears in the table. In 1973, 13.68% of Jews were self-employed businessmen, versus 4.08% in the rest of the population.

 † In the census a distinction was made between "service workers" and "farm laborers."

6
On Thinking, History, and the Social Sciences

But indeed language has succeeded until recently in hiding from us almost all the things we talk about.

I. A. RICHARDS

The first section of this chapter is devoted to a discussion of economic analysis in general. At times the discussion deals with some technical issues, and may be of more limited interest than the previous chapters. In the second section features of the social sciences, of the ways "history" is perceived in particular, are discussed. Both sections will examine the differences and the similarities between my approach and other approaches to human behavior (thinking in particular) and the "meaning" of history.

Economic Theory

In the first chapter a paradigm for economic analysis in particular, and for the analysis of human behavior in general (thus for the social sciences) was presented, which stated that people do their utmost to ensure their self-preservation. This is how I have interpreted "utility maximization." This point and its implications are elaborated here and the similarities and the differences between my approach and traditional approaches in economics will be pointed out. The analysis is based on the following points:

1. First the utility function is defined. It will then be shown that in a model where everything is assumed to be known with certainty (whatever that means) there is no distinction between the implications of my hypothesis and the usual ones in economics, namely, that people maximize the utility of their wealth subject to some constraints. The predictions of both hypotheses are the same, although it is not clear what intuitive interpretation one can give to utility functions in models of "certainty." But these models in economics, as well as in the natural sciences, can be

viewed as reasonable approximations; the arguments presented here show when such approximations are reasonable.

2. Only when one analyzes the choices human beings have to make when facing uncertain prospects—and I think that facing such prospects is what human behavior is all about—does it become clear that my view has greater explanatory power. As shown in the earlier chapters, this view can shed light not only on attitudes toward gambling, insurance, and crime, but also on how human beings think (i.e., gamble on ideas), how the terms "creativity" and "entrepreneurship" can be precisely defined (by mathematical symbols and with testable implications), and how one can distinguish between risk and uncertainty, a distinction both Knight (1921) and Keynes (1921) have tried to make, but without succeeding in giving it any precision. It will also be pointed out that while traditional economic models can deal only with the analysis of human adaptations to *given* rules, my approach can provide systematic analysis that can deal with the question of *how* rules are created to begin with.

3. The role the distribution of wealth plays in my analysis is contrasted with the usual one in mainstream economics, and it is shown that by using it one can get rid of what is called "normative economics" where ad hoc "welfare functions" have been postulated and where comparisons have been made between utilities. This area of economics has been developed in order to make statements about the distribution of wealth in the economy, which is assumed, in general, to have no direct effect on individual behavior. The utility function postulated here introduces in a straightforward way the effects that changes in the distribution of wealth have. Thus there is no need to make ad hoc assumptions about inequality, nor to make interpersonal comparisons between utilities, assumptions, and comparisons that lead only to abstract mental exercises and no falsifiable statements.

If I am not for myself, who will be for me?
If I am for myself only, what am I?
If not now, when?

Talmudic saying

What Does "Utility Maximization" Imply?

Economics explores and tests the implications of the assumption that people maximize the utility of their wealth. What are the implications of this assumption? Surprisingly, there is only one, namely, that people prefer more wealth to less. The "law of demand" that is sometimes seen as an outcome of utility maximization can be shown to be negatively inclined by merely taking into account the limited opportunity sets the individual faces, without making statements about utility functions (see Becker 1971).

The utility function introduced in the first chapter differs from the one usual in economic analysis: first, because a clear intuitive meaning can be given to it, namely, that of a probability of self-preservation; second, because this function depends not only on one's wealth but also on one's relative position in the distribution of wealth; and third because it implies that *unexpected* changes in the wealth distribution have a predictable effect on human behavior. Recall its precise definition: $U(.,.|.)$ represents a probability that depends on one's wealth, W_o, and on the percentage of people in the society whose wealth is greater than W_o, $\alpha(W > W_o)$, given that $\alpha(.)$ is one's expected position in the wealth distribution:

(1) $$U = U(W_o, \alpha(W > W_o)|\alpha(\cdot))$$

and

(2) $$U_1 = \frac{\partial U}{\partial W_o} > 0, \ U_2 = \frac{\partial U}{\partial \alpha} < 0$$

where U_1 denotes the positive marginal utility of wealth and shows by how much one's probability of survival increases if one's wealth increases, while $\alpha(W > W_o)$ remains constant. U_2 shows by how much one's probability of survival diminishes if one's relative wealth diminishes.

This view of the utility function implies that "selfishness" and maximization of utility have nothing to do with one another. For we know that human beings cannot survive alone and thus one's family and friends must appear either implicitly in this "utility" function or as components of one's wealth (recall the discussion and evidence on kin in chapter 2). Moreover, as shown in the previous chapters, this function enables us to define sentiments of love, envy, jealousy, and ambition, or "moral" and "immoral" sentiments in general, as well as one's gambling on ideas or one's creativity, sentiments, and actions that the traditional approach in economics can neither define nor examine. As for altruism (another concept that the traditional approach has difficulties in dealing with), the approach has suggested that traits we perceive today as altruistic might have their origin in circumstances in which gambling on them increased the stability of the society. These are some of the most straightforward differences between the approach presented in this book and traditional ones in economics; there are others.

Economic analysis as practiced today can address only the question of how individuals adapt to changes in either relative prices, opportunities, or legal constraints. It cannot show how new technologies, rules, and laws are created to begin with. What is the role of individuals in the process? (Paradoxically, the most "individualistic" of the social sciences provides no explicit role for individuals in its theories.) The approach presented in the first chapter provides answers to both these questions: it suggests under what circumstances people will gamble more frequently on novel ideas and under what circumstances other people will be more likely to accept these ideas, thus creating a new rule to which the society conforms.

The Law of Demand

As for the law of demand, perhaps *the* cornerstone of economic analysis, the approach here suggests that this law relies on more extensive assumptions that is at first apparent. Let us elaborate the traditional meaning of this law and see how it can be viewed in light of the approach presented in this book.

The law of demand is derived by assuming that "real income" remains constant when relative prices change. The meaning of the mental exercise of keeping real income constant is that when one price goes up, one's income is compensated in such a way as to allow the individual to be able to buy the initial basket of goods he consumed. While for some purposes this exercise might provide a good approximation, for others it might not, and in making it, as shown in the next section, one neglects the most important aspect of human behavior: thinking.

When unexpectedly climate becomes harsher, population increases, or the price of an imported good rises, the assumption that real income is held constant already means that somehow a compensation has been made for the diminished wealth. Unfortunately, except in myths and fairy tales human beings are not given such compensation, but must find them themselves and adjust their behavior to their changed circumstances. In this case, neglecting the income (or more correctly the wealth) and the redistributive effects have grave consequences, since the whole problem of the creation of new rules and new technologies is automatically eliminated from the model.

There are, however, some circumstances in which these effects can be neglected, for example, when the government imposes a tax on one commodity and subsidizes another. If expenditures on both commodities represent a relatively small fraction of people's budgets, one may assume that real income stays constant and that the distribution of wealth has not been changed significantly. Under these circumstances the predictions of the law of demand are likely to be confirmed by the evidence, and the predictions derived from my model and the traditional ones would be the same.

Under other circumstances the law seems irrelevant. If there is a significant increase in the relative price of a commodity on which people spend a relatively large fraction of their income, then simultaneously with this increase, average wealth per capita drops and the wealth distribution changes significantly. Thus if one observes a decreased demand for the commodity whose relative price has increased, one will not be able to attribute this decrease to the law of demand since real income has *not* remained constant. However, when such significant changes occur, one can make far-ranging predictions as to the subsequent expected changes in technology, in the political process, and in gambling activities in general. These predictions are discussed below.

> *If it is the world you seek, there can be no justice. If it is justice you seek, there can be no world.*
>
> LEVI, A FOURTH-CENTURY RABBI

The Consequences of Changing Wealth Distribution

What predictions can one make from the model as to the events that might occur when relative prices change significantly? In order to predict what the effects of such an alteration will be, one must distinguish between two cases. Assume that a mechanism exists by which the groups whose relative position has been changed expect to be compensated by groups whose situation has improved so as to maintain everybody's real income at approximately the expected levels, thus leading to expectations of no significant alterations in the distribution of wealth. In this case the evidence will support the predictions of the law of demand and other disturbances might be neglected.

But assume now that *no* mechanism exists by which wealth is expected to be redistributed, or that wealth has diminished. Then a change in relative prices which changes the distribution of wealth *significantly* will have additional consequences. Individuals whose relative wealth has diminished now have a greater incentive to gamble, to commit crimes, *and* to offer novel ideas in business, technology, science, the arts, or politics. At the same time, individuals whose relative wealth has increased have a smaller incentive to gamble, but have a greater incentive to insure themselves and spend more on either law enforcement or on charities (and thus become "conservatives").

One particular implication of this argument: it has been frequently pointed out that a change in relative prices results in greater incentives to make technological innovations in the direction of the goods whose relative price has increased, although no rigorous mechanism has been presented as to how this might occur. The hypothesis and the evidence presented in the previous chapters provide the missing link: individuals whose relative wealth has diminished now have a greater incentive to gamble on novel ideas in that direction.

But it is useful to reemphasize that this prediction stems from the same model that also predicts greater social unrest as a result of the significant change in relative prices. Moreover, the same model predicts the emergence both of new slogans in the political market against groups that have benefited from the change in relative prices, and of charges of "monopoly" power being used, even if it has not. These charges might be mere words behind which expectations for redistributing wealth are hidden. This view does not imply that redistribution should not be carried out; it implies only that we can sometimes understand the underlying mechanism behind the façade of words and understand their hidden message, since the emergence of such charges and of the torrent of words can be predicted.

All the aforementioned predictions show the greater power of the hypothesis on human attitudes toward risks presented here relative to other theories that have been offered. They stem from statements on human behavior that are straightforward, that can be translated to one line of mathematical symbols, and that show why by making assumptions on maintaining real income constant one eliminates the discussion on the most interesting aspect of human behavior, namely, thinking.

In contrast to this positive approach toward the question of wealth distribution, let us briefly present some of the traditional views on income distribution in economic theory.

Economists have approached this issue from two viewpoints: normative and the so-called positive. In the normative framework some ad hoc welfare functions have been postulated, making interpersonal comparisons between utilities and retreating to the concept of "Pareto efficiency," a concept that means essentially "more is better than less." In formulating these welfare criteria, economists have begun with some assumptions that seemed "widely acceptable." Thus, unsurprisingly, this field consists of mental exercises with mathematical symbols, but no verifiable hypothesis. Within the so-called positive framework the usual approach has been to start from the marginal productivity theory and examine the effects that various economic variables have on wages, profits, and rents, assuming that social, cultural, and political institutions are exogenous or unchanging. This is hardly an appealing approach for explaining the facts, since changes in income distribution are strongly related to changes in both political and social institutions.

To the question "Are people equal?" economists on both the right and the left have answered no. But to the question "Why are they not equal?", their answer is longer. For those on the left, the answer is that society makes them unequal. For those on the right, inequality is perceived as being inherent in the human condition.

These two views prompt the left and right to give different answers to the question of what should be done about inequality. The right holds that nothing should be done, since attempts to alleviate inequality can lead only to oppression. The left maintains that social reforms should be carried out.

What do the views and the evidence presented here have to say about this controversy? First, that both social conditions *and* factors inherent in the human condition (I call the latter "chance") play roles in explaining inequality, and that one cannot separate the effects of the two. Thus, it is not true that one cannot do anything about inequality, nor is it true that social reforms can eliminate it. They can diminish it, but they can never eliminate chance from the human condition.

How far should social reforms go in order to diminish inequality? For the moment, my answer is irrelevant for the simple reason that this book deals only with positive questions.

On Risk and Uncertainty

Before discussing the social sciences in general, I would like to emphasize that according to my hypothesis one *can* make a distinction between risk and uncertainty.

The term "risk" refers to situations where the estimated probabilities can be the same for all the people involved (as in lotteries), and so a comparison can be made between different people's reactions toward the same "risky" situation. When probabilities can be only *subjectively* estimated and there is no way to compare people's reactions, uncertainty prevails. The second situation refers to circumstances in which the diminishment of one's relative wealth increases one's incentive to gamble on novel ideas. This uncertainty is inherent in the human condition.

When this distinction between "risky" and "uncertain" situations is made, Knight's two famous arguments, that thinking and positive profits are both due to uncertainty and not risk, are easy to understand and prove. The proofs, carried out in chapter 1 and its appendix, were simple: since risk refers to attitudes toward property that has already been allocated, engagement in risky activities can lead only to redistribution of wealth but not to the creation of wealth. In contrast, uncertainty deals with property that has not yet been allocated. Thus an outsider will measure positive economic profits when lucky hits on novel ideas are made. Such lucky hits can be made when people gamble on novel ideas, an activity defined here as "thinking."

If this view of creativity (or entrepreneurship, or thinking) is correct, one can understand what policies firms might adopt to encourage such activity, and what policies to abandon if the entrepreneurial trait (one could also call it productivity) is to be encouraged. Automatic promotions and job security might be the best means of stifling ideas and diminishing productivity. In contrast, a hierarchical structure that provides fewer positions as one advances in a profession, and significant discrepancies between wage rates for individuals with similar education, provide incentive to the lower-paid employees to gamble more frequently on novel ideas (since in this case some of these employees' expectations will at times be frustrated).

But since more frequent gambling on novel ideas is the outcome of one's increased misery and increased suffering, one cannot argue that abolishing automatic promotions, job security, or tenure is "good." These arrangements make one's life more secure and more convenient, if less innovative or productive. But the question is what do we want? Happy people or creative people?[1]

> *Life's but a walking shadow, a poor player*
> *That struts and frets his hour upon the stage*
> *And then is heard no more. It is a tale*
> *Told by an idiot, full of sound and fury,*
> *Signifying nothing.*
>
> *Macbeth 5.5.24–28*

On History, Thinking, and the Social Sciences

Creativity, or what I call the gamble on ideas, is a subject that has fascinated many scientists: mathematicians, psychologists, sociologists, as well as economists (whose synonym for this term is entrepreneurship). The question of how we know has been raised frequently, but while no agreement has been reached on the precise mechanism that leads us to "know," agreement *has* been reached on the definition of science, one of the methods by which we try to know. This activity is characterized by three features, as the Goldsteins (1978) define it:

1) It is a search for understanding, for a sense of having found a satisfying explanation of some aspect of reality.
2) The understanding is achieved by means of statements of general laws or principles—laws applicable to the widest possible variety of phenomena.
3) The laws or principles can be tested experimentally. [p.6]

The word "experimentally" does not refer to the ability to carry out controlled experiments to test theories: astronomy, one of the most exact of the "exact" sciences, cannot control experiments, nor can geology or biology (when features of evolution are analyzed). Most of the evidence is already in our past and in nature.

In this book I have tried to follow the three principles mentioned above: a general hypothesis has been provided which is consistent with the assumptions we make about the biological world, and an attempt has been made to try to find a satisfactory explanation for a wide variety of phenomena. While features of primitive societies, of development, and of the occupational structure of some discriminated groups have been analyzed in depth, it has also been shown how a uniform approach can shed light on "larger" issues such as anti-Semitic outbursts, behavior in the political market, features of religions, and the way we think.

Since the principle postulated is a general one concerning human behavior, instead of one emphasizing the effects that the cultural environment has on human behavior (although when discussing how ideas are transferred from one generation to another and how they become custom attention was paid to this point), the analysis has concentrated on the *emergence* of some ideas, that is, why people have suddenly gambled on them. This view of human behavior enables us to make comparisons between different places and times and to make predictions both about "big" historical events and occurrences of everyday life. The same model has been used to make both predictions. Dare I say then that there is a theory of history in these chapters? I would prefer merely to say that a general theory of human behavior is presented here, which makes predictions about a wide variety of human activities, which is supported by the empirical evidence (statistical and nonstatistical), and which seems to shed light on various historical events that no other approach can.

In contrast to my uniform approach to all aspects of human behavior, even a superficial look at various disciplines in the social sciences reveals a human being who is schizophrenic. In economics he maximizes his profits or the utility of his wealth, has rational expectations, is always better off when having greater choice, and encounters no conflicts. In psychology, the same human being is stressed, depressed, obsessed, has Oedipus complexes, dreams, and escapes from freedom (according to Fromm). In anthropology primitive man is sometimes viewed as living near starvation, as maintaining his traditions, and as having no aspirations.

As for history, there seem to be many ways of viewing it. In high school we are taught to view it as not much more than a succession of dynasties, laws, and wars, all given some "political" interpretation. Some historians who look for "causes" seem to emphasize geography and climate as factors determining historical events, while the "new historians" seem to speak about "collective mentalities" as determining the course of history.[2] Marxists seem to be saying that history is determined by the way goods are produced: they argue that if a feudal society is being transformed into a capitalist one, then the "capitalistic mode of production" will change the society's institutions, religious, social, exchange, and otherwise (although Marxists neither define what a "capitalistic mode of production" means precisely, nor do they explain the causes for the transition from one mode of production to another). Paradoxically, Marxists have dealt so much with classes, movements, and materialistic interpretations that the accomplishments of individuals have been lost. I say "paradoxically" since Marx, a true entrepreneur according to my views, can play no role in his or his followers' theory of history. Other historians seem to view historical events solely in terms of psychological behavior (as shown in chapter 3), and still others, whom we may call the philosophical interpreters of history (Hegel, Spengler), seem to look for some common elements that can explain continuity in historical events. According to Hegel, for example, "history" seems to have a purpose, a kind of march of "mind" toward "freedom."

If the view of historical events presented here is correct, then history seems to be something quite different. Sudden fluctuations in human populations combined with the resulting random gambling on ideas can shed light on some historical events. According to this view there seems to be no continuity in our history, nor do methods of production effect religious beliefs, nor does "civilization" represent "progress," nor do classes determine the path of history. Rather, many of the features we view as "progress" seem to represent adaptions to our increasing numbers. The new rules, new technologies, and the arts seem to represent some individuals' novel ideas which the rest of the population has gambled on when the distribution of wealth has changed and people have suffered more. Methods of production do not effect religious beliefs; rather, both can be expected to change when population increases and the wealth distribution changes. Thus it appears that "chance happeneth to them all," since our thinking, or our gambling on ideas, seems to be a random event.[3]

Do such very divergent views of the same facts characterize empirical disciplines besides the social sciences?[4] Looking back at the history of science one can see that a situation where many schools try to explain the same phenomena is characteristic of the early stages of a science. An example taken from the history of physical optics will illustrate this point.[5] Today physics textbooks tell students that light is composed of photons which exhibit characteristics of both waves and particles. This characterization, however, is only half a century old. Until the end of the seventeenth century there was no single generally accepted framework for analyzing light. Instead there were three schools: the Epicurean, the Aristotelian, and the Platonic. One group assumed that light consisted of particles emanating from material bodies, another that it was a modification of the medium that intervened between the body and the eye, and the third explained it in terms of the interaction of the medium with an emanation from the eye. Each school emphasized the particular phenomenon that its own theory could best explain while other observations were dealt with by ad hoc assumptions and remained open problems for further research.

The lack of a uniform framework in a discipline has several immediate implications: each writer in the discipline feels forced to build his field from its foundations, and the choice of observation and experiment is free since there are no standard methods or even sets of phenomena that are accepted by every scientist in the field. This imposes constraints on the scientist's behavior, as is evident, for example, in the history of the development of the theory of electricity (an example originally given by Kuhn 1970). Although Franklin's theory of electricity was unable to explain all the known cases of electrical repulsion, his theory seemed better than those of other schools because it explained more of the facts it had to deal with. The acceptance of Franklin's theory suggested which experiments were worth performing and which were not. This made the constant reiteration of fundamentals unnecessary and enabled scientists to undertake more precise work and to work out their theories in more detail.

But the acceptance of a uniform framework changes the scientists' allocation of time. Instead of attempting to build up their field from the first principles and then justify the use of each concept introduced (tasks that can now be left to writers of textbooks), scientists can allocate their time to research that takes up where others have left off. This is the process that explains why an earlier stage of science is characterized by books such as Franklin's *Experiments . . . on Electricity,* Darwin's *Origin of Species,* or Adam Smith's *Wealth of Nations,* while later, when there is a common framework, the results of research will generally appear as brief, technical articles. These examples show why the range of questions I have tried to deal with is broader: the social sciences lack a uniform paradigm and I have tried to provide one. Another reason for the wider topics has already been mentioned: it can show the greater explanatory power of my hypothesis. However, the reader should be reminded of the price paid for covering so many issues: I would be dishonest to pretend to a complete mastery of all the relevant sources, although they were selected carefully following discussions with scientists from various fields.

With regard to uniform principles in the social sciences, historians and political scientists have rarely claimed that they share a general theory that can be used to explain all historical or political events. Demographers have never claimed to have a general approach that can explain changes in fertility, death rates, or patterns of marriage. Hollingsworth (1969) writes that a demographer should be deeply versed in economics, sociology, religious observance, archeology, anthropology, climatology, epidemiology, and gynecology. But the purpose of the demographer is to collect data and analyze them with the help of theories provided by other disciplines, and not to explain all facts by some uniform "demographical" approach. The absence of a paradigm in legal studies is also evident: legal scholars have been unable from remote antiquity to define justice clearly although the assumption that individual as well as society's behavior must be guided by some principle of justice seems to be the paradigm of this discipline. In spite of the many books written on justice, the notion itself remains obscure. Rawls (1971) writes:

> Justice is the first virtue of social institutions, as truth is of systems of thought. A theory however elegant and economical must be rejected or revised if it is untrue; likewise laws and institutions no matter how efficient and well arranged must be reformed or abolished if they are unjust. [p. 3]

But the two problems are not the same: while a theory will be rejected if untrue (the criterion being the empirical evidence), what evidence could ever show that a law or an institution is unjust? Moreover, if by "systems of thought" Rawls means sciences in general, then he is again mistaken,[6] for "truth" is not their virtue—degrees of belief would be the more appropriate term. "Truth" is a mere feature of our language; explaining facts is the virtue of the sciences. There are no "truths" in systems of thought. In mathematics one finds logic and exactitude. But exactitude is not truth: by translating words to the abstract symbols of mathematical language one only checks consistency. As for sociology, in a recently published book, *What Is Sociology?*, Norbert Elias (1978) writes:

> To trace back everything observed as mobile and changing to something changeless and eternal was the central task of all science, and the criterion for the scientific status of any field of research. Consequently, many academics, especially sociologists, feel a certain disquiet and perhaps even an uneasy conscience: on the one hand they lay claim to being scientists, yet on the other hand they are not in a position to comply with the declared philosophical ideal of science. [p. 114]

This principle was followed in this book, suggesting that doing our utmost to ensure our self-preservation may be our changeless, eternal task. I hope that I have presented enough evidence so that the reader knows that this idea is no longer a gamble.

I promised not to raise philosophical questions and I shall not. But a few words must be said on some philosophers who, although they never looked systematically at facts, seemed to arrive at conclusions similar to the ones reached in this book (although to agree with their views would have been a gamble). Schopenhauer saw behind both nature and human life the struggle of blind forces, a striving without purpose, a meaningless effort that creates and destroys in vain. According to him the hope of mankind lies in the realization that struggle and achievement are illusions.

If one calls Schopenhauer's blind forces "chance", and if one is persuaded by the views and evidence presented here that our thinking is due to the perception of inequality, Schopenhauer's conclusions seem very close to the ones put forth in this book.

Even closer to my views are Henri Bergson's. In *Creative Evolution*, he argues that intellect is merely a factor in biological adaptation, which has a pragmatic use in the struggle for life; that utility rather than attainment of "truth" is the role of science; and that only by our intuition do we understand the world. If one defines "intuition" as the gamble on novel ideas, the similarity between Bergson's views and mine is evident.

But my analyses differ from these philosophers', since the discussion has been presented in positive (that is, falsifiable) terms. This methodology enables us to reach the conclusion that while we are all endowed biologically with the ability to gamble on novel ideas, we will use this ability only when our relative position in the wealth distribution fluctuates significantly; otherwise this trait will remain latent.

It may also be useful to mention that my views on the way the human mind works seem consistent with those of some physicists, who, relying on the physics of quantum mechanics, and relativity, argue that one cannot separate the observer from the observed in any act of perception.[7] The system the two form is one entity, each influencing and defining the other. They draw a similarity between the randomness of brain processes and the indeterminism of quantum mechanics, arguing that chance and necessity, randomness and structure blend into one in the human brain and that no logical distinction can be drawn between these two properties. This is exactly the meaning of my discussion on creativity in the first chapter and of the mathematical proof in its appendix. Further comparison between quantum mechanics and my views shows that the distinction between the way probability appears in my model, i.e., as inherent in the human condition, and the way mainstream economics seems to deal with it, i.e., as reflecting mere ignorance of initial conditions, is similar to the distinction made between the meaning of probability in quantum mechanics and in classical physics. Finally, these arguments indicate that the viewpoint frequently expressed by some neuroscientists—that the brain is the product of determinate processes that at least in principle are discoverable (and thus that even emotion could be built in a computer)—is incorrect.

One major conclusion from the discussion and evidence presented in this book is that the human trait called "thinking" or "creativity" can neither be reduced to rules of scientific research nor be taught at universities.[8] It is the toughest of disciplines, and can be taught only by chance and suffering.[9]

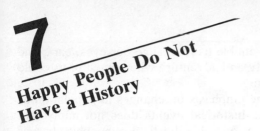

7
Happy People Do Not Have a History

Pain that cannot forget
falls drop by drop
upon the heart
until in our despair
there comes wisdom
through the awful grace of God.

AESCHYLUS

Economic development as conventionally understood and measured might not tell us much about either wealth per capita or general welfare. One of the major points of this book is that much of what we consider to be signs of progress or development—the rise of markets and of social institutions, literacy, legislation, and so forth are, in a historical perspective, an illusion. These new institutions substitute for the trust, customs, and beliefs that are shared when human populations are much smaller and are maintained at stable levels, while innovations and discoveries, or the gambling on novel ideas in general, are due to people's suffering. It should then be clear that development, as measured by a rising gross national product, cannot be equated with either progress, an evolutionary process, or increased welfare, as is done now by most Western minds. The data suggest that human populations have moved to riskier environments and harsher climates because of their increased numbers, that all eat food of diminishing quality, and that technology, which some of us tend to view as a random outcome of the human genius, appears in a historical perspective as the means by which people try to approximate and hold their position in the wealth distribution stable. However, it must be clear that what constitutes "wealth" changes considerably: paintings and music evoke the memories of lost landscapes; legislation and money substitute for lost trust; babysitters and books on fairy tales for grandparents who no longer live with their grandchildren; and central authorities on earth in part for lost beliefs in divine authority. We owe a great debt to artists and writers, entrepreneurs who enable us to change our eyes, ears, and minds so that we may find beauty and adventure where most of us could perceive only ugliness and gloom.

But it should be noted that the emphasis on changes in population as a means of understanding some historical events does not imply that "demography is destiny"; it implies only that drastic demographic changes due to factors beyond human control have led to unexpected and significant changes in the wealth distribution and to the emergence of new ideas, political ideas in particular. The subsequent gamble on such ideas assigns a central role to individuals and to political systems in shaping the course of history. Also, the emphasis on population does not imply that increased creativity is necessarily associated with rising population: the major thrust of my views is that people's increased creativity is due to the perception that they are "outdone" by their fellows, whether or not these "fellows" are one's countrymen. Such a process can thus occur when some nations are suddenly opened up to international trade or receive more information on what is happening in other nations. While such discoveries lead to increased suffering among people who view suddenly themselves as inferior, and may lead to increased creativity among them, the process is not necessarily related to a rising population, but may be due to technological change (the introduction of television, for example).[1]

There is no such thing as a free lunch.

MILTON FRIEDMAN

Wealth, Welfare, and Population

Wealth, Population, and Political Instability;
or, What Caused the Rise of the West?

Rarely have social scientists asked why markets have risen, why agriculture emerged, why some particular occupations exist, why some social institutions have arisen, or why people have gambled on new ideas. We should focus our attention on the problem of changed incentives and the emergence of ideas rather than either on the behavior of already existing firms or on descriptions of where and when certain events have occurred. The work of some social scientists who have followed this line of research is summarized below.

North (1981) argues that the social sciences lack a theory of demographic change, that the model of the state is deficient, and that a positive theory of the sociology of knowledge is lacking. He also considers that the materials needed to fill the gap are "1) a theory of property rights that describes the individual and group incentives in the system; 2) a theory of the state, since it is the state that specifies and enforces property rights;

3) a theory of ideology that explains how different perceptions of reality affect the reaction of individuals to the changing "objective" situation" (pp. 7–8). The first two chapters in this book can be viewed as attempts to construct these materials.

As already noted, Schultz (1980) argues that disequilibrium is the causative factor for the emergence of the entrepreneurial trait, although he does not define precisely either the concept of the entrepreneur or the mechanism that leads to change. The argument that "stress" (which seems to be the psychologists' synonym for the economists' disequilibrium) is a causative factor has been applied by a large number of social scientists, who thus explain the rise of agriculture in general and of specific technological innovations in this sector in particular. The works are summarized in Mark Nathan Cohen's (1977) splendid book, *Food Crisis in Prehistory,* in which he argues and presents extensive evidence that the shift from hunting and gathering societies to agricultural ones came *in response* to population pressure:

> The idea that population growth or pressure may contribute to technological change is of course not new. Demographic stress as a cause of domestication was suggested by Leslie White (1959). And a number of recent studies have attempted to show that population growth and pressure are contributors to the process of culture growth rather than simply results of technological change. (See Drummond 1965; Smith 1972a, b; Harner 1970; Spooner [ed.] 1972; Meyers 1971; Kunstadter 1972; Flannery 1969, 1973; Binford 1968; Harris in press; Cohen 1975a, b; Sanders and Price 1968; Carneiro 1961, 1970, 1972; and others). The basic discussion of the role of population growth as a determinant of technological change, and the study which prompted much of the later work, however, was the work of Ester Boserup (1965). It is Boserup who was primarily responsible for challenging the traditional Malthusian models of population growth and reversing our perspective on the cause and effect relationship between growth and technological change. In her analysis of agricultural systems she argues that it is not so much technological progress as population density that determines what type of agriculture will be employed. She argues in fact, that the relative efficiency of various agricultural technologies is largely a function of population density and that various known technologies represent a continuous series of more or less elastic responses to growing population. [p. 13]

Barbara Bender (quoted in Leakey 1981), a British anthropologist, rejects the idea and argues that changes in social structures might provide the explanation for the shift to agriculture. She argues that there is a correlation between the appearance of hierarchies and what she defines as "surplus" goods. As the discussion and evidence in the first two chapters suggest, there is not really a contradiction between the two views. When population increases, the wealth distribution changes and people begin to gamble more frequently, the result of which is the appearance of what some social scientists define as "surplus goods."

In another context it was shown that some social scientists share the view that many of the features of the early and late Middle Ages can be viewed as adjustments to fluctuations in population, taking into account already existing levels of technology. McNeill (1976) makes an even stronger point: he applies his argument not only to the Middle Ages but to a variety of historical circumstances (the puzzling fall of some empires) and shows that contacts due to migrations among previously disconnected populations and their respective lack of immunity to new disease shed light on some dramatic fluctuations in populations (e.g., in Europe when the Black Death struck and in Central and South America when the Europeans arrived) and the consequent changes in economic structure, customs, and taboos. The approach here in the previous chapters has been similar, only first a uniform framework relating changes in *individual* behavior to changes either in the expected number of people with whom future interactions are expected or in the wealth distribution has been provided. Only later was this analysis applied to some strikingly different subjects that no one, so far, has tried to analyze from a unified viewpoint or by pointing out the similarities between them.

It may be helpful at this point to reemphasize the role population has played in this book. In chapter 2 the relationship between the structure of exchange and some demographic variables was discussed. In chapters 3 and 4 an additional variable emerged, namely, how exactly population grows: is it a slow trend or are there abrupt, unexpected fluctuations? It was shown that when population fluctuates wildly (either because of lack of immunity to diseases or changes in climate), customs and methods of exchange are abruptly altered. In contrast, in societies where population is either stable or rises slowly, customs either remain unaltered or are gradually adjusted. Since customs channel expectations as to one's relative position in the distribution of wealth, one would expect that in a society where customs are either unaltered or change slowly and continuously there will be less fluctuation in the individual's relative position in the wealth distribution.[2] This implies that there will be a smaller supply of innovative ideas in business, science, and the arts as well as fewer crimes, for it is significant change in one's relative position in the distribution of wealth that leads one to gamble. One would thus expect both a more turbulent social structure in societies where population has fluctuated wildly *and* a more spectacular record of achievement in science, technology, and the arts. This would seem to be the explanation for the "rise of the West."

At this point one may ask whether it is not true that today "developed" countries have lower rates of population growth than less developed ones and yet still provide a disproportionate supply of novel ideas in technology, science, and the arts. In order to answer this question, it must be seen in a historical perspective. To begin with, the higher rate of population growth in the less developed countries is a recent phenomenon. From the nineteenth century until the 1930s the rate of population growth in these countries was markedly below that of Europe (see Kuznetz 1966). The current rise in population in the less developed countries is not in small part due to the intervention of the "developed" countries, which have introduced their medical technologies into societies in which neither custom nor the political structure has been adjusted to absorb the abrupt and unexpected changes.

It is important to emphasize that from the point of view of the members of local populations in less developed countries, their increased numbers can be viewed as an unexpected event; the evidence in the previous chapters makes it clear that people adapt to new circumstances slowly. How can an illiterate population understand that the new medical technology of the West will diminish the mortality rate of their children and that they can thus limit the number of children they have and still expect to have the same number of *surviving* children as they had before? Indeed, several social scientists have pointed out that parents' expectations of childhood mortality are only slowly altered when changes in health technology are forced upon them (see Kuznetz 1979). These slow changes in expectations lead to the high increase in population.

Population growth is due not only to slowly changing expectations concerning childhood mortality, but also to the fact that parents' perceptions of what a "child" means changes slowly. Recall that in many societies children have provided not only insurance against old age (substituting for social security) but also the means by which property can be protected. In developed societies children are no longer expected to play these roles. Indeeed, the word "child" is one further example of a semantic problem: we continue to use the same word for something whose content has been drastically altered, or which means different things in different societies.

On Literacy and Education

I have argued that when the number of people with whom future interactions are expected increases, it becomes more likely that people will gamble on the idea of literacy. But as the discussion on anti-Semitism has revealed, literacy has costs as well as benefits. These costs come to the fore when we look at the more rigid behavior of literate people and at the consequences of a lack of communication between oral and literate cultures, events that occur because the original meaning of the words is either lost, drastically altered, or totally misunderstood.

One must therefore be very careful when advocating education, and literacy in particular, in oral cultures (i.e., some of the Third World countries today). Exposing them simultaneously to the Bible, Marx, and Freud, or teaching them some of the confused notions of literate societies ("efficiency," "justice," "capitalism," "socialism," "freedom," "exploitation") might have totally unpredictable consequences. This is one reason I have tried to avoid these popular concepts as far as possible: they are vague and have a normative connotation. Instead I have tried to use ordinary, everyday language (but with precision) and make statements which can be verified or rejected, even when discussing features of religions.

That literacy does not always lead to "economic development" and is not a causative factor was one of the points made earlier, the conclusion being based on evidence from the anthropological literature. One would expect that, in communities that are still relatively isolated and have faced stable circumstances for long periods of time, even if education is exogenously introduced by a central authority or a benevolent foreign country, it will not necessarily change behavior. In contrast, if the community becomes less isolated so that both the potential number of participants in exchange increases (decreasing the frequency of transactions between any two particular individuals) *and* the relevant distribution of wealth according to which people shape their behavior changes, education (as the West understands this term) will become one of the entrepreneurial activities people will have a greater incentive to gamble on.

The relationship between education and methods of production has been analyzed in the agricultural literature. Schultz (1975) has argued that education facilitates the reallocation of resources in agriculture when disequilibria occur. Patrick and Kehrberg (1973) have found that education makes no contribution to farm output in areas of Brazil considered traditional, while Haller (1972) has found that in regions described as traditional in Colombia education has not had a statistically positive effect on farm production, but in regions considered "modern" a positive effect has been found. Similar evidence provided by anthropologists and psychologists was presented in chapter 2.

On Growth and Political Instability

The relationship between economic growth (by which I mean the measurement of increased gambling activity and the adaptation of the population to its increased numbers) and the introduction of new technologies and changes in the organization of social institutions must be analyzed in terms of the individuals who bring these changes about. Algebraic formulas and mechanistic models of the economy will provide no help. The question is how individuals' incentives can be altered so as to induce them to introduce these changes, at the same time trying to avoid both an increased crime rate and the greater political instability that may accompany them.

The arguments and evidence presented in the previous chapters suggest a way, however imprecise. Consider a typical less-developed country in which population has either unexpectedly increased or more extensive contacts have suddenly been established between it and the rest of the world. As a result, the distribution of wealth is altered and the social fabric weakened. Under these circumstances (if there is no way back) the predictions of my hypotheses are that the supply of entrepreneurial acts will in general increase. But whether the entrepreneurship in education or technology will be put to use in that country or whether there will be a "brain drain" (another word for migration, an entrepreneurial strategy that some people will gamble on) depends on the amount of entrepreneurial activities that are undertaken in the local criminal or political "markets."

The increased political instability is due to the fact that groups whose relative wealth has dropped are more willing to gamble on ideas that some individuals (politicians) are always ready to provide. In order to diminish the resulting political instability, methods of redistributing wealth through central authority must replace the weakened customs: this is the way governments can correct their own previous mistakes in introducing new, Western technologies in health and education, technologies that are foreign to the population's habits. However, one must be careful when deciding how much to redistribute from the relatively rich to the relatively poor, for as both my views and the empirical evidence indicate, expectations of such redistributions, while they may diminish the crime rate and the probability of revolutions, simultaneously diminish the incentive to engage in entrepreneurial acts in general. However, there is a range in this policy where a pragmatic political entrepreneur can move in a way that diminishes fluctuations in the wealth distribution (thus increasing political stability and diminishing the crime rate) but still maintains enough incentives to supply novel ideas in business, science, and the arts.

I do not argue in this book that "small is beautiful"; what I argue is that both "small" and "big" can be beautiful, but the transition from one to the other is painful and takes time. How "big" can be perceived as "beautiful" is shown in the final section of the book.

On Methods of Redistributing Wealth

In the previous chapters it was shown that in primitive societies where population is stable, customs exist that help to maintain inequality at stable levels. Growing up under these customs leads to expectations for redistributing wealth that simultaneously diminish crime rates *and* the supply of novel ideas. What happens when population increases but it remains stable at the new higher level? The evidence has suggested that a higher level of economic development will be measured in such a society and that there will be more frequent changes in the individual's position in the wealth distribution, although inequality could still be maintained at a stable level by a new set of customs.

In other chapters it was shown how religions and political mechanisms substitute for customs that have guided the redistribution of wealth where populations have been smaller and stabler. What are the institutions today that redistribute wealth in a society?

As one would expect, when population increases the government will play a greater role in redistributing wealth by either progressive income taxes, direct subsidies to the relatively poor, social security for the elderly, or a variety of legislation.[3] In another study, with Gabrielle Brenner, I analyzed how the emergence of progressive income tax systems can be explained by relying on the arguments presented in this book, without making any normative statements about "justice," "fairness," or ad hoc assumptions about "welfare functions," concepts that seem to justify these tax schedules today. The argument is straightforward: since those who became relatively poor are the more likely to commit crimes, the relatively rich have an incentive either to increase expenditures on methods of self-protection or on law and order, expenditures that decrease the probability of one's becoming a victim of crime. Alternatively, they may transfer wealth through charity or taxation so as to diminish the relatively poor's incentives to commit crimes. All these strategies impose some costs on the relatively rich, and a combination of penalties for committing crimes and of subsidies for the poor will be chosen to diminish the crime rate and increase the stability of the society.

But taxes and charities (the latter *not* being due to altruism) are not the only methods for redistributing wealth in society. Legislation preventing entry to some occupations, constraints on migration, tariffs, and subsidies to farmers, scientists, and artists all raise the relative wealth of some groups while diminishing that of others. Olson (1965, 1978) has analyzed the emergence of interest groups in general, and of unions and of lobbying organizations in particular, which under various ideological banners have favored the introduction either of legal restriction that indirectly raises their relative wealth or of direct means of redistributing wealth through a central authority. One may view the emergence of such groups as an institutional adaptation to increased population that substitutes for the weakened customs, family ties, and religious beliefs that carried out redistribution in the relatively smaller and stabler societies of the past. This substitution takes time: one must first find the ideas around which the new groups can be organized. In primitive societies fear of God and of sorcery leads to the redistribution of wealth, and we do not know how long it took for these ideas to emerge and to be institutionalized. Today accusations of "exploitation," "greediness," "disregarding social justice," and of being "unfair" or "discriminatory" are expected to lead to similar outcomes. Making use of these words, formulating theories around them, and then using them as political slogans for passing legislation all take time. It must be clear, however, that people follow such slogans, even though they are imprecise, since they reflect at the moment of their invention a strong yet inarticulated human sentiment, a sentiment I have tried to articulate in this book.[4]

Art is a lie which reveals reality.

PICASSO

On the Arts

How do the arts fit into the view of human behavior presented here? We may see "artists" as individuals who offer novel ideas, invent new languages (musical in particular) that enable us to perceive the world in a new way. Art is the term used to sum up the ideas that have come to life because the public, past and present, has been willing to gamble on them. It follows that if artists are the "entrepreneurs" who gamble on novel ideas, the broad predictions made in the previous chapters about the circumstances in which people will more likely gamble should also hold true for this particular type of human activity. Two main predictions have been made: first, that the arts should flourish when people also gamble on a wide variety of new activities (i.e., when the wealth distribution suddenly changes); second, that many features of what now is considered to be art can be viewed as a substitute for wealth lost because of an unexpected rise in the population.

If the first prediction is accurate, it implies that novelty in the arts should not appear regularly, but should be concentrated during periods of increasing instability, whether political, economic, or social (to make the traditional but improper distinction). This observation has been made by many historians (as shown in chapter 1), and, as Arieti (1976) summarizes, by many psychologists and other social scientists as well. They have all pointed out that the phenomena of "geniuses" appearing in clusters have been observed since antiquity, and that the possibility that these occurrences are due to either chance or genetics is infinitesimal.

According to Arieti (1976), Valleius Paterculus, a Roman historian (19 B.C.–A.D. 30 ?), was among the first who raised the question of why men of great talent appear in certain periods. Valleius suggested that once a talented man appears, envy and admiration will induce other people to imitate his work and become creative. This view seems consistent with that presented here. Suppose that an individual breaks with tradition in the arts and the public gambles on his new ideas. Others who have until now followed the traditional schools now perceive the threat of their wealth (and status) diminishing. This induces them, as well as others, to gamble on new ideas (albeit not only of "positive" but also "negative" types: remember Salieri's intrigues against Mozart).

More recently, Kroeber (1944) and Gray (1958, 1961, 1966) have tried to deal with the phenomena of a concentration of great talent appearing in a few periods. Kroeber admits however, that he is not seeking for explanations. Gray, on the other hand, proposes an "epicyclical theory," according to which history consists of well-defined political, economic, and social cycles and subcycles. The peaks of these cycles coincide with bursts of creativity. (I must admit that Gray's theory is not very clear to me, thus the interested reader should look at the original work and then choose between the various explanations.)

Let us turn now to the second prediction and see how some features of what we consider art can be related to our fluctuating numbers. "Art" is another word whose content has changed greatly. While we subsume painting, sculpture, music, and literature under this term, the interpretation we give to paintings, sculptures, and music from the Renaissance, for example, is very different from that given by the medieval or Renaissance societies that gave birth to these works. Did Michelangelo's paintings and sculptures represent "art"? Were medieval paintings "art"? Were the passion plays and epic tales "literature"? I think (that is, I gamble on the idea) they were not; at least they were not intended to be either "art" or "literature"—not as we interpret these terms today.

Recall the picture of medieval societies drawn in the previous chapters. How could one get information about the world and how did one interpret it until the fifteenth or even the seventeenth century in Western Europe? The population was mainly illiterate, which left only two channels of information open: oral and visual (but not written). Thus, unsurprisingly, music, plays, paintings, and sculptures provided information as well as misinformation to most of the population. The images of medieval and Renaissance paintings depict ancient legends and religious myths from Greek and Roman mythology or the Old and New Testaments, and sometimes images of war and public figures. If nature appears in these images, it is rather abstract and seems only to fill out the picture, without however being the *subject* of the study itself. Neither is much attention paid to the daily occurrences of everyday life.

The idea that looking at nature is self-rewarding or that looking at landscapes devoid of action is enjoyable is new, as is landscape painting. This is not very surprising: when populations were small, nature was at everybody's back and front doors—views of woods, swamps, rivers, and birds were part of one's daily life. Only when this activity became relatively rare (because of our increased numbers) did we suddenly, but predictably, "discover" nature's beauty. This is what some artists succeeded in doing. Koestler (1964) notes these changes as well as the simultaneous ones in literature:

> Considering the bulk and value of Greek literature and the artistic brilliance of Athens, the feeling for nature . . . was poorly developed among a people whose achievement in the dramatic and sculptural arts has been unsurpassed; it is seriously lacking in Homer, even when he refers to the sea or to the famous garden of Alcinous, and it can hardly be said to enter Greek drama save in the *Oedipus at Colonnus* and in some of the lyrical choruses of Euripides. Indeed, the continent of nature had to wait for a thorough and minute exploration until the romantic movement of the nineteenth century: Byron, Shelley, Wordsworth, Goethe, first brought the ocean, the rivers and the mountain ranges into their own. . . . [p. 367]

Thus, by evoking memories, words and paintings replaced lost landscapes, and artists conditioned our ears and eyes to the new environments. To translate this statement into the more technical language of the previous chapters, artists are the entrepreneurs who gamble on novel ideas when our wealth diminishes (that is, when our landscapes are lost) and the rest of the population gambles on their interpretation. Thus, while the composition of "wealth" changes considerably, these entrepreneurs help maintain our perception that "wealth" has not diminished.

Not only is nature absent from painting and literature until the Renaissance (at least in Western Europe; in China, as one would expect, it appears earlier), so are people and the occurrences of everyday life. The reason is clear: when people lived in relatively closed, small communities, they had more than enough information on their neighbors' behavior. Thus the images of daily life were too familiar to need additional visual reminders.

But let us return to the great pre-Renaissance panels depicting scenes of religious life and myths of the period that we so much admire. The artists in this case gave an interpretation to written words, words that most of the population had no incentive to learn how to read. The Church and central authorities subsidized paintings on religious subjects or paintings glorifying their victories and benevolence. This is not surprising: if the Church and the ruling families wanted to promote their views, how could they do so if not by visual images, plays, and music? In illiterate societies the only way to attract the population's ears and eyes was through music, drama, and painting. Indeed, Pope Gregory the Great, who lived at the end of the sixth century, said that many members of the Church could neither read nor write, and that for the purpose of teaching them "painting can do for the illiterate what writing does for those who can read." What better testimony to the cunning of Church and prince than the fact that we still enjoy the paintings, music, and great cathedrals of that period? We even sometimes still enjoy the Passion plays, the epic tales, and the *Chanson de Roland*. How these tales and chants glorified certain leaders and how the Passion plays glorified the ideas of the New Testament and taught the population to hate the Jews are all well-known features of the "literature" of this period.

Today, while we still apply the word "art" to painting and sculpture and the word "literature" to poetry and plays, we expect these works to reflect the artists' personal views. However, the "informational" component of the arts has been diminished if not totally eliminated (is this the reason that today's paintings are abstract?). Information is conveyed to us by the relatively more objective newspapers, photographs, and television; we would be suspicious of artists who tried to sell us "information" or propaganda for a regime. At least, this seems now to be the view in the West; in the communist East and not so long ago even in the West under fascist regimes, the arts have been used as tools of propaganda, and with considerable success. Thus if telling a story and providing information are no longer the goal of art, what do we expect artists to do? As the word "impressionism" suggests, we expect them to give us their impressions, their interpretations of the world, and let us decide whether or not we want to gamble on them.

Matisse expressed his views on art very clearly: he wanted it to have the effect of a good armchair on a tired businessman. Other painters have stated their goals differently, although the content of their statements is similar. Vrubel, a Russian painter of the nineteenth century, stated that "the eye of the people must be trained to see beauty everywhere—in streets and railroad stations," and this is what he painted. Do not we admire his and Manet's paintings of gray streets and railway stations clouded in mists? Viewers of an earlier period would probably have been unable to perceive beauty in those dark structures and in the noise of the locomotives. Van Gogh seemed to share Vrubel's views:

> This morning I visited the place where the streetcleaners dump the rubbish. My God, it was beautiful! Tomorrow they are bringing a couple of interesting pieces from that garbage pile, including some broken street lamps, for me to admire or, if you wish, to use as models. . . . It would make a fine subject for a fairy tale by Andersen, that mass of garbage cans, baskets, pots, serving bowls, metal pitchers, wires, lanterns, pipes and flues that people have thrown away. I really believe I shall dream about it tonight, and in winter I shall have much to do with it in my work . . . it would be a real pleasure

to take you there, and to a few other places that are a real paradise for the artist, however unsightly they may be.

And indeed, we admire Van Gogh's *The Huth Factories at Clichy* (1887), in which factories with their smoking chimneys intrude into the pastoral landscape. Are the chimneys ugly? For Van Gogh's contemporaries, whose eyes were conditioned to more pastoral surroundings, they probably were and they diminished the viewers' wealth. This transformation of ugliness into beauty has been repeated many times in the history of art: the Eiffel Tower was considered ugly, but can we imagine Paris today without it after generations of photographers, film makers and painters, Delaunay in particular, have succeeded so well in accustoming our eyes to it? And even New York, with its square buildings, square streets, and square illuminated windows has some appeal: Mondrian's colorful squares, which were intended to depict this feature, probably had their effect. As for the increased level of noise we are exposed to, perhaps Rossini's contemporaries were right when they mentioned his masterly handling of "patter" in his music, his ability to make the audience smile at human noise rather than feel it to be unbearable (recall the finale of the first act of *L'Italiana in Algieri*).

If artists are entrepreneurs who provide us with novel ideas on which we gamble, we may apply the conclusions of this book about entrepreneurship in general to this case as well. We may see then that success and wealth destroy the creativity that they induce. Recall that Giordano never wrote another *Andrea Chenier* after he married a wealthy heiress, and that Van Gogh said that success is the artist's worst enemy (one need only take a look at Picasso's, Miro's, and Chagall's later paintings). And did not Haydn compose his most beautiful symphonies in London rather than under Eszterhazy patronage? That Rossini suddenly stopped composing may not be so surprising after all: not only did he succeed very well in monetary terms, but most of the critics found him beyond comparison. This is a very dangerous situation: if comparison is disallowed, what incentive is left? Indeed, Rossini is alleged to have explained his retirement as a composer by stating that further success could hardly increase his existing fame, while a failure could only diminish it. Verdi, on the other hand, returned to compose the two masterpieces of his old age after being frequently and unfavorably compared with Wagner, a comparison that troubled him. And Camus once wrote: "Sadness of success. Opposition is necessary. If everything was more difficult for me, as before, I should have more right to say what I say. It remains that I can help many people—while waiting." It may thus indeed be true that happy people do not have a history.

Chapter 1

1. See the appendix for a more precise and detailed discussion on the differences between my approach and the standard ones in economics.

2. The empirical part in this section is drawn from Brenner and Brenner (1981).

3. More evidence of this comes from a survey carried out by the Massachusetts State Lottery Commission, which found that "the public prefers a game offering a relatively small number of large prizes to one offering a single very large prize and a great many very small ones. It overwhelmingly favors a single top prize of $100,000 over a large number of top prizes of $1,000 each. . . . By 15 to 1, the public would rather have one chance in 1,000 of winning $300 than one chance in 2 of winning 50 cents. . . . The Massachusetts lottery has no competition as the public favorite form of betting. Betting at race tracks is a distant second. The 44% of bettors who prefer the lottery choose it because of its good chance of winning big prizes at low cost to play."

4. See Lazear and Michael (1980), for example.

5. See Adam Smith (1776), p. 120, and Arrow (1970). It is not clear on what evidence they base their opinions. In the surveys carried out, as mentioned in the text, it was found that gamblers knew very well that the odds were against them.

6. One could argue that the probability of criminals' being caught depends not only on luck—one can specialize in crime. Changing this assumption of the model would not change its qualitative results as long as it is assumed that luck plays a greater role in this activity relative to the customary ones.

7. A variation on Sellin's views is summarized in Horowitz (1973), who writes that violence may be produced by a threat to the continued enjoyment of a status already achieved or by conduct that seems to foreshadow some deprivation in the future, and that many of the events which precipitate ethnic riots are of this character. These statements reflect those I prove formally. In the model it is one's worsened position in the wealth distribution, relative to what is expected, that leads to a greater probability of crime. Bell (1961) makes a similar point: "Crime is a form of resentment, a desire for gain, an act of violence against a person who has more" (p. 156).

8. The rest of this section, on the Canadian data on crimes, is drawn from Brenner and Brenner (1982a).

9. Anthropological studies are filled with descriptions of such mechanisms. One provided by Gluckman (1965) is worth quoting: "Among the Nyakyusa . . . people are protected against [witches] by 'defenders' who punish the witches. . . . The defenders punish not only witches, but also those who fail to provide prescribed feasts, and those who behave dis-

respectfully towards parents and parents in law as well as women who act thus to their husbands'' (p. 267).

10. As for more recent evidence on this issue, it has frequently been noted that in Japan, in contrast to Britain, the U.S., and other Western countries, violent crime has been declining in the per capita incidence of reported murders, robberies, rapes, and assaults. In 1978, fewer than 2,000 robberies were reported in all Japan, compared with 1977 figures of 14,000 in Britain, 21,000 in West Germany (each with roughly half of Japan's population), and 400,000 in the U.S. (with twice the population of Japan). The explanation criminologists give for the difference focuses on the close social ties in Japanese communities, and the strong social sanctions (as opposed to legal sanctions) against those who stray from traditional norms and values. My explanation for the difference will become evident in the last chapter.

11. Paradoxically, the most "individualistic" of the social sciences has no well-defined roles for individuals.

12. See the mathematical appendix for a more precise discussion.

13. The similarity between Merton's (1957) views and those views presented here is thus clear. In a different context, the view that all aspects of creativity may have a uniform cause has been suggested by Paulos (1980), a mathematician. His thesis is that the logic of creative process is the same in art, science, and humor, and that only the emotional climate differs. But Paulos does not define "emotional climate."

14. Another paradox: Marx, whose writings have had such influence on some minds, and who has thus shaped history, provided no role for himself in his own view of history.

15. See Kirzner (1973).

16. It is also interesting to note that the Chinese word for "crisis" is the same as that for "opportunity," and that the verb "to think" has the same root, in some languages, as the verb "to weigh possibilities" (in French, *penser* comes from *peser*) or the verb "to worry" (in Hungarian *gondolkozni* means "to think" and *gond* means "worry"). The relationship between thinking and worrying appears in Kissinger's (1982) recent memoirs. Kissinger tells us that Nixon was convinced that his (Kissinger's) special talents would flourish under conditions of personal insecurity, and that Nixon saw to it that he developed some doubts about his standing with the president. This idea is a precise translation of the mathematics of the model.

17. The list of individuals whom we now hold in high esteem for their creativity and who claimed to suffer in their lives is endless: Weber, the composer, seems to have had trouble getting along with the authorities. Verdi lost his family before composing *Nabucco*. Sarah Bernhardt complained about the lack of attention and warmth from her mother (why this is equivalent to less "wealth" will become clear in chapter 2). Leonardo da Vinci complained about being unappreciated. Wagner, Beethoven, Schubert, Modigliani, Van Gogh, and Toulouse-Lautrec are just some of the others whose lives are associated with suffering and creativity. Others include Chopin, who, at seventeen, watched his sister succumb to tuberculosis, and already detected the symptoms in himself (a recognition that lowers life expectancy and thus diminishes one's wealth), and the classic writers of children's literature, whose early happiness seems to have ended suddenly (because of the loss of one or both parents, and being abruptly sent from one home to another). The best known of these writers are Louisa May Alcott, Mark Twain, F. H. Burnett, E. Nesbit, Tolkien, Lewis Carroll, and Kipling. Thus the conclusion stated in chapter 6 seems to fit well this somewhat circumstantial evidence: that chance and suffering teach creativity.

18. Notice that no comparison is made here between utilities: $\alpha(.)$ denotes an individual's perception of the fraction of people who are richer than he is.

19. More precisely, the term is neglected because of the following reason: $\alpha(.)$ refers to an individual's perception of the wealth distribution. It is assumed that there is no way that an individual can estimate either others' wealth or his own within ranges of $\pm$ \$10 (chapter 2 makes it clear why one's wealth can never be known with precision). In contrast, the

probability of winning big prizes can be precisely known. As noted in the text, the empirical evidence suggests that people buy lottery tickets because of the probability, however small, of winning these prizes. It is also useful to note that where the dynamic analysis concerning gambling, crimes, and creativity is made, no approximations are made in this model.

Chapter 2

1. Some anthropologists have indeed criticized the application of standard economic analysis to anthropology, pointing out that economic analysis deals with *impersonal* exchange, while in primitive societies exchange is, to a large extent, personal (see Schneider 1974 for unsuccessful attempts at using standard demand and supply analysis in anthropology, and Herskovits 1940, pp. 61–62, for criticism). But neither have anthropologists provided a uniform framework for approaching their subject matter, nor have they related their arguments to the stability of the population of primitive tribes. In addition to the extensive literature quoted in the text, also see Firth (1970), Le Clair and Schneider (1968), Pryor (1977), and Posner (1980) for summaries on various aspects of primitive societies.

2. Also see Malinowski (1948), p. 80, on the ownership of tales. This and the evidence quoted in the text suggest that the difference between primitive and developed societies is not really whether property rights are allocated or not, but rather the way they are defined. When population is small and stable, customs can define them. When population is larger and fluctuates, laws will define them and they will be enforced by police as well as by custom.

3. As Herskovits (1940) points out: "Because with but few exceptions, [primitive folk] have developed no written language, the word [primitive] thus became synonymous with 'non-historic' or 'non-literate' " (p. 25). One possible answer to the question of why they are nonliterate is suggested in the section. Why they are "nonhistoric" will become evident at the end of the book.

4. In other words, the point made here is that culture too is a relative concept.

5. How to analyze memory within a formal framework is presented in the mathematical appendix. For an application of that model to the issue of advertising, see Brenner and Brenner (1982b).

6. Frederic Pryor pointed this out to me.

7. Goody (1968) makes a similar point: "The transmission of the verbal elements of culture by oral means can be visualized as a long chain of interlocking conversations between members of the group. Thus, all beliefs and values, all forms of knowledge, are communicated between individuals in face-to-face contact . . . and they are only stored in human memory" (p. 29). Goody, however, does not relate the reliance on memory to the stability of populations in primitive societies.

8. See Goody (1977), p. 30. Also notice that prayers today still consist of monotonous singing and a good deal of repetition.

9. Here, however, I must note a rather startling theory that has been offered by Julian Jaynes (1976) to explain this same set of phenomena: the fact that people in the past memorized the ornamented language of the Homeric epics, and so forth. He writes: "When musical accompaniment is no longer used, as it is not in later Greek poetry, it is, I suggest, because the poem is no longer being sung from the right hemisphere. . . . It is instead being recited from left hemispheric memory alone, rather than being recreated in the true prophetic trance. This change in musical accompaniment is also reflected in the way poetry is referred to. . . . More early poetry is referred to as song (as in the Iliad and the Theogeny), while later poetry is often referred to as spoken or told" (p. 369). Jaynes explains this change, as well as the start of civilization, by a rather abrupt biological mutation. He emphasizes the role memory plays in primitive societies and the role "rational" thinking plays in modern societies. The analysis shows that no such drastic (and rather implausible) assumption is necessary to explain the fact that primitive man relied primarily on memory.

10. Lord (1960) shows how a young man becomes acquainted with the art of metrical singing, not by verbatim remembering but by constructing a song out of phrases, themes, and narratives that he has heard before: "The singer cannot and does not remember enough to sing a song: he must and does learn to create phrases" (p. 43).

11. It is useful to note Goody's (1977) observation that the first written documents are neither "literature" nor "poetry." Rather, they are lists, accounting sheets, and laws: "literary documents in any quantity did not appear till the first half of the second millennium, that is, at a time when Sumerian was no longer a spoken language but only a written (or 'dead') one. . . . Even in Assyrian times it is not the main 'stream of tradition,' either in the form of literary creations or the recording of myth and folktale, but rather the administrative and economic documents . . . including deeds of sale and purchase, rental, loan, adoption, marriage bonds, and wills together with the ledgers, lists and memoranda of shopkeepers, secretaries and bankers . . . [that are recorded] (pp. 79–80).

12. In previous research, "primitive societies" have been preselected according to the criteria of either being bound by tradition or "illiterate." But the arguments in the text suggest that both characteristics can be related to the success of maintaining population and wealth distribution stable by a set of customs. Thus these arguments are different from those of Posner (1980), in which population plays no explicit role and where immobility seems to be both a result and an assumption. The question that arises is why in primitive societies there are no incentives to build doors and partitions or to develop literacy. The answer to these questions is given in the first chapter.

13. There is no difference, in principle, between betrayal in this case and betrayal that is due to unexpected fluctuations in the demand for one's services. If the demand for some services unexpectedly diminishes, people who specialize in providing these services are "betrayed" as much as someone who invests in "trust," but who fails to receive the insurance it customarily provides.

14. For additional evidence on how collective responsibility diminishes contract uncertainty in primitive societies see, Herskovits (1940) and Schechter (1935).

15. Herskovits (1940) also emphasizes that a "gift" is not really perceived as an act of altruism: "In Malekulah, the idea that anything may be freely given is unknown. A gift is at most a venture, *a hopeful speculation*. The native looks to receive an advantage at least equal to the value of his yam" (p. 160, italics added). Herskovits also quotes Mauss's conclusions on this issue: "Mauss shows that no matter how freely a gift may be tendered, or how unsought it may be, the very fact of its having been presented carries an obligation of equivalent or increased return that can be ignored only on penalty of social disapprobation and the loss of prestige" (p. 155). Herskovits then makes the following observation about the Busama, a tribe in New Guinea: "Each type of object has its traditional equivalent—a pot of certain size being worth so many taro or mats . . . and most of the visitors go home with items at least as valuable as those which they brought. . . . A careful count is kept, however, and the score is evened up later" (p. 194).

16. More on this concept of debt will be said in chapter 3.

17. The distinction economists have made between public and private implicitly assumes both anonymous exchange and that in some exchanges an individual's behavior has no significant effect on others. Both assumptions make sense only if the population is large enough; otherwise exchange cannot be anonymous.

18. Similar points are made by Cohen (1977, p. 285). It should be noted that when Cohen states that the costs of food go up he means costs for food *holding* quality constant; this is one major point he elaborates in the second chapter of his book. He also notes that "the prospect of altering our food supply might be more constructively faced if we realised that it is the prevailing notion of 'progress' rather than the contemporary 'crisis' which is the historical anomaly. Perhaps it will aid us in our economic transition to realise that human populations once faced the notion of eating oysters and later the prospect of eating wheat

with much the same enthusiasm that we now face with the prospect of eating seaweed, soy protein and artificial organic molecules'' (pp. 285–86).

19. In economics the emergence of money is attributed to the saving of transaction costs when the amount of goods exchanged becomes large, without, however, relating transaction costs to the lack of trust. This view of the emergence of money does not seem to be consistent with the evidence. The greatest number of exchanges are carried out within the family, yet there money is either not used or used to a lesser degree. The empirical evidence supporting the views expressed here appears in the statistical section in this chapter.

20. For conceptual difficulties in defining "markets" or "lack of markets," see Pryor (1977), chap. 5.

21. For the precise definition of all the dependent and independent variables used here, see Pryor (1977).

22. See Dhrymes (1978, pp. 324–53): notice the discussion on the inapplicability of OLS (ordinary least square) procedure.

23. This percentage can be compared to the R^2 in ordinary regression analysis.

24. It may be useful to note that the English word "trade" is akin to an old German word referring to the path of a ship (*trade* or *trâ*), so that trade originally had the connotation of foreign commerce. See Pryor (1977), p. 110, and note that "foreign" trade means that less frequent transactions are expected among partners in trade.

25. For the precise definition of interest rates in primitive societies, see Pryor (1977).

26. That the bosses of the Mafia receive rather than give gifts is a feature of the literature on this subject (although empirical investigation cannot be expected). Perhaps the reason is the same as the one mentioned in the text: they provide insurance. Also, the fact that the Mafia is organized into families seems to be an empirical implication of the arguments presented in the text.

27. In one country donating blood is a custom, in another there is a market for it. In one country grandparents still live with their children and grandchildren, providing (with love) a wide range of services; in another similar services are purchased from maids and babysitters or provided by dishwashers and television. In one place grandparents still sit by the bedside of their grandchildren and tell them stories; in another books on fairy tales are bought and read by the babysitter. Which countries are the richer? As measured by the GNP, the richer countries are those in which money is exchanged for services. As the arguments in the first two chapters and these examples show, this conclusion can be very misleading. For a serious treatment of these issues see North (1981).

28. I paraphrase here a segment from Schultz (1961).

29. Murdock (1968) notes that many activities related to hunting and gathering are apparently perceived as less arduous and more prestigious than agricultural labor, hence the persistence of what Murdock calls "hunting mentality."

30. The arguments presented in these first two chapters may provide an answer to the question of why civilizations have developed fortuitously in those places where, because of geographical conditions, contacts between people were more frequent (the Mediterranean, China) and, as a result, people's positions in the wealth distribution changed more frequently since customs were more difficult to enforce. But, as will become clear in the next chapter, significant fluctuations in population rather than population size per se seems to have had an effect on the turbulent histories of some societies.

31. The arguments presented in this chapter may also shed light on a recent case brought before the Supreme Court in the U.S. concerning Amish employers' refusal to pay social security taxes. According to the views presented here, the Amish are right and the IRS is wrong, for it is part of Amish religious customs to take care of people of their own religion. Thus the Amish provide one another with insurance that the rest of the U.S. population does not. Why then should they pay twice?

32. This appendix is drawn from Brenner and Brenner (1982b).

Chapter 3

1. Most of the information on the history of usury in this section is drawn from Nelson's (1949) classic study.

2. The Amoraim (from the Hebrew word *amar,* which means "to say" or "to interpret") were Jewish scholars at Caesaria and Tiberias in Palestine (ca. A.D. 200–ca. 350), and at Sura and Pumbedita in Babylonia (ca. A.D. 200–ca. 510) who interpreted the Mishnah and other collections.

3. This is the title of chapter 6 in Homer's (1963) book, for example.

4. A similar interpretation was already given by Wilson (1572). Tawney, in the introduction to a reprinted edition of the book, writes: "[Calvin changed] the plane on which the discussion has been conducted, by treating the question of the ethics of money lending, not as a matter to be decided by an appeal to a special body of doctrine on the subject of usury, but as a particular case of the general problem of the social relations . . . which must be solved in the light of existing circumstances. The Mosaic Law may have suited the special conditions of the Jews, but it is irrelevant to the life of commercial communities" (p. 119).

5. As quoted in Nelson (1949), p. 157.

6. In a broader context, Goody (1968) has noted that "literate religions tend to . . . place greater emphasis on individual paths to righteousness. Though this difference is one of degree, it does link up with the 'individualizing' tendency of a literate technology and an elaborate division of labor" (p. 3). Goody, however, does not mention that literacy, "individualizing" tendencies, and the division of labor can all be linked to a fluctuating population around a rising trend and the changes in wealth distribution.

Chapter 4

1. See Becker (1959), Phelps (1962).

2. The sources used to describe fragments of Jewish history in this section, as well as in the rest of the chapter, are the *Encyclopedia Judaica* (1971), Gross (1975), Dimont (1962), Arendt (1951), Sombart (1913), Kochan (1977), Sachar (1977), Steinsaltz (1976), Eidelberg (1977), and, to a large extent, Poliakov (1955, 1961, 1968, 1977, 1980).

3. Recent experiences with conversions among illiterate people seem to be similar: in Bolivia, for example, missionaries have observed that Mormons baptized dozens of Indian families a month only to discover that the next missionary on the circuit was rebaptizing them in his own faith (see *Newsweek,* 27 April 1981, pp. 87–88).

4. See Steinsaltz (1976).

5. Although the facts are reinterpreted and, at times, just as in oral societies, some facts plunge down history's "memory hole" (to use Orwell's phrase). For example, after 1960 the 1881 pogroms episode in Russia disappeared from history textbooks in the U.S.S.R., and anti-Semitic outbursts receive very favorable and understanding treatment by Vladismir Begun in *The Creeping Counter Revolution* and Lydia Modzhorian in *Zionism as a Form of Racism and Racial Discrimination.*

6. Goody (1968) writes: "What specific factors prevent the realization of the full potentials of literacy? First, there is a tendency to secrecy, to restrict the circulation of books. In West Africa, such secrecy even gathers round the Qur'an itself, increasing its magical efficacy as well as the power of its custodians. The magical books of medieval Europe acquired a similar character. Many of the ceremonial texts of Egypt and Mesopotamia 'were not intended to be read by human eyes' for they were essentially communications between man and god, not man and man. . . . Such restrictive practices tend to arise wherever people have an interest in maintaining a monopoly of the sources of their power" (pp. 11–12).

7. Once, we are told, the word of many people was "worth its weight in gold." Such statements are rare today.

8. Julian the Apostate, one of the tolerant Roman emperors, wrote, "While striving to gratify their own God, they [the Jews] do not, at the same time, serve the others." According to him this was their error.

9. It may be useful to point out the link between the analysis in this section and that in the previous chapter. In both places the same question is raised: How can central authorities maintain the bonds among an increasing number of people when kinship and existing religions no longer prove sufficient to maintain the stability of societies? The answer in both places is the same: under such circumstances shifts will occur toward more "impersonal" methods of exchange, supported by laws and police. This does not imply that the roles of kinship and religion disappear, but only that their value decreases relatively in diminishing contract uncertainty. The next example shows that even today, when populations have "exploded," kinship and religion diminish contract uncertainty. Murray Schumach (1981), in *Diamond People,* describes the mainly Jewish New York based diamond industry of the twentieth century and shows how social and religious bonds diminish uncertainty. Exchange is based on complex rules that go back 1000 years and contracts are still based on a code of honor that traces its roots to the Old Testament, the Talmud, and the teachings of the Maimonides. Contracts of millions of dollars are concluded by only a handshake and the Hebrew-Yiddish *"Mazel and Brucha"* (luck and blessing) rather than being written, and some degree of hostility exists between religious and nonreligious Jews. Finally, some anecdotal evidence: Heine's father warned him not to express atheistic theories in school: "It would harm my business were people to discover that my son does not believe in God. Particularly the Jews would stop buying velvets from us, and they are honest folk and pay promptly."

10. One tends to forget that the first Spanish and Sicilian ghettos of the medieval era were actually requested by the Jews themselves as a symbol of their autonomy. The first official ghetto was created only in 1555 by Pope Paul IV.

11. Regulation of dress is by no means a feature related to Jews. In many illiterate societies dress codes exist in order to provide information. For example, in the stratified society of the Ming dynasty, the shape, color, fabric, and motifs of a robe indicated the wearer's status at court. Yellow, for example, could be worn only by the highest ranking members of the imperial family, while subdued colors were reserved for concubines of a certain age.

12. See Poliakov (1955), p. 53.

13. See Shapiro (1981).

14. In a letter to the *New York Review of Books* (16 August 1979) entitled "Anti-Semitism in Spain," it is mentioned that the heavy influx into the Spanish job market of highly skilled Latin American refugees   some of them Jewish   has helped revive Spanish xenophobia.

15. Thus it may not come as much of a surprise that anti-Semitic incidents in the U.S. doubled in 1981 and that racism is on the rise throughout Canada. In both countries the national pies have diminished relative to the expected one, and the wealth distributions have changed. I should also note that when this book was already finished, *The Economist* (15 January 1983, p. 91) reviewed two books: Stephen Wilson's *Ideology and Experience: Anti-Semitism in France at the time of the Dreyfus Affair,* and Robert Wistrich's *Socialism and the Jews: The Dilemmas of Assimilation in Germany and Austria-Hungary.* The reviewer states that both books arrive at the same conclusion: "The anti-semite constituency was heterogenous, but largely based on groups, like the status-conscious lower middle class, threatened by the new economic situation. The anti-semites regretted a world they had lost. . . . Their anti-semitism was a mythology, a magic event, a form of reassurance at a time when society was changing and seemed to be leaving them behind." These conclusions are consistent with the model present here.

16. See Campbell (1964), p. 336.

17. Some people may say that winter causes people to wear fur coats; in the tropics fur coats are not worn, and argue that in this case the causal relationship is identified although no unexpected events occur. But this statement is misleading. For winter does not cause anything. The fact that people are cold (and thus have lost part of their wealth) causes them to start wearing fur coats. In order to examine this causal statement, it must either suddenly become hot where once was cold, or the contrary. Otherwise this statement cannot be

verified. The reason we say that winter causes an event is because this statement saves words (i.e., transaction costs): people don't have to state the obvious.

18. One may say that an individual may commit suicide by lighting a match in such a place. In this case, however, no causal statement can be made.

19. Between Simon and Granger there was a period when some social scientists tried to clarify the notion of "causal relationship" within the system of *simultaneous* equations (see Bassman 1963, L'Esperance 1972, and Strotz and Wold 1963). Why these writers did not note that the word "cause" has no meaning when everything is simultaneously determined is hard to understand. Besides, their models have nothing to say about human behavior.

20. It is this central point that seems to have been vaguely treated by the writers on causality, Feigl (1953) and Russell (1953), for example. Moreover, Russell also introduces into his article the "free-will" problem. I have showed that the arguments here shed light on this term in chapters 1 and 2; that is, that it is not very meaningful in the context of creativity. For before an individual gambles on an idea, chance and society (which induce the changing wealth distribution) must create the conditions necessary for creativity.

Chapter 5

1. See Becker (1959).

2. In addition to the sources on Jewish history mentioned in the previous chapter, other sources used here include Kahan (1964, 1978), Glaser (1972), Kuznets (1972), and Ellman (1970).

3. On the interaction between the "quality" and "quantity" of children, see Becker (1975b).

4. On the similarities between Armenians and Jews see the *Encyclopaedia Judaica*, pp. 471–76.

5. The information on Parsis is drawn from Karaka (1858, 1884) and Kulke (1974).

6. The similarity between the adjustments Palestinians and other people have made in "diaspora" has been noted by Peretz, Wilson, and Ward (1970), and detailed numerical evidence has been presented in Brenner and Kiefer (1981), on which this segment of this chapter is based. That study was written more than four years ago and the model presented there is not satisfactory. However, the sources for the data can be found there.

7. See Bell (1961). As for the crime of ethnic groups in general, Horowitz (1973) observes that violence may be produced by a threat to the continued enjoyment of status already achieved or by conduct that seems to foreshadow some deprivation in the future, and that many events that precipitate ethnic riots are of this character. Notice that the model in chapter 1 lends precision to these statements.

8. Alfred Marshall, in his *Principles of Economics* (1910), writes: "In every country, but especially in Germany much of what is most brilliant and suggestive in economic practice and in economic thought is of Jewish origin. And in particular to German Jews, we owe many daring speculations as to the conflict of interests between the individual and society and as to their ultimate economic causes" (p. 753). Thorstein Veblen tries to explain the same phenomenon. In "The Intellectual Pre-Eminence of Jews in Modern Europe" (1948), he attributes the higher intellectual level to the very act of breaking with an ethnic world view. In his opinion, men who discard one tradition become skeptical of all "conventional realities." This alienated vantage point sparks intellectual revolution. In a recent interview, Isaac Stern, the violinist, said that the reason for the Jewish success in music is the greater willingness of Jews to "rebel"—which is exactly the meaning of entrepreneurship. Also, in a recent article in the *Jerusalem Post* (28 January–3 February 1979, p. 21), a member of the Israel Institute for Innovations said that 80% of new ideas came from Russian immigrants. His explanation was that "Russian immigrant engineers don't have a more inventive mind than other people. . . . But many of them were forced to think up new ideas in Russia if they wanted to hold on to their jobs in failing plants."

9. This segment is again based on Brenner and Kiefer (1981), where the detailed data source can be found.

Chapter 6

1. I do not suggest that the choice is totally ours: if the Earth's climate were suddenly to become harsher, whatever institutions have we built to increase our security would be altered. When the alterations are made there will be unhappiness and creativity. See also Brenner and Brenner (1982c).

2. See Braudel (1979) and Stone (1981), for example.

3. Thus the folk saying, "If Cleopatra's nose was different, history would be different," seems correct. Who can say how the shape of Cleopatra's nose affected her behavior? What seems irrelevant is the work of historians who deal with "counter-factual analysis," i.e., analysis that raises "what would happen if" questions. It may also be useful to note that my methodology in this book is that employed in all empirical science (biology, paleontology, physics), and relies on the principle that "exceptions prove the rule." This is the reason that so much of the analysis deals with features of Jewish history.

4. The next paragraphs are in part based on Brenner (1980).

5. See Kuhn (1970), pp. 12–15.

6. It should be noted that Rawls's theory has no empirical content: his whole viewpoint is based on the mental exercise of asking individuals what wealth distribution would they prefer. His argument that people would prefer more equal distribution has not much meaning in light of the theory presented here.

7. See the works of Pagels (1982), Hunt (1982), and Jastrow (1981).

8. A similar conclusion is also reached by Isaiah Berlin (1980), although from a different approach.

9. What do the views presented here suggest about evolution? At times it is argued that a climatic switch to drier conditions about two million years ago appears to have been a continent-wide and possibly a global phenomenon. Such circumstances might have triggered the increased gambling activity of the human mind. This statement, however, already assumes the existence of "human" minds. Recent theories and findings suggest that these conditions may also have led to the appearance of new species: these new models of evolution are called "punctuated equilibrium" (in contrast to the traditional theories of evolution which view evolution as a gradual process).

Chapter 7

1. See Brenner (1982).

2. Notice that custom is one form of taxation in that it "taxes" people's behavior.

3. See Brenner and Brenner (1982a).

4. The methodology used in this book, namely, concentrating on the effects of significant changes, is not unusual either in the social sciences or in biology. Stephen Gould (1980) summarizes its rationale as follows: "It is nature's richness that permits us to establish a science of natural history in the first place—for the variety virtually guarantees that appropriate exceptions can be found to probe any rule. Oddities and weirdnesses are tests of generality, not mere peculiarities to describe and greet with awe or a chuckle" (p. 72). It is also useful to note McNeill's (1963) observation: "Compared to the civilized societies of Asia, European civilization exhibited marked instability. Rising to an extraordinary peak in classical times, it declined in equally extraordinary fashion following the fall of the Roman Empire in the West. By contrast, Chinese, Indian . . . history presents a far smoother curve. Despite . . . changes in modes of religious, artistic and intellectual expansion, the . . . peoples of Asia always maintained a fairly stable institutional base on the local level." (p. 538).

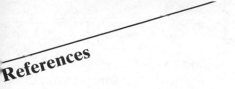

References

Abu Lughod, A. I. 1973. Educating a community in exile: The Palestinian experience. *Journal of Palestine Studies* 2.

Akerlof, George A. 1970. The market for 'lemons': Quality uncertainty and the market mechanism. *Quarterly Journal of Economics* 84:488–500.

Alchian, Armen A. 1953. The meaning of utility measurement. *American Economic Review* 42:26–50.

Alchian, Armen A. and Reuben Kessel. 1962. Competition, monopoly and the pursuit of money. In H. G. Lewis, editor, *Aspects of labor economics*. Princeton: Princeton University Press.

Allais, Maurice and Ole Hagen. 1979. *Expected utility hypothesis and the Allais paradox*. London: D. Reidel.

Allan, W. 1965. *The African husbandman*. Edinburgh: Oliver and Boyd.

Arendt, Hannah. 1951. *The origins of totalitarianism*. New York: Harcourt Brace Jovanovich.

Arieti, Silvano. 1976. *Creativity: The magic synthesis*. New York: Basic Books.

Arrow, Kenneth J. 1963. *Social sciences and individual values*. New Haven: Yale University Press.

———. 1970. *Essays in the theory of risk bearing*. Amsterdam: North Holland.

Barnicot, N. A. 1969. Human nutrition: Evolutionary perspectives. In P. J. Ucko and G. W. Dimbleby, editors, *The domestication and exploitation of plants and animals*. London: Duckworth.

Bassman, R. L. 1963. The causal interpretation of non-triangular systems of economic relations. *Econometrica* 31:439–48.

Bate, W. Jackson. 1975. *Samuel Johnson*. New York: Harcourt Brace Jovanovich.

Bates, M. 1955. *The prevalence of people*. New York: Scribner's.

Baumol, William J. 1968. Entrepreneurship in economic theory. *Economic Review* 59:64–71.

Becker, Gary S. 1959. *The economics of discrimination*. Chicago: University of Chicago Press.

————. 1965. A theory of the allocation of time. *Economic Journal* 75:493–517.

————. 1971. *Economic theory.* New York: Alfred A. Knopf.

————. 1974. Crime and punishment: An economic approach. In G. S. Becker and W. M. Landes, editors, *Essays in the economics of crime and punishment.* New York: National Bureau of Economic Research.

————. 1975a. *Human capital.* New York: Columbia University Press.

————. 1975b. *The economic approach to human behavior.* Chicago: University of Chicago Press.

Bell, Daniel. 1961. *The end of ideology.* New York: Collier Books.

Ben-Porath, Yoram. 1968. Some economic characteristics of a refugee camp. In *Middle East Development,* Truman Center Publications 3. Jerusalem: Truman Center.

————. 1980. The f-connection: families, friends and firms and the organization of exchange. *Population and Development Review* 6:1–30.

Bergson, Henri. 1911. *Creative evolution.* New York: Holt.

Berlin, Isaiah. 1980. *Against the current: Essays in the history of ideas.* New York: Viking Press.

Birdsell, J. B. 1953. Some environmental and cultural factors influencing the structure of Australian aboriginal populations. *American Naturalist* 87:171–207.

————. 1968. Some predictions for the Pleistocene based upon equilibrium systems among recent hunters. In R. B. Lee and I. DeVore, editors, *Man the hunter.* Chicago: Aldine.

Bloch, Marc. 1940. *Feudal society.* Vols. 1 and 2. Reprint 1961. Chicago: University of Chicago Press.

Bloch, Maurice. 1973. The long-term and the short-term: The economic and political significance of the morality of kinship. In J. Goody, editor, *The character of kinship.* London: Cambridge University Press.

Block, M. K. and J. M. Heineke. 1975. A labor theoretical analysis of criminal choice. *American Economic Review* 65:314–25.

Borrill, J. 1975. Study of gamblers and drug-takers in H. M. prison Pentonville. Paper prepared for discussion at the consultation on compulsive gambling, 22 May.

Bose, S. 1964. Economy of the Onge of Little Andaman. *Man in India* 44:298–310.

Boserup, Ester. 1965. *The conditions of agricultural growth.* Chicago: Aldine.

————. 1981. *Population and technological change.* Chicago: University of Chicago Press.

Braudel, Fernand. 1979. *Civilization matérielle, économie et capitalisme, XVᵉ–XVIIIᵉ siècle,* Vols. 1–3. Paris: Armand Colin.

Brenner, Gabrielle A. and Reuven Brenner. 1981. Why do people gamble? Rapport de recherche no. 81–11, Ecole des Hautes Etudes Commerciales.

————. 1982a. The easy case for progressive taxation? Cahier 8220, Département de Science Economique et Centre de Recherche en Développement Economique, Université de Montréal.

————. 1982b. On memory and markets, or why are you paying 2.99 for a widget? *Journal of Business* 55:147–58.

————. 1982c. Why do productivity and profits decline? Theory and evidence. Rapport de recherche no. 82-09, Ecole des Hautes Etudes Commerciales.

Brenner, Reuven. 1980. Economics—an imperialist science? *Journal of Legal Studies* 9:179–88.

————. 1982. Why do nations engage in wars? Cahier 8228, Département de Science Economique et Centre de Recherche en Développement Economique, Université de Montréal.

Brenner, Reuven and Nicholas M. Kiefer. 1981. The economics of diaspora. *Economic Development and Cultural Change*. 29:517–34.

Brinner, Roger E. and Charles T. Clotfelter. 1975. An economic appraisal of state lotteries. *National Tax Journal* 28:395–404.

Buchanan, James M. 1965. An economic theory of clubs. *Economica* 32:1–13.

————. 1975. *The limits of liberty: Between anarchy and leviathan.* Chicago: University of Chicago Press.

Campbell, Joseph. 1981. *The masks of god: Occidental mythology.* New York: Penguin Books.

Carr-Hill, R. A. and N. H. Stern. 1979. *Crime, the police and criminal statistics.* New York: Academic Press.

Carr-Saunders, A. M., H. Mannheim, and E. G. Rhodes. 1942. *Young offenders.* London: Cambridge University Press.

Chiswick, Barry R. 1978. The effects of Americanization on the earnings of foreign born men. *Journal of Political Economy* 8:897–923.

Cipolla, Carlo M. 1976. *Before the industrial revolution: European society and economy, 1000–1700.* New York: W. W. Norton.

————. 1979. *Faith, reason and the plague.* New York: W. W. Norton.

————. 1981. *Fighting the plague in seventeenth century Italy.* Madison: University of Wisconsin Press.

Cohen, Mark N. 1977. *Food crisis in prehistory.* New Haven: Yale University Press.

Cornish, D. B. 1978. *Gambling: A review of the literature and its implications for policy and research.* London: HMSO.

Danziger, Sheldon and David Wheeler. 1975. The economics of crime: Punishment or income distribution. *Review of Social Economics* 33:113–31.

Darby, Michael R. and Adi Karni. 1973. Free competition and the optimal amount of fraud. *Journal of Law and Economics* 16:67–88.

Davison, William I. and James E. Harper. 1972. *European economic history: The ancient world.* Vol. 1. New York: Appleton-Century-Crofts.

Denham, W. W. 1974. Population structure, infant transport and infanticide among Pleistocene and modern hunter-gatherers. *Journal of Anthropological Research* 30:191–98.

Devereux, G. 1955. *A study of abortion in primitive societies.* New York: Julian.

Devereux, G. 1955. *A study of abortion in primitive societies.* New York: Julian.

———. 1967. A typological study of abortion in 350 primitive, ancient and preindustrial societies. In Rosen, editor, *Abortion in America.* Boston: Beacon.

Dhrymes, P. J. 1978. *Introductory econometrics.* New York: Springer-Verlag.

Dimont, Max F. 1962. *Jews, God and history.* New York: New American Library.

Divale, W. T. 1972. Systematic population control in the Middle and Upper Paleolithic: Inferences based on contemporary hunter-gatherers. *World Archeology* 4:222–43.

Downes, D. M., B. P. Davies, M. E. David, and P. Stone. 1976. *Gambling, work and leisure: A study across three areas.* London: Routledge and Kegan Paul.

Duesenberry, James S. 1949. *Income, saving and the theory of consumer behaviour.* Cambridge: Harvard University Press.

Dunn, F. L. 1968. Epidemiological factors: Health and disease in hunter-gatherers. In R. B. Lee and I. DeVore, *Man, the hunter.* Chicago: Aldine.

Durkheim, Emile. 1911. *De la division du travail social.* 3d edition. Paris.

Easterlin, Richard A. 1974. Does economic growth improve the human lot? Some empirical evidence. In P. David and M. Reder, editors, *Nations and households on economic growth.* New York: Academic Press.

Ehrlich, Isaac. 1974. Participation in illegitimate activities: An economic analysis. In G. S. Becker and W. M. Landes, editors, *Essays in the economics of crime and punishment.* New York: National Bureau of Economic Research.

———. 1975. The deterrent effect of capital punishment: A question of life and death. *American Economic Review* 65:397–417.

Eidelberg, Shlomo. 1977. *The Jews and the crusaders.* Madison: University of Wisconsin Press.

Elias, Norbert. 1978. *What is sociology?* New York: Columbia University Press.

Ellman, Yisrael. 1970. The economic structure and the characteristics of American Jewry. *Bitfutzot Hagolah:* 101–95 [in Hebrew].

Encyclopaedia Judaica. 1971. Jerusalem: Keter Publishing.

Engelman, Uriah Z. 1944. *The rise of the Jew in the western world.* New York: Behrman's Jewish Book House.

Epstein, T. S. 1962. *Economic development and social change in south India.* New York: Humanities Press.

Erickson, Edwin E. 1977. Cultural evolution. *American Behavioral Scientist* 20:669–81.

Evans, Bergen. 1978. *Dictionary of quotations.* New York: Avenel Books.

Evans-Pritchard, E. E. 1940. *The Nuer.* Oxford: Clarendon Press.

———. 1963. *Essays in social anthropology.* London: Faber and Faber.

Feigl, H. 1953. Notes on causality. In H. Feigl and M. Brodbeck, editors, *Readings in the philosophy of science.* New York: Appleton-Century-Crofts.

Final report: Gambling in America. 1976. Washington, D.C.: U.S. Government Printing Office.

Firth, Raymond, editor. 1970. *Themes in economic anthropology.* London: Tavistock.

Fortes, M. 1945. *The dynamics of clanship among the Tallensi.* London: Oxford University Press.

Foster, George M. 1967. Peasant society and the image of limited good. In J. M. Potter, M. N. Diaz, and G. M. Foster, editors, *Peasant society: A reader.* Boston: Little, Brown.

Friedman, Milton. 1975. *Price theory.* Chicago: Aldine.

Friedman, Milton, and L. J. Savage. 1948. The utility analysis of choices involving risks. *Journal of Political Economy* 56:279–304.

Fromm, Erich. 1969. *Escape from freedom.* New York: Discus Books.

Gage, Nicholas. 1978. Cypriots need unity, but still won't compromise. *New York Times,* 23 April.

Gambling in Britain. 1972. London: Gallup Social Surveys.

Gandz, S. 1936. Oral tradition in the Bible. In S. W. Baron and A. Marx, editors, *Jewish studies in memory of George A. Kohut.* New York: Alexander Kohut: Memorial Foundation Publication.

Genesis, with interpretations. 1963. Edited by M. D. Kassauto. Tel-Aviv: Yavneh [in Hebrew].

Glaser, Nathan. 1972. *American Judaism.* Chicago: University of Chicago Press.

Gluckman, Max. 1965. *Politics, law and ritual in tribal society.* New York: Mentor Books.

Glueck, E. T., and S. Glueck. 1950. *Unravelling juvenile delinquency.* New York: Harper and Row.

Goldstein, Martin, and Inge F. Goldstein. 1978. *How we know.* New York: Plenum Press.

Goody, Jack. 1962. *Death, property and the ancestors.* Stanford: Stanford University Press.

———, editor. 1968. *Literacy in traditional societies.* Cambridge: Cambridge University Press.

———. 1971. *Technology, tradition and the state in Africa.* London: Oxford University Press.

———. 1977. *The domestication of the savage mind.* Cambridge: Cambridge University Press.

Gough, Kathleen. 1968. Literacy in Kērala. In J. Goody, editor, *Literacy in traditional societies.* London: Cambridge University Press.

Gould, Stephen J. 1980. *The panda's thumb.* New York: W. W. Norton.

Granger, C. W. J. 1969. Investigating causal relations by econometric models and cross-spectral methods. *Econometrica* 37:424–38.

Granger, C. W. J., and P. Newbold. 1977. *Forecasting economic time series.* New York: Academic Press.

Gray, C. E. 1958. The epicyclical evolution of Graeco-Roman civilization. *American Anthropologist* 60:13–31.

———. 1961. An epicyclical model for western civilization. *American Anthropologist* 63:1014–37.

————. 1966. A measurement of creativity in western civilization. *American Anthropologist* 68:1384–1417.

Gregory, Nathaniel. 1980. Relative wealth and risk taking: A short note on the Friedman-Savage utility function. *Journal of Political Economy* 88:1226–30.

Griliches, Zvi. 1964. Research expenditures, education and the aggregate agricultural production function. *American Economic Review* 54:961–74.

Gross, Nachum, editor. 1975. *Economic history of the Jews.* New York: Schocken Books.

Gunning, Patrick J. 1972. Toward a theory of the evolution of government. In G. Tullock, editor, *Explorations in the theory of anarchy.* Blacksburg, Va.: Center for Study of Public Choice.

Hagen, Everett E. 1975. *The economics of development.* Homewood, Ill.: Richard D. Irwin.

Hagopian, E., and A. B. Zahlan. 1974. Palestine's Arab population. *Journal of Palestine Studies* 3:32–74.

Haller, Thomas. 1972. Education and rural development in Colombia. Ph.D. dissertation, Purdue University.

Hambly, W. D. 1926. *Origins of education among primitive people.* London: Macmillan.

Handler, Jerome S. 1979. Joseph Rachell and Rachael Pringle Polgreen: Entrepreneurs in eighteenth century Barbados. Working paper, Department of Economics, University of Chicago.

Handy, E. S. C. 1923. *The native culture in the Marguesas.* B. P. Bishop Museum, bulletin 9. Quoted in Herskovits (1940).

Hassan, F. 1973. On mechanisms of population growth during the Neolithic. *Current Anthropology.* 14:535–42.

Hatcher, John. 1977. *Plague, population and the English economy, 1348–1530.* London: Macmillan.

Hayami, Yujiro, and Vernon W. Ruttan. 1971. *Agricultural development: International perspective.* Baltimore: Johns Hopkins University Press.

Hayden, B. 1972. Population control among hunter-gatherers. *World Archaeology* 4:205–21.

Herskovits, Melville J. 1940. *Economic Anthropology.* Reprint 1965. New York: W. W. Norton.

Hicks, John. 1969. *A theory of economic history.* London: Oxford University Press.

Higgins, Benjamin. 1968. *Economic development.* New York: W. W. Norton.

Hobbes, Thomas. 1651. *Leviathan.* Edited by C. B. Macpherson, 1980. Penguin Books.

Hoebel, Adamson E. 1954. *The law of primitive man.* Reprint 1974. New York: Atheneum.

Hoffer, Eric. 1951. *The true believer: Thoughts on the nature of mass movements.* New York: New American Library.

Hollingsworth, T. H. 1969. *Historical demography.* Ithaca, N.Y.: Cornell University Press.

Homer, Sidney. 1963. *A history of interest rates*. New Brunswick: Rutgers University Press.
Horney, Karen. 1945. *Our inner conflicts*. New York: W. W. Norton.
———. 1950. *Neurosis and human growth*. New York: W. W. Norton.
Horowitz, Donald. 1973. Direct, displaced and cumulative ethnic aggression. *Comparative Politics* 6:1–16.
Hoselitz, Bert F. 1968. Entrepreneurship and capital formation in France and Britain since 1700. In M. E. Falkus, *Readings in the history of economic growth*. London: Oxford University Press.
Howell, F. G., and F. Bourlière. 1963. *African ecology and human evolution*. Chicago: Aldine.
Hunt, Morton. 1982. *The universe within*. New York: Simon and Schuster.
Inventive Russian immigrants. 1979. *Jerusalem Post* 3 February 1979, p. 21.
James, William. 1880. Great men, great thoughts and environment. *Atlantic Monthly*, 46:441–59. Quoted in Arieti (1976).
Jastrow, Robert. 1981. *The enchanted loom: The mind in the universe*. New York: Simon and Schuster.
Jaynes, Julian. 1976. *The origins of consciousness in the breakdown of the bicameral mind*. Boston: Houghton, Mifflin.
Johnson, Paul. 1979. *A history of Christianity*. New York: Atheneum.
Kahan, Arcadius. 1964. A note on methods of research on the economic history of the Jews. In *For Max Weinreich on his seventieth birthday*. The Hague: Mouton.
———. 1978. Economic opportunities and some pilgrims' progress: Jewish immigrants from eastern Europe in the U.S., 1890–1914. *Journal of Economic History* 38:235–51.
Karaka, Dosbhai F. 1858. *The Parsees: Their history, manners, customs and religion*. London: Smith, Elder.
———. 1884. *History of Parsees*. London: Macmillan.
Keynes, John M. 1921. *A treatise on probability*. London: Macmillan.
Kirzner, Israel M. 1973. *Competition and entrepreneurship*. Chicago: University of Chicago Press.
Kissinger, Henry. 1982. *Years of upheaval*. Boston: Little, Brown.
Knight, Frank. 1921. *Risk, uncertainty and profit*. New York: Houghton Mifflin.
———. 1935. *The ethics of competition*. New York: Harper Brothers.
Kochan, Lionel. 1977. *The Jew and his history*. New York: Schocken Books.
Koestler, Arthur. 1964. *The act of creation*. London: Hutchinson.
Kornhauser, William. 1959. *The politics of mass society*. Glencoe, Ill.: The Free Press.
Krader, Lawrence, editor. 1966. *Anthropology and early law*. New York: Basic Books.
Kroeber, A. 1944. *Configurations of culture growth*. Los Angeles: University of California Press.
Kuhn, Thomas S. 1970. *The structure of scientific revolutions*. Chicago: University of Chicago Press.

Kulke, Eckerhard. 1974. *The Parsees in India*. Munich: Welforum Verlag.

Kuznetz, Simon. 1966. *Modern economic growth: Rate, structure and spread*. New Haven: Yale University Press.

———. 1972. *Economic structure of U.S. Jewry: Recent trends*. Jerusalem: Hebrew University Press [in Hebrew].

———. 1977. Notes on the study of economic growth of nations. In M. Nash, editor, *Essays on economic development and cultural change in honor of Bert F. Hoselitz*. Chicago: University of Chicago Press.

———. 1979. *Growth, population and income distribution*. New York: W. W. Norton.

Landa, Janet. 1976. An exchange economy with legally binding contract: A public choice approach. *Journal of Economic Issues* 10:905–22.

———. 1979a. Money and alternative institutional arrangements for achieving ordered anarchy. *Munich Social Science Review* 2:5–29.

———. 1979b. The economics of the ethnically homogeneous middlemen group. Working paper no. 7924, Institute for Policy Analysis, University of Toronto.

Laughlin, W. S. 1968. Hunting: An integrating biobehavior system and its evolutionary importance. In R. B. Lee and I. DeVore, *Man the hunter*. Chicago: Aldine.

Lazear, Edward P., and Robert T. Michael. 1980. Family size and the distribution of real per capita income. *American Economic Review* 70:91–107.

Leakey, Richard E. 1981. *The making of mankind*. New York: E. P. Dutton.

Le Clair, Edward E., Jr., and Harold K. Schneider, editors. 1968. *Economic anthropology: Readings in theory and analysis*. New York: Holt, Rinehart, and Winston.

Lee, Richard B. 1968. What hunters do for a living, or how to make out on scarce resources. In R. B. Lee, and I. DeVore, editors, *Man the hunter*. Chicago: Aldine.

———. 1969. !Kung bushman subsistence: An input-output analysis. In Vayda, editor, *Ecological studies in cultural anthropology*. New York: Natural History Press.

Lee, Richard B., and I. DeVore. 1976. *Kalahari hunter-gatherers: Studies of the Kung san and their neighbors*. Cambridge, Mass.: Harvard University Press.

Leibenstein, Harvey. 1957. *Economic backwardness and economic growth*. New York: John Wiley.

Le Roy Ladurie, Emmanuel. 1966. *Les paysans de Languedoc*. Paris: S.E.V.P.E.N.

L'Esperance, W. L. 1972. Interdependence vs. recursiveness: A review of the debate and notions of causality in economics. In K. Brunner, editor, *Problems and issues in current econometric practice*. Columbus: Ohio State University Press.

Le Vine, Robert A. 1960. The internalization of political values in stateless societies. *Human Organization* 19:51–59.

Lévi-Strauss, C. 1968. The concept of primitiveness. In R. B. Lee and I. DeVore, editors, *Man the hunter*. Chicago: Aldine.

Lewis, I. M. 1968. Literacy in a nomadic society: The Somali case. In J. Goody, editor, *Literacy in traditional societies*. London: Cambridge University Press.

Lipset, Seymour M. 1960. *Political man: The social bases of politics*. Garden City, N.Y.: Doubleday.

Loeb, Edwin M. 1926. *History and traditions of niue*. B. P. Bishop Museum Bulletin no. 32. Quoted in Herskovits (1940).

Loftus, Elisabeth. 1976. *Memory*. Reading, Mass.: Addison-Wesley.

———. 1979. *Eyewitness testimony*. Cambridge, Mass.: Harvard University Press.

Lord, A. B. 1960. *Singer of tales*. Cambridge, Mass.: Harvard University Press.

Luce, Duncan R., and Raiffa, Howard. 1966. *Games and decisions*. New York: John Wiley and Sons.

Maine, Henry S. 1905. *Ancient Law*. London: John Murray.

Malinowski, B. 1926. *Crime and custom in savage society*. London: Kegan Paul, Trench and Trubner.

———. 1948. *Magic, science and religion*. Glencoe, Ill.: The Free Press.

Mansfield, Edwin. 1971. Technical change and the rate of imitation. In N. Rosenberg, editor, *The economics of technological change*. Middlesex: Penguin Books.

Markham, T. M. 1978. Palestinians: People in crisis. *New York Times*, 19 February.

Markowitz, Harry. 1952. The utility of wealth. *Journal of Political Economy* 80:151–58.

Marshall, Alfred. 1910. *Principles of economics*. London: Macmillan.

Marshall, L. K. 1962. !Kung bushmen's religious beliefs. *Africa* 32:221–52.

Marty, P. 1922. *Etudes sur l'Islam en Côte d'Ivoire*. Paris.

McClelland, David G. 1953. *The achievement motive*. New York: Appleton-Century-Crofts.

McGagg, William O. 1972. *Jewish nobles and geniuses in modern Hungary*. New York: Columbia University Press.

McKern, W. G. 1922. Functional families of the Patwin. University of California publication, vol. 13:235–58. Quoted in Herskovits (1940).

McNeill, William H. 1963. *The rise of the west*. Chicago: University of Chicago Press.

———. 1976. *Plagues and people*. New York: Anchor Books.

Merton, Robert K. 1957. *Social theory and social structure*. New York: Free Press.

Murdock, George P. 1967. *Ethnographic atlas*. Pittsburgh: University of Pittsburgh Press.

———. 1968. The current status of the world's hunting and gathering people. In R. B. Lee and I. DeVore, editors, *Man the hunter*. Chicago: Aldine.

Nelson, Benjamin. 1949. *The idea of usury: From tribal brotherhood to universal otherhood.* 2d edition. Reprint 1969. Chicago: University of Chicago Press.

North, Douglass C. 1981. *Structure and change in economic history.* New York: W. W. Norton.

North, Douglass C., and Robert P. Thomas. 1973. *The rise of the western world.* London: Cambridge University Press.

Olson, Mancur. 1963. Rapid growth as a destabilizing force. *Journal of economic history* 23:529–52. Reprinted in R. J. Art and R. Jarvis, editors (1973), *International politics: Anarchy, force, imperialism.* Boston: Little, Brown.

———. 1965. *The logic of collective action.* Cambridge, Mass.: Harvard University Press.

———. 1978. The political economy of comparative growth rates. Working paper, University of Maryland.

Ong, Walter J. 1971. *Rhetoric, romance and technology.* Ithaca, N.Y.: Cornell University Press.

Orwell, George. 1946. Politics and the English Language. *Horizon* no. 76, Reprinted in *Inside the whale and other essays* (1957). New York: Penguin Books.

Pagels, Heinz R. 1982. *Quantum physics and the language of nature.* New York: Simon and Schuster.

Parry, M. 1951. *Serbo-Croatian folk song.* New York: Columbia University Press.

Patrick, George, and E. Kehrberg. 1973. Costs and returns of education in five agricultural areas of eastern Brazil. *American Journal of Agricultural economics* 55:145–53.

Paulos, John A. 1980. *Mathematics and humor.* Chicago: University of Chicago Press.

Peretz, D., A. M. Wilson, and R. J. Ward. 1970. *A Palestine entity.* Washington, D.C.: Middle East Institutions.

Phelps, Edmund S. 1962. The statistical theory of racism and sexism. *American Economic Review* 62:659–61.

Pitt-Rivers, Julian. 1973. The kith and the kin. In J. Goody, editor, *The character of kinship.* London: Cambridge University Press.

Polgar, S. 1964. Evolution and the ills of mankind. In Sol Tax, editor, *Horizons of anthropology.* Chicago: Aldine.

———, editor. 1975. *Population, ecology and social evolution.* The Hague: Mouton.

Poliakov, Léon. 1955. *Du Christ aux juifs de cour.* Paris: Calmann-Lévy.

———. 1961. *De Mahomet aux Marranes.* Paris: Calmann-Lévy.

———. 1968. *L'histoire de l'antisémitisme de Voltaire à Wagner.* Paris: Calmann-Lévy.

———. 1977. *L'histoire de l'antisémitisme: l'Europe suicidaire: 1870–1933.* Paris: Calmann-Lévy.

———. 1980. *La causalité diabolique.* Paris: Calmann-Lévy.

Posner, Richard A. 1980. A theory of primitive society with special reference to primitive law. *Journal of Law and Economics* 23:1–55.

Pryor, Frederic L. 1977. *The origins of the economy.* New York: Academic Press.

Qubain, F. I. 1966. *Education and science in the Arab world.* Baltimore: Johns Hopkins University Press.

Rattray, R. S. 1913. *Hausa folk-lore.* Oxford: Oxford University Press.

Rawls, John. 1971. *A theory of justice.* Cambridge, Mass.: Harvard University Press.

Report of the royal commission on betting, lotteries and gaming. 1951. London: Royal Commission, H.M.S.O.

Rosen, Sam, and Desmond Norton. 1966. The lottery as a source of public revenue. *Taxes* 44:617–25.

Rosenberg, Nathan. 1976. *Perspectives on technology.* London: Cambridge University Press.

Rostow, W. W. 1960. *The stages of economic growth.* London: Cambridge University Press.

Russell, Bertrand. 1953. On the notion of cause with applications to the free-will problem. In H. Feigl and M. Brodbeck, editors, *Readings in the philosophy of science.* New York: Appleton-Century-Crofts.

Russell, J. G. 1969. Population in Europe 500–1500. In C. M. Cipolla, editor, *The Fontana economic history of Europe.* Vol. 1, chapter 1.

Sachar, Howard M. 1977. *The course of modern Jewish history.* 2d edition. New York: Delta Books.

Sahlins, M. 1972. *Stone age economics.* Chicago: Aldine.

Sapir, E., and M. Swadesh. 1939. *Nootka texts.* Philadelphia: Dwight Whitney Linguistic Series. Quoted in Herskovits (1940).

Schechter, Frank I. 1935. The law and morals of primitive trade. In *Legal essays in tribute to Orrin Kip McMurray.* Berkeley: Berkeley University Press.

Schmookler, Jacob. 1971. Economic sources of inventive activity. In N. Rosenberg, editor, *The economics of technological change.* Middlesex: Penguin Books.

Schneider, Harold K. 1974. *Economic man.* New York: The Free Press.

Schultz, Theodore W. 1961. Investment in human capital. *American Economic Review* 51:1–17.

———. 1975. The value and the ability to deal with disequilibrium. *Journal of Economic Literature* 13:827–47.

———. 1980. Investment in entrepreneurial ability. *Scandinavian Journal of Economics* 82:437–48.

Schumach, Murray. 1981. *Diamond people.* New York: W. W. Norton.

Schumpeter, Joseph A. 1934. *The theory of economic development.* Reprint 1969. Oxford: Oxford University Press.

Scribner, Sylvia, and Michael Cole. 1981. *The psychology of literacy.* Cambridge, Mass.: Harvard University Press.

Sellin, T. 1938. Culture, conflict and crime. *Social Science Research Council Bulletin* no. 44.

Sewell, R. 1972. Survey of gambling habits of a short-term recidivist prison population. In G. E. Moody, editor, *The facts about the 'money factories.'* London: The Churches' Council on Gambling.

Shapiro, Max. 1981. *The penniless billionaires*. New York: Times Books.

Simon, Herbert A. 1952. On the definition of the causal relation. *Journal of Philosophy* 49:517–28.

Sims, Christopher A. 1977. Exogeneity and causal ordering in macro-economic models. In *New methods in business cycle research: Proceedings from a conference*. Federal Reserve Bank of Minneapolis.

Smith, Adam. 1776. *The wealth of nations*. Reprint 1976. Chicago: University of Chicago Press.

———. 1762. *Lectures on policy, justice, revenue and arms*. In Herbert W. Schneider, editor, *Adam Smith's moral and political philosophy* (1948). New York: Hafner Publishing.

Smith, S., and P. Razzell. 1975. *The pool winners*. London: Caliban Books.

Solow, Robert M. 1967. Income inequality since the war. In E. G. Budd, editor, *Inequality and poverty*. New York: Norton.

Sombart, Werner. 1913. *The Jews and modern capitalism*. New York: Burt Franklin.

Sowell, Thomas. 1975. *Race and economics*. New York: David McKay.

Spencer, Herbert. 1860. The physiology of laughter. In *Macmillan's Magasine*, 395–402. Quoted in Arieti (1976).

Spiro, Michael H. 1974. On the tax incidence of the Pennsylvania lottery. *National Tax Journal* 27:57–61.

Steinsaltz, Adin. 1976. *The essential Talmud*. London: Weidenfeld and Nicholson.

Stigler, George J. 1975. *The citizen and the state*. Chicago: University of Chicago Press.

Stini, W. A. 1971. Evolutionary implications of changing nutritional patterns in human populations. *American Anthropologist* 73:1019–30.

Stone, Lawrence. 1981. *The past and the present*. Boston: Routledge and Kegan Paul.

Strotz, R. H., and H. Wold. 1960. Recursive vs. Non-recursive systems: An attempt at synthesis. *Econometrica* 28:417–27.

Sullivan, Harry S. 1940. Conceptions of modern psychiatry. *Psychiatry* 3.

Sumner, William G., and Albert G. Keller. 1927. *The science of society*. Vol. 1. New Haven: Yale University Press.

Sussman, R. M. 1972. Child transport, family size and increase in human population during the Neolithic. *Current Anthropology* 13:258–59.

Thompson, J. W. 1939. *The literacy of the laity in the Middle Ages*. Berkeley: University of California Press.

Thomson, D. F. 1949. *Economic exchange and the ceremonial exchange cycle in Arnhem land*. London: Macmillan.

Toynbee, Arnold J. 1966. *Change and habit: The challenge of our time*. London: Oxford University Press.

Turnbull, C. 1966. *Wayward Servants*. London: Eyre and Spottiswoode.

———. 1968. The importance of flux in two hunting societies. In R. B. Lee and I. DeVore, editors, *Man the hunter*. Chicago: Aldine.

Umbeck, John. 1977. A theory of contract choice and the California gold rush. *Journal of Law and Economics*. 20:421–37.

United Nations Relief and Work Agency (UNRWA). Reports 1951–73.

Van Den Haag, E. 1969. *The Jewish mystique*. New York: Dell.

Veblen, Thorstein. 1899. *The theory of the leisure class*. Reprint 1953. New York: The New American Library.

————. 1948. The intellectual pre-eminence of Jews in modern Europe. In M. Lerner, editor, *The Portable Veblen*. New York: Viking Press.

Von Neumann, J., and O. Morgenstern. 1947. *Theory of games and economic behavior*. Princeton: Princeton University Press.

Waardenburg, Jean-Jacques. 1966. *Les universités dans le monde arabe actuel*. Paris: Mouton.

Walker, N. D. 1965. *Crime and punishment in Britain*. Edinburgh: Edinburgh University Press.

Weber, Max. 1904–5. *The Protestant ethic and the spirit of capitalism*. Reprint 1958. New York: Charles Scribner's Sons.

Weinstein, David, and Lilian Deitch. 1974. *The impact of legalized gambling*. New York: Praeger.

West, E. G. 1976. *Adam Smith: The man and his work*. Indianapolis: Liberty Press.

White, L. A. 1949. *The science of culture*. New York: Farrar, Straus.

Wilson, Edward O. 1978. *On human nature*. Cambridge, Mass.: Harvard University Press.

Wilson, Thomas. 1572. *A discourse upon usury*. Reprint 1925, with a historical introduction by R. H. Tawney. London: Frank Class.

Wiser, William H., and Charlotte V. Wiser. 1963. *Behind mud walls*. Los Angeles: University of California Press.

Wolf, Eric R. 1959. *Sons of the shaking earth*. Chicago: University of Chicago Press.

Woodburn, J. 1968a. An introduction to Hadza ecology. In R. B. Lee and I. DeVore, editors, *Man the hunter*. Chicago: Aldine.

————. Stability and flexibility in Hadza residential groupings. In R. B. Lee and I. DeVore, editors, *Man the hunter*. Chicago: Aldine.

Yudkin, J. 1969. Archeology and the nutritionist. In P. J. Ucko and G. W. Dimbleby, editors, *The domestication and exploitation of plants and animals*. London: Duckworth.

Zellner, Arnold. 1979. Causality and econometrics. In K. Brunner and A. H. Meltzer, editors, *Three aspects of policy and policy making: Knowledge, data and institutions*. Amsterdam: North-Holland. Carnegie-Rochester Conference Series on Public Policy, supplementary series to the *Journal of Monetary Economics* 10, pp. 9–55.

Index

246 ◆ Index